SlutWalk

Also by Kaitlynn Mendes

FEMINISM IN THE NEWS: Representations of the Women's Movement since the 1960s

FEMINIST ERASURES: Challenging Backlash Culture (*edited with Kumarini Silva*)

SlutWalk

Feminism, Activism and Media

Kaitlynn Mendes
University of Leicester, UK

palgrave
macmillan

First published 2015 by
PALGRAVE MACMILLAN

Palgrave Macmillan in the UK is an imprint of Macmillan Publishers Limited, registered in England, company number 785998, of Houndmills, Basingstoke, Hampshire RG21 6XS.

Palgrave Macmillan in the US is a division of St Martin's Press LLC, 175 Fifth Avenue, New York, NY 10010.

Palgrave Macmillan is the global academic imprint of the above companies and has companies and representatives throughout the world.

Palgrave® and Macmillan® are registered trademarks in the United States, the United Kingdom, Europe and other countries.

ISBN 978–1–137–37889–7 hardback
ISBN 978–1–137–37890–3 paperback

This book is printed on paper suitable for recycling and made from fully managed and sustained forest sources. Logging, pulping and manufacturing processes are expected to conform to the environmental regulations of the country of origin.

A catalogue record for this book is available from the British Library.

Library of Congress Cataloging-in-Publication Data
Mendes, Kaitlynn, 1983–
Slutwalk : feminism, activism and media / Kaitlynn Mendes.
pages cm
ISBN 978–1–137–37890–3 (paperback)
1. Women's studies.   2. Feminism.   3. Feminism and mass media.   I. Title.
HQ1180.M46 2015
305.42—dc23   2015012284

Typeset by MPS Limited, Chennai, India.

This book is dedicated to all those who have participated in, and contributed to SlutWalks around the globe. Your work has helped make rape culture visible.

Contents

vii

List of Figures and Tables

Figures

Tables

Acknowledgments

Firstly, I would like to thank all of those SlutWalk organizers who agreed to speak with me for my research. Without the generosity of their time and insights, this project would have been lacking.

Secondly, I would like to thank my family, Ben, Brayden and Adam, for all the support and love they provide. Boys, I hope my work enables you to grow up as proud feminists who understand the importance of consent, and the ways slut shaming perpetuates sexual abuse.

Thirdly, I would like to thank my parents, Helder and Lynn, who have always been there for me, and have been willing to listen to me and engage with my work. Your conversations helped me to develop and defend my own ideas, for which I am very grateful.

Finally, I would like to thank the many colleagues and friends who took time to offer feedback on my work. Jessalynn Keller, Jessica Ringrose, Helen Wood and Shannon Gormley – I admire and respect you all, and appreciate your feedback.

List of Abbreviations and Acronyms

CPS	Crown Prosecution Service
FGM	Female Genital Mutilation
FURIE	Feminist Uprising to Resist Inequality & Exploitation
LA	Los Angeles
MLB	Major League Baseball
MP	Member of Parliament
NBA	National Basketball Association
NFL	National Football League
NGO	Non-Governmental organization
NOW	National Organisation for Women
NYS	New York City
PAC	Political Action Committee
PAP	People Action's Party
PC	Police Constable
RAINN	Rape, Abuse and Incest National Network
RCC	Rape Crisis Centre
SNS	Social Networking Site
UCLA	University of California at Los Angeles
UFC	Ultimate Fighting Championship
UK	United Kingdom
UN	United Nations
US	United States

1
Introduction

In January 2011, Toronto Police Constable Michael Sanguinetti addressed a small group of York University students on campus safety. Prefaced by the statement 'I'm told I'm not supposed to say this' he went on to advise that, 'women should avoid dressing like sluts in order not to be victimized' (Kwan 2011). While his intention might have been to protect women, his comments that 'slutty' women attract sexual assault perpetuated the long-standing myth that victims are responsible, or somehow 'are asking' for the violence used against them. In response to PC Sanguinetti's comments, Toronto residents Heather Jarvis and Sonya Barnett translated their anger at the ways women were slut-shamed and victim-blamed, into political activism. Creating a website and Facebook and Twitter accounts, the women invited the public to join them for a 'SlutWalk' to the Toronto Police Headquarters to vent their frustration. On 3 April 2011, the first SlutWalk set off from Queen's Park in Toronto, attended by thousands. Although the organizers asked people to dress in their normal, everyday clothing to demonstrate the ways that sexual assault occurs no matter what women wear, a number of attendees showed up in 'provocative' attire to make a statement that no matter how they dress, they do not deserve to be assaulted.

Before the first march even took place, the movement went 'viral,' attracting much initial publicity via the feminist blogosphere, including popular sites such as *Rabble.ca, Jezebel* and *Feministing* (McNicol 2012). By the end of the 2011, SlutWalks emerged organically in over 200 cities and 40 nations, mobilizing tens of thousands of women, men and children (Carr 2013). In 2014, although the movement had slowed, SlutWalks continued to take place in major cities such as Baltimore, Bloomington, Denver, Edmonton, Guelph, Jerusalem, Johannesburg, Melbourne, Miami, Milwaukee, Munich, Orlando, Ottawa, Philadelphia,[1] Portland,

Reno, Rio De Janeiro, Rochester, Salt Lake City, Seattle,[2] Toronto, Vancouver, Victoria (Canada), Warsaw and Washington DC. In July 2014 a record breaking 11,000 people turned up to the fourth annual SlutWalk in Reykjavík, Iceland (Kaaber 2014).

Because there has been an erasure of (Western) news coverage of feminist activism and protest since the Second Wave (Mendes 2012), with feminism frequently being labelled 'dead' or 'redundant' (see Douglas 2010; Gill 2007; McRobbie 2009; Mendes 2011a), SlutWalk's global reach and its ability to generate international headlines provides an opportunity to assess how modern feminism, and feminist activism is represented in a global context. Specifically, how has an anti-rape movement been represented not only by the mainstream news media, but by the thriving feminist blogosphere, across a range of cultures where women's equality differs greatly? While post/Third Wave feminism is regularly assessed in popular culture, less research explores its representation in the news media (for exceptions, see Gill 2007; Mendes 2012; Varvus 2002, 2007), and few to date have examined its representations in feminist media (see Carr 2013; Dow & Wood 2014).

At the same time, an abundance of research is emerging which focuses on the rise of a new protest culture, and its relationship to social media (see Atkinson 2009; Castells 2012; Gerbaudo 2012; Harlow 2011; Juris 2012; Lim 2013; Madianou 2013; Marmura 2008; Penney & Dadas 2014; Wolfson 2012). Yet, despite this, most studies are concerned with anti-globalization, anti-capitalism, or the Arab Spring, and pay little attention to the ways in which feminists have harnessed social media and the internet to challenge sexism, misogyny and 'rape culture' (for exceptions, see Chattopadhyay 2011; Harp et al. 2014; Keller 2011, 2013, 2015; Puente 2011; Rapp et al. 2010; Shaw 2012a; Zobl & Drueke 2012). As Chandra Mohanty argued: 'Because social movements are crucial sites for the construction of knowledge, communities, and identities, it is very important for feminists to direct themselves toward them' (2003, p. 528). And while the mainstream news undoubtedly remains an important vehicle through which people come to learn about and understand modern protest, the rise of blogs, online magazines and social media platforms opens up new spaces which are increasingly necessary to explore.

As a result, this book will present findings from research on eight English-speaking nations which held SlutWalk marches between 2011 and 2014 (Australia, Canada, India, New Zealand, South Africa, Singapore, the UK and the US). The analysis will examine representations of SlutWalk in mainstream news and online feminist media sites. These findings will be enriched with insights gathered from interviews with

22 SlutWalk organizers from around the world. My aim is not to provide a complete 'history' of the movement, but to add insight into some of the ways it has been represented, choreographed and experienced, all of which contributes to a wider political project of the 'storying' of feminism (Hemmings 2005) and feminist activism (Mendes 2011a). In order to contribute to the storying of feminism, however, one must first understand how SlutWalk came about.

The genesis and development of SlutWalk

In January 2011, Toronto resident Heather Jarvis was on Facebook when she came across an article from York University's student newspaper *The Excalibur*, recounting PC Sanguinetti's comments about how women could avoid being 'victimized' by not dressing like 'sluts.' Angered by the perpetuation of rape myths – particularly the idea that women who dress provocatively, drink alcohol, or who enjoy sex, are regularly blamed if sexually assaulted – Jarvis shared the story on Facebook, creating an online dialogue between friends. In one exchange with Sonya Barnett, Jarvis stated she wanted to go to the Toronto police headquarters to share her anger, and was immediately supported. After exchanging a few messages, Jarvis and Barnett agreed to stage a protest. The idea for the name emerged when Barnett told a colleague about their protest, who jokingly asked if they were going to call it 'SlutWalk'. Both Barnett and Jarvis liked the name, and plans for the first SlutWalk began with the creation of a website, Facebook page and Twitter account (Jarvis 2012).

Although the numbers of protesters said to have attended the march range from 1,000 to 3,000 people (McNicol 2012; 'Toronto's Slutwalk sparks blogosphere feminism debate'; Onstad 2011), it not only attracted local media attention, but was reported across Canada and the world, fuelling the emergence of this grassroots political movement. News records indicate that marches first began springing up in Canada and the US before moving across the Atlantic to the UK, Australia, Singapore, New Zealand, South Africa and a range of other non-Western and non-English-speaking nations (see also Carr 2013; Dow & Wood 2014). Significantly, the movement also went 'viral' amongst the feminist blogosphere and received much publicity and attention. SlutWalks generally consist of a march, ending with a range of speeches from sexual assault survivors, sex workers and members of anti-rape organizations. In several cases, the march is either preceded or followed by a range of events including consent workshops, flashmobs, film screenings, poetry readings and more.

Defining SlutWalk

As a grassroots political movement, operating without an equivocal 'leader' or base (Carr 2013), it is difficult to provide a universal definition of SlutWalk, its key aims, message or goals. Instead, the movement has been shaped by its geographical and temporal settings, local issues, current events and organizers' personal understanding of sexual violence and rape culture. As a result, the movement's message and key aims have at times varied and, like feminism itself, there is no monolithic SlutWalk (Genz & Brabon 2009). That said, despite operating in a number of regions with differing cultural, social and political contexts, an examination of various Facebook pages, websites and Twitter accounts reveals the following priorities:

- A movement that challenges 'rape culture' and the idea that victims are to blame for sexual violence
- A movement that seeks to reclaim or re-appropriate the word 'slut'
- A movement which promotes the idea that no one 'asks' to be raped or sexually assaulted
- A movement which encourages a 'do not rape,' rather than a 'don't get raped' culture
- A movement to improve the current judicial and police systems regarding sexual assault
- A movement to increase the public's awareness and education surrounding issues of sexual violence and to provide support and outreach for survivors
- A movement that promotes respect for the individual and the variety of choices they make (including freedom to dress how they want)
- A movement which fights for women's rights
- A movement that is inclusive of all genders, ages, ethnicities, classes and sexual orientations

Although the above is not a comprehensive list, nor do all of the items on it apply to *all* SlutWalk satellite groups, it gives a flavour and provides context for some of the most mentioned goals or explanations provided by SlutWalk organizers themselves, which are important to know as we move through this book.[3] And while helping us understand how SlutWalk emerged and what it stands for is important, these items don't make sense without first understanding the cultural context in which they emerged – namely what feminists and scholars call 'rape culture.'

SlutWalk in a time of rape culture

For several decades, feminists and academics have increasingly talked about the development of a 'rape culture,' or a socio-cultural context in which male dominance is eroticized, and where young men and women are taught that male aggression is a 'healthy' and 'normal' part of sexual relations (Herman 1978). As a result, rape culture not only fosters the belief that men are *entitled* to women's bodies, but that rape 'makes sense' in certain scenarios, and is an inevitable part of life (see Buchwald et al. 2005; McNicol 2012; Valenti 2007). Tired of the routine objectification of their bodies and the ways that women are told to accept violence as a 'natural' part of sexuality, the SlutWalk movement emerged at a time when the absurdity or 'dislocation' of this culture was becoming increasingly evident to large sections of society (see Shaw, F. 2011). Although they might not have been familiar with the term 'rape culture,' there is no doubt that women (and many men), had become increasingly frustrated by the ways they were being policed and held accountable for other people's actions. As co-founders Heather Jarvis and Sonya Barnett articulated on the SlutWalk Toronto website:

> We are tired of being oppressed by slut-shaming; of being judged by our sexuality and feeling unsafe as a result. Being in charge of our sexual lives should not mean that we are opening ourselves to an expectation of violence, regardless if we participate in sex for pleasure or work. No one should equate enjoying sex with attracting sexual assault. (SlutWalk Toronto 2011)

And while a number of high profile articles have been published in recent years, denying the existence of rape culture (see Kitchens 2013, 2014; Roiphe 1994), below are some recent examples which provide the emotional fodder for large scale resistance to it, including SlutWalk.

Rape culture exists in a town near you

In March 2011, a month before the first SlutWalk took place, an 11-year-old girl in Cleveland, Texas was gang raped by 18 men while the attack was filmed on a mobile phone. In its report of the crime, *The New York Times* included quotes from the community, stating the girl wore makeup and fashions 'more appropriate to a woman in her 20s' (McKinley 2011), thus suggesting she was responsible for her attack. Furthermore, local residents were quoted talking about how the perpetrators would 'have to live with this for the rest of their lives,' while ignoring the impact the assault would have for the victim.

In August 2012, while SlutWalks were marching into their second year, a 16-year-old high school student in Steubenville, Ohio was raped by two classmates while passed out at a party. Over a six hour period, the girl was undressed, transported and sexually assaulted while other party-goers captured and disseminated images and texts about the assault via social media. Although there were many witnesses to the assault, no one attempted to intervene. As one witness explained, he didn't stop it because: 'It wasn't violent. I didn't know exactly what rape was. I thought it was forcing yourself on someone' (Carter & Harlow 2013). Not only is men's entitlement to a woman's body symptomatic of rape culture, but so too is the lack of knowledge of what rape actually is or looks like (Meyer 2010).

At the trial of the men who were charged with the 2012 gang rape and murder of a 23-year-old Delhi student on a moving bus, their lawyer stated he had never heard of a 'respected lady' being raped in India, and that, as an unmarried woman, she should not have been out in the streets at night (MacAskill 2013). Rape culture supports the policing of women's behaviour (they shouldn't be out at night), and justifies male violence if a woman is (perceived) to be out of line. In this way, rape culture serves as a reminder for women to remain in their 'proper' place, and demonstrates that if they fail to do so, they will be (threatened with) rape, battery or murder.

This line of thought is also responsible for the views that some women *cannot* be raped – such as sex workers, 'sluts,' or women of colour, who are always thought to be 'up for it.' At the same time, the disabled or those not conventionally beautiful are thought to be so undesirable that they would be grateful for any sexual attention at all. Yet rape culture also excuses sexual assault as an inherent part of masculinity, as we saw in 2014 when two teenage cousins were raped, strangled and then hung from a tree in Uttar Pradesh, India. In a country where it is estimated that a woman is raped every 22 minutes, not only were two of the attackers police officers, but the leader of the region's governing party told an election rally that in cases of gang rape, 'boys will be boys' (Blake 2014), thus constructing male violence as 'natural' and 'inevitable.' This routine excuse of rape is a key feature of rape culture.

'Legitimate' rape or 'bad sexual etiquette'?

One key feature of rape culture is the qualification of rape in terms of its legitimacy. Scholars have noted that when most people think of rape, they think of a stranger attacking a woman in a dark alley – a scenario in which the victim puts up a valiant fight and sustains visible injuries (Meyer 2010). Research has found that any other type of rape is likely to be classified as 'sex gone a bit wrong' (see Benedict 1992; Meyer 2010). It is therefore perhaps no surprise that when commenting on the 2012 rape accusations filed against Wikileaks founder Julian Assange by two Swedish women, British MP George Galloway insisted that one of the crimes in question – Assange having sex with one of the women while she slept – was merely a case of 'bad sexual etiquette.' Galloway went on to state that even if Assange's actions were captured on camera, they would not constitute rape 'as anyone with any sense can possibly recognize it.' This is because, as the two had previously engaged in consensual sex, 'not everybody needs to be asked prior to each insertion' ('George Galloway attacked over Assange "rape" comments' 2012). Similarly, when the US government tried to extradite film director Roman Polanski, who was accused of drugging and raping a 13-year-old girl in the 1970s, *The View* host Whoopi Goldberg declared: 'I know it wasn't rape-rape. It was something else but I don't believe it was rape-rape' (Robertson 2009). This is despite the fact that Polanski admitted his actions and even apologized to the victim (Hare 2011). When rape is downplayed as 'bad sexual etiquette,' when rapists are forgiven for their crimes because of their celebrity status, or when qualifications are made about 'real,' and 'legitimate' rape, these discourses downplay the nature of the crime, and therefore set the context for how it will be handled. This informs what is known as the 'second assault' (see Wolburt Burgess et al. 2009), which is another key feature of rape culture.

The second assault

For many victims, the post-assault experience can be just as traumatic as the assault itself. This is credited to the veracity of *rape myths* – or generalized, false ideas or beliefs about rape which trivialize it, suggests that it did not occur, or can only occur in certain contexts. Rape myths serve to redirect blame for this crime on the victims, or to reduce the perpetrators' culpability (Bonnes 2013, p. 210; Meyer 2010). Franiuk et al. (2008) argued that rape myths are key to the perpetuation of sexual assault in our culture because they make people question the legitimacy of rape cases (cited in Bonnes 2013, p. 211). The cultural acceptance of rape myths mean that when victims report the assault (to friends, family or the authorities), they are often questioned about their appearance, behaviour, profession, or sexual past, as a way of transferring blame to them (Benedict 1992; Bonnes 2013; Meyer 2010; Worthington 2008).

With this in mind, it is no surprise that, for example in the British and American context, figures show that between 80 and 90 percent of rape is never reported (Campbell 2013, p. 84; Dodd 2014; The White House Council on Women and Girls 2014). The underreporting of this crime is often due to women's own internalization of rape myths, which either prevents them from seeing the crime as rape (e.g. if it was done by an intimate partner), or makes them believe that they were responsible (see Bonnes 2013). Yet despite the chronic underreporting of rape, it is commonly believed that women 'cry rape' because they are ashamed about the encounter and want to save face (Meyer 2010), or because they want to punish or get revenge on the suspected assailant (Benedict 1992). In 2013, Britain's Crown Prosecution Service (CPS) found that, in fact, false rape accusations are 'extremely rare' – mounting to around two per month, but are extremely damaging to the credibility of all victims who seek justice (Crown Prosecution Service 2013). Other research has similarly suggested that false rape accusations are around two percent, the same as most other crimes (Lonsway & Fitzgerald 1994 cited in Bonnes 2013, p. 211; Lisak et al. 2010).

In Britain, of the estimated ten to 20 percent of cases that *are* reported, the complaint is withdrawn (often from pressure from the police or family), or the accusation is not acted upon (amidst lack of evidence) 80 percent of the time (Dodd 2014; The White House Council on Women and Girls 2014). In Britain, the Metropolitan Police's specialist sexual violence unit has been accused of persuading women to drop their cases to help improve their performance record (Dodd 2014). At present, of the 14 percent of reported rape cases that go to trial in Britain, only half result in a conviction (Campbell 2013, pp. 84–85). This means that only an estimated six or seven percent of all rapes will ever lead to a conviction. These statistics are unsurprising when studies such as the Sexual Assault Research Summary Report (2005) found that one in three Britons believe rape victims are partly responsible for their rape (cited in Meyer 2010, p. 26).

As a result, most rapists get away with their crimes, or receive light sentences if charged. For example, in 2013 a Montana judge gave a 44-year-old male teacher a 30-day sentence for raping a 14-year-old pupil (who later committed suicide in the run up to her trial, after enduring years of slutshaming). Amidst protests over the sentence, the judge defended his actions by claiming that the *defendant* had 'suffered enough,' and that the victim was 'older than her chronological age' (Brown 2013). The following year, an Indiana judge gave no jail time for a man convicted of repeatedly drugging and raping his own wife. In his ruling, he advised that *she* 'needed to forgive' her attacker (Pearce 2014). That same year a Dallas judge gave a light sentence to a man who admitted raping a 14-year-old girl, because she neither a virgin nor 'the victim she claimed to be' (Belle 2014). These are the cases which at least made it to court. In New Zealand, a group of youths calling themselves 'Roast Busters' plied underage girls with alcohol, gang raped them and bragged about it on Facebook. Although several victims have come forward, to date, no one has been charged.

These are but a few examples of the ways in which perpetrators of sexual assault receive impunity for their crimes. As a result, it is no surprise that a thriving rape culture operates in most of the world – a culture not only in which women are raped, but in which assaults can be photographed, recorded and shared, and yet perpetrators either completely avoid punishment, or receive light sentences. And this rape culture is not only evident in the ways that actual violence is acted upon, managed and discussed, but is embedded in our culture. Feminist commentators, activists and scholars alike have highlighted the ways in which sexual violence surrounds us – through images, advertisements, jokes, language and laws. Cumulatively, all of these things serve to validate and perpetuate rape, and result in it 'making sense' in certain contexts (such as if a woman is wearing 'slutty clothing,' drinks alcohol, isn't a virgin, or flirts with her attacker beforehand) (Benedict 1992; Bonnes 2013; McNicol 2012; Meyer 2010; Worthington 2008).

That rape culture thrives in its celebration of aggressive masculinity, misogyny and sexism, is evidenced by one of the most popular songs of 2013. In Robin Thicke's 'Blurred Lines,' he sings about the supposed 'grey area' between consensual sex and rape for 'good girls.' Although these girls may say 'no,' the lyric 'I know you want it' is repeated throughout, implying that they really mean 'yes.' Although the song was banned from several UK university campuses, the fact that this response was seen by many as an 'overreaction' only serves to highlight how normalized and embedded rape culture is (see Walmsley 2013).

Resistance to rape culture

All of the above examples are evidence that rape culture is not just a Western/Eastern, northern/southern, first world/third world problem, but one which is experienced, albeit in different ways, around the globe. Although it is only just starting to attract mainstream media attention, women (and men) are beginning to fight back against rape culture and challenge the naturalness of such conventions. This applies to so-called 'honour killings,' street harassment, rape jokes, sexualized imagery and more. And while people continue to occupy the streets and public spaces, much activism is taking place online. For example, in 2013, an international group of feminists successfully initiated the #FBrape campaign demanding that companies pull their advertisements from the social media company due to Facebook's refusal to remove misogynist content encouraging violence against women and girls. The one-week campaign resulted in a promise from Facebook to change their policies on hate speech and make it easier to remove offensive pages. In 2014, the #Yesallwomen hashtag trended on Twitter after 22-year-old Elliot Rodger murdered six people in California, saying he was bent on 'punishing' women for rejecting him. The hashtag was both a response to the narrative that 'not all men' are like Rodger, and as a means of sharing stories about the ubiquitous nature of sexual violence which *all* women encounter.

Similarly, the grassroots initiatives Hollaback! and The Everyday Sexism Project seek to raise awareness and catalogue the everyday experiences of sexism. As The Everyday Sexism Project explained, by sharing your stories, 'you're showing the world that sexism *does* exist, it *is* faced by women *everyday* and it *is* a valid problem to discuss' (Bates 2014, italics original). Other online efforts to raise awareness of, and end rape culture, include the 'I Help End Rape Culture By...' page on Facebook, in which participants are invited to upload photos of themselves carrying a sign of how they help end rape culture. While the internet opens up a range of possibilities for challenging rape culture, activism is taking place in offline spaces, too. For example, the feminist group FORCE: Upsetting Rape Culture, seeks to disrupt rape culture by creating an environment in which sexual violence is addressed. Actions include creating a mock Victoria's Secret line of 'consent-themed, anti-rape panties' (FORCE n.d.), as well as creating public monuments in which rape survivors share their stories (FORCE 2014). Universities across the world, but particularly in the US, are also taking the lead in campaigns to end rape culture. Whitman College in Washington is home to the 'All Students for Consent' group which has launched campaigns such as 'Ask for it,' in which the 'it' stands for consent (All Students for Consent, n.d.). The group 7000 in Solidarity at UCLA in California frequently produces posters, events and art which challenge rape myths. In 2014, Columbia student Emma Sulkowicz's 'mattress protest' went viral, as she vowed to carry a single mattress around campus until college administrators expelled a student she accused of raping her (Grigoriadis 2014).

There have also been a number of marches which protest rape culture. Reclaim the Night, which first began in the US in the 1970s and spread

across the world, has experienced a sort of revival in
or so. Since 2004, the London Feminist Network has
Reclaim the Night march which attracts thousands.
of women in Johannesburg attended a Mini-skin
women were assaulted at a taxicab rank for wearing short
2012). In New Zealand, thousands of people attended protests over
Roast Busters scandal discussed above, in which groups of young men
were drugging and raping underage girls and then posting videos brag-
ging about it online (Manning 2013). In 2013 and 2014, the One Billion
Rising for Justice movement held marches in cities all around the world,
demanding an end to violence against women. In 2014, hundreds of
Israelis protested against what they saw as the incompetent handling
of sexual assault cases (Chai 2014). And in India, thousands of people
have come together to protest both the gang rape and murder of a
23-year-old student in 2012, and the 2014 gang rape and murder of two
teenage cousins.

It is amidst this wider rape culture, and the ways feminists are fighting back, that SlutWalk not only emerged, but exploded as a global
grassroots movement. What is significant about SlutWalk is not the
premise; after all, women have been protesting against sexual violence
for decades. What is striking about SlutWalk was its ability, *despite* its
feminist roots, to capture the mainstream media's attention. While it is
impossible to refute the fact that feminism is experiencing a revitaliza-
tion, this was certainly not the case in 2011. In fact, I, along with many
of its organizers, argue that SlutWalk has been instrumental in bringing
feminism and feminist issues *back* onto the public's consciousness. Not
only did it make it onto the mainstream news, but it became widely
discussed amongst news presenters, radio hosts, political and social
pundits, bloggers and DJs. As someone who is deeply interested in representations of feminism in mainstream news media (Mendes 2011a,
2012, 2015), I couldn't help but be interested in this movement, and
the complex ways in which it was being discussed.

As a result, Chapter 2, 'Contextualizing the Issues,' establishes a
theoretical and methodological framework for the study. It discusses key
developments in the anti-rape movement, situating SlutWalk amidst
theories on Third Wave and postfeminism. The chapter also provides an
overview of previous research on representations of sexual violence and
anti-rape activism. It then moves on to a discussion about the development of social networking sites, and their relationship with contemporary social movements. The chapter concludes with a discussion about
the specific methods used to conduct this research, including content

alysis, frame analysis, critical discourse analysis, online ethnography and in-depth interviews.

Chapter 3, 'Situating SlutWalk,' analyzes the movement's temporal and geographic contexts, assessing what SlutWalk is said to stand for, as well as where and when it is represented as taking place. This includes examining which phases of SlutWalk's cycle are reported – its planning stages, the march or its aftermath. I argue that, unlike historic representations of feminism, SlutWalk is unique because it received a lot of pre-march attention. This is significant because instead of reporting on aspects such as the march's success or failure, how many and who attended, this coverage not only alerted the public to the movement's existence, but provided potential participants with information on how to become involved. The chapter also explains regional and national variations in the movement, including the use of parallel or alternative names, and ways in which it was made locally and culturally relevant.

Importantly, this chapter also addresses some key critiques of the movement, particularly from women of colour who argued that the movement (unintentionally?) marginalized them, demonstrating the ways feminism still has issues with white privilege, despite its increasingly intersectional nature. Rather than ignoring these critiques, the chapter outlines the various strategies used to address these legitimate concerns. The chapter concludes with a discussion about intersectionality, namely my surprise that this was not more widely discussed outside of North America, where issues of colonialism, capitalism and racism abound.

Chapter 4, 'Representing the Movement: SlutWalk Challenges Rape Culture,' focuses on the overwhelmingly supportive frames employed in both my mainstream and feminist media samples. This chapter specifically focuses on articles and posts which frame the movement as one which seeks to end rape culture, sexual violence and victim-blaming. While this is undoubtedly a positive development, I argue that much coverage, particularly in the mainstream news, was superficial and did not adequately explain causes of and solutions to rape culture. In contrast, unburdened by professional, political, organizational or economic constraints, the feminist media did a much better job of explaining, dismantling and challenging common rape myths. As a result, the chapter raises questions about the effectiveness of mainstream news vs. alternative, feminist and mostly non-commercial accounts of the movement, which acted as an important site for *discursive politics* and *activism,* which is necessary when trying to enact cultural change.

Following on from this, Chapter 5, 'Representing the Movement: SlutWalk is Misguided or Opposed,' examines the smaller proportion of articles/posts which represent the movement as misguided or opposed. The chapter documents the specific discourses used to construct this frame, such as how it conforms to patriarchy, and ignores issues of 'real' feminist concern. Rather than dismissing all articles which oppose the movement as inherently 'bad,' I instead argue that many such critiques are in fact necessary for the movement's development and growth. In particular, it is important to question the movement's tactics, message and goals, and ensure necessary dialogues about the intersectional nature of oppression, patriarchy's hegemonic hold in a 'postfeminist' context, and the possibility of collective social change in neoliberal times.

At the same time, I argue that SlutWalk provides evidence of a departure away from a postfeminist 'sensibility' (Gill 2007), in which feminism has been 'taken into account' only to be depoliticized and rejected. Instead, many of the texts recognize the need to challenge rape culture, and the issues of contention revolve around which strategies are the most appropriate or effective. Following on from this, the chapter presents a critique of the *visual* representations of SlutWalk, particularly in the mainstream news, arguing that it contributed to postfeminist constructions of a movement which fights for individual freedoms such as the right to dress like a 'slut.' Yet at the same time, I demonstrate the ways that feminists used personal blogs and photosharing sites such as Flickr, to disrupt the mainstream 'storying' of SlutWalk, and create their own 'counter-memories' of the movement as one with more radical and patriarchy-shattering potential. The chapter concludes with an examination of discourses which sought to discredit the movement and its supporters, picking apart the logic in these common backlash discourses.

Chapter 6, 'SlutWalk Hierarchy and Organizers' Roles,' presents findings from interviews with 22 organizers from around the world. Organizers shared their experiences with various aspects of the movement, such as how they became involved, divided responsibilities, learned the ropes and reached out to mainstream and alternative media outlets. What became clear from my research is the ways in which, unlike other modern social movements which scholars claim are 'horizontal' (Castells 2009, 2012; Juris 2008), hierarchies exist and were at times actively embraced by satellite groups.

Carrying on with an analysis of interviews with organizers, Chapter 7, 'SlutWalk, Connectivity and Cyberactivism,' focuses on the ways satellite groups used social media, particularly Facebook, to connect with other satellite groups, individual feminists and feminist organizations, to create networked counterpublics in which sexual assault was identified as a key problem in need of addressing. A key theme running through both Chapters 6 and 7 is the importance of social media platforms, particularly Facebook. Not only were they instrumental in recruiting organizers and participants, but they were often the primary means through which organizers communicated and shared information about SlutWalk and rape culture in general. And while social media provided organizers with easy access to networked communities, they also opened up space for organizers to become targets for online abuse and trolling. Organizers not only shared their experiences of getting trolled, but detailed their strategies for managing them, which varied from satellite group to satellite group. The chapter concludes with views about organizers' overall experiences with the movement.

Chapter 8, 'Conclusion,' finishes the book with a re-statement of my key arguments as well as a discussion about SlutWalk's legacy and impact, and the hope of change for the future.

2
Contextualizing the Issues

Chapter 2 provides an overview of literature, theories and concepts relevant to finding out how SlutWalk was represented in the media and experienced by organizers in eight nations (Australia, Canada, India, New Zealand, Singapore, South Africa, the UK and the US) which hosted marches between 2011 and 2014. This includes a scholarly review of modern feminism, violence against women, the anti-rape movement and post and Third Wave feminism. It also includes scholarly work on representations of violence against women, and representations of feminist activism. The chapter will then move on to examine literature on social media and its use in modern social movements, and pays particular attention to concepts of *discursive activism* and *networked counterpublics*, which I found extremely useful in explaining the movement's online activism and communities. The chapter concludes with an explanation of the how the study was conducted, using methods such as qualitative content analysis, critical discourse analysis, frame analysis, semi-structured interviews and close observation of online feminist communities.

Modern feminism

According to Puente (2011) 'Feminism today is a diverse panorama constructed out of historic, individual, and collective efforts that seek to redefine the condition of women' (pp. 334–5). This is particularly true when examining the histories and state of feminist activism in the eight nations included in this study: Australia, Canada, India, New Zealand, Singapore, South Africa, the UK and the US. Although it is not possible to provide a detailed history of feminist activism in each nation, all have experienced feminist campaigns – with greater or lesser visibility – around similar issues, such as equal citizenship and pay, law and moral reform, reproductive control and bodily rights (see Anderson 1991; Bouchier 1983; Coote & Campbell 1982; Gangoli 2007; Mitra 2013; Sawer 2013; van Acker 1999). Yet despite campaigning on similar issues, often in similar periods, the specific forms of women's activism, and the shape of each women's movement, are marked by national distinctiveness arising from their own histories, culture, and experience with various forms of oppression (Forestell & Moynagh 2014). As we will see in Chapter 3, these national and cultural distinctions were also reflected in the way SlutWalks developed across the world.

Although much of the 'storying' of feminism situates it as a Western phenomenon or something 'imposed' on Third World women (Carr 2013; Jayawardena 1986), scholars have contested such beliefs, and have instead noted the ways that various nations around the world have in fact developed their own feminisms, emerging out of specific historic circumstances and ideological and material changes in women's lives (Jayawardena 1986). These include, but are not limited to imperialism, colonialism, racism and capitalism, and explain why feminist activism around the globe is not monolithic, although much activity intersects and connects in important ways (de Haan et al. 2013; Forestell & Moynagh 2014). Rather than documenting the histories of feminist activism in each of the eight nations included in this study, the section below will instead provide a background to activism which has specifically centred around sexual violence – a problem women all around the world experience, albeit in different ways.

Violence against women and the anti-rape movement

According to the UN (1992), violence against women is 'Violence that is directed at a woman because she is a woman or that affects women disproportionately.' It includes domestic violence, rape and sexual assault, (so-called) honour crimes, forced marriages, female genital mutilation and human trafficking (Järvinen et al. 2008). Around the globe, millions of women will experience violence each year, and most violence will be committed by someone the victim knows (Järvinen et al. 2008, p. 7). In the 1970s, feminists began to challenge the notion that sexual violence was a rare, individual problem, committed by a few 'bad apples.' Through consciousness-raising sessions, radical feminists were the first to politicize rape as a feminist issue, and to argue that (sexual) violence was a structural tool used to maintain men's dominance over women (Bevacqua 2001). As such, feminists worked to re-conceptualize rape from a crime of sex and passion, to one of power and control used to enforce women's subordination in a patriarchal society (Brownmiller 1975; Moffett 2006).

Although mainly white, Second Wave feminists in the West are responsible for the theoretical understanding of rape as presented above, the development of black feminist and postcolonial theory re-imagined rape as a tool used to maintain not only gendered hierarchies, but other forms of control as well (see Hill Collins 2000; hooks 1984). For example, these contributions helped shape understanding of the ways rape has been a tool used to regulate sexuality ('corrective rape' for lesbians in South Africa), a means of establishing racial, political and class hierarchies (systematic raping of black slaves in the US, or black women in South African apartheid), and as a weapon of war and imperialism (a means of pillaging, punishing and humiliating the enemy).

In the UK, it is estimated that 2,000 women a week are raped or sexually assaulted (Järvinen et al. 2008, p. 8), while in India, the estimates are one person every 22 minutes (Blake 2014). In South Africa, the supposed rape capital of the world, the figure jumps to one person assaulted every 27 seconds (cited in Hancox 2012). Other countries such as Singapore do not release official statistics on rape or sexual assault, perhaps to bolster the view that rape is not a problem, and that Singaporeans are law-abiding citizens (Gwynne 2013; Ward 1995). Although my point here is to highlight that rape is a *global* phenomenon, it is worth pointing out there are many issues with international rape statistics, namely that statistics are based on estimates because most victims are reluctant to come forward for fear they won't be believed, that they will be blamed for their assault, or that they won't receive justice (see Campbell 2013; McDuff et al. 1977). Furthermore, not all countries collect data on a national scale – India, for example, does not – while others such as Singapore do not release official statistics at all (Gwynne 2013).

Others have pointed out how question wording about sexual assault has a dramatic influence on people's responses. This is in part because many people lack the understanding of what rape actually is. For example, in their 2011 annual survey, the US Justice Department's Bureau of Statistics found that nearly 250,000 people admitted they had been victims of rape or sexual assault over the previous 12 months. The previous year, the Centers for Disease Control and Prevention also conducted a survey in which they asked individuals if they had engaged in sex either without their consent, or where it was not possible. When phrased as 'sex without consent,' as opposed to 'rape,' the response jumped to 1.3 million over the previous 12 months (see 'Statistics Shed Little Light on Rape Statistics' 2013). These vastly different figures clearly show the continued need to educate the public on what rape is, to identify it as a social problem, and to shatter the myth that rape only occurs between strangers in a dark alley in which there are outward physical marks from the attack. This has been, and continues to be a key goal of anti-rape movements around the world.

Anti-rape activism

Although feminism may have different goals, histories and understandings about the nature of women's oppression in different parts of the world, one common concern has been violence against women. In some places, such as Canada, Australia, New Zealand, the US and the UK, anti-rape campaigning grew out of Second Wave feminist organising, and became a 'submovement,' developing its own organizations and strategies (Bevacqua 2008, p. 164). In other places, such as India and South Africa, anti-rape activism developed out of anti-colonial and anti-apartheid movements (Bonnes 2013; Gangoli 2007; Mitra 2013; Rosenthall 2001), while in Singapore, where social protest and activism is generally discouraged, it developed with academic and government support (Ward 1995).

Although women around the globe have participated in anti-rape activism, research indicates different areas of focus. For example, in India, anti-rape activism was often initially targeted towards the police, who as representatives of the State, frequently used brutality and sexual violence as a means of subordinating women (Gangoli 2007). As a result, the focus was not on the interpersonal nature of rape, but its use as a structural form of violence. In the American context, there was an initial divide between black and white feminists, resulting in the under-representation of black women in the anti-rape movement (Matthews 1989). Black women did not join the largely white anti-rape movement in the US, not because they lived lives free from sexual violence, but because many white feminists ignored issues central to black women's experiences with rape and the criminal justice system (Bevacqua 2001, 2008). While there is evidence that black and white feminists did eventually come together, in some cities such as LA, there were separate rape crisis centres for white, Latina and black women (Matthews 1989).

Despite these differences, most scholarship focuses on how these anti-rape movements have scored some major successes, including recognizing rape as a common problem, identifying it as a political (read sexist, racist, imperialist, etc.), rather than a personal issue, changing legislation, establishing rape crisis centres and hotlines, challenging the judicial and police processes, and having rape recognized a serious crime (see McNickle Rose 1977; Wolburt Burgess et al. 2009). There is, however, evidence that more needs to be done, particularly in shattering myths surrounding what rape is, why rape happens, who rapists are, who victims are, and who is to blame. In places like Singapore and India, for example, marital rape is still not a criminal offence (Gwynne 2013), while in South Africa marital rapes are given lighter sentencing if the husband followed customary laws that regard a woman's body as her husband's property (Hancox 2012). In general, women of colour are less likely to report rape than white women (Gavey 2005), and women of all races are less likely to report rape when there is a relationship between the woman and the assailant – a particular problem given that around 97 percent of women who seek help from rape crisis centres know their assailant (Berrington & Jones 2002).

There are also clear biases within judicial systems, as men of lower socio-economic groups and those of colour are much more likely to be convicted of rape due to ingrained stereotypes portraying them as inherently sexual and bestial (Benedict 1992; Matthews 1989; Moorti 2002). These issues are in continual need of addressing, and highlight the ways that sexual violence is a result not only of sexism and misogyny, but of racism, colonialism, poverty and imperialism (Bevacqua 2001; Rapp et al. 2010). And although consciousness-raising has been crucial for the development of these nuanced understandings of sexual assault, anti-rape activism has been most visible in the development of public actions such as Reclaim the Night marches, and the establishment of rape crisis centres, hotlines and prevention programmes.

Take Back/Reclaim the Night

In the 1970s, as sexual violence became increasingly recognized as a systemic issue, women began to develop strategies aimed at raising public awareness of this violence. In 1975, while walking back at night to her home in Philadelphia, microbiologist Susan Speeth was stabbed to death. In response, a group of women organized the first Take Back the Night event in an attempt to reclaim the streets as safe spaces for women (Take Back the Night 2014). Two years later, women in Leeds, UK were angered by police response to the Yorkshire Ripper murders and organized the first Reclaim the Night to 'highlight that they should be able to walk anywhere and that they should not be blamed or restricted because of male violence' (London Feminist Network 2014; Mackay 2014). In the years that followed, a number of Reclaim/Take Back the Night marches ensued, and became particularly popular events on college/university campuses. Although their popularity faded for a time, a number of cities across the US, Canada, Britain and Australia have recently revived them as annual events (see London Feminist Network 2014; Reclaim the Night Australia 2014; Take Back the Night Calgary 2014).

Rape crisis centres, hotlines and the self-defence movement

For nearly 40 years, rape crisis centres (RCC) have provided services for victims of sexual assault, and are now standard fare in many communities in the US, UK, Canada, South Africa, Australia and New Zealand (Wolburt Burgess et al. 2009). In places like India, however, where they are known as rape crisis cells or crisis intervention centres, they are generally underrepresented and under-resourced (Sharma 2014). Although the services vary from centre to centre, in general RCCs provide shelter for victims, advocacy through information about medical and legal systems, accompaniment to medical and legal appointments or court appearances, and post-rape counselling (Wolburt Burgess et al. 2009). The first rape crisis centre was established as early as 1972 in Washington, DC, and other centres began to emerge towards the end of the decade across the US, UK, Australia, South Africa, Canada and New Zealand (Gavey 2005; Rosenthall 2001). According to McNickle Rose (1977), the establishment of the RCC is one of the biggest accomplishments of the anti-rape movement.

Another brainchild of the anti-rape movement was the establishment of 24-hour hotlines, which often act as victims' first point of contact after their assault. Like RCC, rape hotlines provide counselling, information about medical issues, the criminal justice process, local resources, and support for family and friends of victims (see RAINN 2009a). Unlike rape crisis centres, however, hotlines might be preferable because victims are able to remain anonymous. While these holiness have been established in the US, Canada, Australia, South Africa, New Zealand and the UK since the 1970s and 80s, the Indian government only introduced one in 2013 after the much publicized gang rape and murder of a student on a moving bus (Gottipati 2012). Just over a year later, however, reports emerged that it was under threat of closure after lack of government funding (Nelson 2014).

While RCC and rape hotlines provide services *after* an attack, many feminists from the 1970s onwards became involved in the feminist self-defence movement, which, although a smaller subset of the feminist anti-rape movement, has been seen as a credible victim-prevention strategy (Searles & Berger 1987). This movement, which was most active in the US in the 1980s, advocated for women to attend feminist-led self-defence classes, which could teach specific physical and psychological skills that might come in useful during an attack (McCaughey 1997; Searles & Berger 1987). The movement emerged partly in response to a context in which women, the 'weaker sex,' were seen as 'natural' victims (McCaughey 1997), incapable of resisting rape. In fact the movement was a response to common advice given to women by so-called experts, to reason or plead with attackers, and then submit to rape (and even enjoy it) if these were unsuccessful to avoid further harm (Storaska 1975 cited in Searles & Berger 1987, p. 62). Critical of many 'rape prevention' tips such as staying indoors after dark, wearing baggy clothing, carrying mobile phones, walking with dogs or husbands or friends, those in the feminist self-defence movement rejected these tactics which place the onus of being safe in women's hands, and instead focused on providing women with physical and psychological skills which make them harder targets for men's abuse (McCaughey 1997).

Although the self-defence movement focused on teaching women how to use their bodies as 'weapons,' it also placed a strong focus on overcoming psychological barriers that might prevent them from fending off their attackers (Searles & Berger 1987). For instance, classes taught women to overcome their need to feel polite and not make a fuss, and instead to make lots of noise – both as a means of startling the attacker, but also to solicit help (Jenni 2010; Sanford & Fetter 1979). Classes also focused on teaching women to fend off an attacker at close quarters, recognising that rape often happens at home from family, friends or acquaintances (Jenni 2010). Although the movement gained popularity in the 1970s and 80s, its demise ultimately came from a lack of funding, as local and national governments, private foundations, churches and other women's organizations were more willing to pay for rape hotlines, RCCs and counselling than for victim-prevention programmes (Searles & Berger 1987, p. 78). Although there aren't many specific feminist self-defence classes around anymore, McCaughey (1997) argued that a cultural shift has occurred in which it is more acceptable for women to defend themselves – whether this is through the purchase of a firearm, or through some knowledge of self-defence derived from popular classes such as boxercize or cardio combat. In any case, McCaughey (1997) noted how participation in these activities challenged traditional gender norms which suggest that women are no physical match for men, and therefore presents a new form of feminist consciousness.

As evidenced above, although feminists have worked tirelessly since the 1970s to prevent sexual assault, support survivors, and keep sexual

violence on the public agenda, I argue that the global SlutWalk movement has played an important role in bringing issues of sexual assault,
rape culture and slut-shaming back onto the public agenda. Although
certainly not the only contemporary example (see the introduction
for recent initiatives), it's provocative name, sexy photo opportunities,
carnivalesque atmosphere, and appeal to a younger generation has captured the media and public's imagination in a way that long-standing
initiatives such as Reclaim the Night have failed to do, despite promoting similar messages. As London Reclaim the Night organizer Finn
Mackay (2012) explained, she found it 'depressing' that the media only
became interested in violence against women when their 'breasts are on
display and she has "slut" written across her chest in lipstick.'

As we will see in Chapters 3–5, SlutWalk has attracted not just supportive media attention, but a range of criticisms, from those accusing
the movement of everything from inherent (and sometimes blatant)
racism and perpetuating the male gaze to promoting neoliberal notions
of women's sexuality and empowerment. That SlutWalk wouldn't have
'made sense' in the 1970s or 80s, but does today is largely a result of
the postfeminist context in which this sort of Third Wave activism takes
place. These two concepts will be explored next.

Postfeminism

Over the past several years, a range of scholars around the world have
documented a shift towards a 'postfeminist' cultural climate or 'sensibility' (Douglas 2010; Gill 2007; Gwynne & Mueller 2013; McRobbie 2007,
2009; Tasker & Negra 2007). Although postfeminism can be characterized by a number of themes, including the construction of femininity as
a bodily property and the rise of makeover paradigms, more relevant to
this research is the ways this sensibility includes: a rhetoric of individualism, choice and empowerment; the resurgence of ideas about biological sexual difference; and an emphasis on surveillance, monitoring and
self-discipline (Gill 2007, p. 255). Scholars note that the current postfeminist sensibility only 'makes sense' in a culture in which feminism
has *already* been taken into account, and where women are viewed as
'autonomous agents no longer constrained by any inequalities or power
imbalances whatsoever' (Gill 2007, p. 260). As Susan Douglas (2010)
argued, in a postfeminist era, women are presented with the 'seductive
message that feminism's work is done' and are told 'empowerment' is
achieved through purchasing and sexual power rather than economic
and political power. This is perhaps most clearly identified through
discourses of empowerment, or 'Girl Power' feminism which emerged

in the 1990s as a reaction to the stereotype of ugly, unfeminine, man-hating 'women's libber' of the 1970s and 80s.

According to scholars, those embracing Girl Power celebrated their femininity/sexuality as potential sites of empowerment, while often ignoring the ways they uphold various types of oppression (Genz & Brabon 2009; Taft 2004; Zaslow 2009). For example, Girl Power feminism celebrates women's freedom to engage in sexual activity and expression, while ignoring the ways that these types of activities and expressions are tightly policed, and serve to enhance male pleasure.

As a symptom of this postfeminist sensibility, Girl Power derides tradi-tional feminist activism and theory, which are made to seem redundant either because feminist goals have already been achieved, or because feminism is thought to have failed women and created a string of new 'problems' (see Faludi 1992; Gill 2007; McRobbie 2007, 2009; Mendes 2012; Tasker & Negra 2007). Consequently, while postfeminism appears to celebrate women's new found freedoms, critics note that it wilfully misrepresents feminist goals instead (Negra 2008), and is part of an overall backlash which serves to undercut feminism's progress (Genz & Brabon 2009). It does this by increasingly drawing upon neoliberal discourses which equate consumption with freedom, liberation and empowerment, rather than collective or political action (Douglas 2010; Mendes 2012; Taft 2004; Zaslow 2009). While postfeminism and Girl Power are generally written about in a Western context, the rise of global capitalism and neoliberal ideologies means that this sensibility is increas-ingly common around the world (see Gill & Scharff 2011; Lazar 2011).

Although much research on postfeminist culture analyzes chang-ing tropes and discourses found in books (Gwynne 2013; Harzewski 2011; McRobbie 2007), magazines (Projansky 2007), film (Gwynne & Muller 2013; Negra 2008; Schreiber 2014) and TV (Munford & Waters 2014), others have paid attention to its circulation in mainstream news and feminist media production (see Darmon 2014; Gill 2007; McNicol 2012, 2015; Mendes 2011b; 2012; Shaw, F. 2011, 2012a, 2012b, 2012c, 2013; Varvus 2002, 2007). For example, these scholars note that feminists' insistence that 'personal' issues such as domestic violence and rape be considered 'political' issues are being reversed, as media commentators and journalists reframe these as unconnected, personal injustices (see Darmon 2014; Gill 2007; McNicol 2012). This is because the postfeminist focus on individualism rejects any notion that structural inequalities exist (Negra 2008), and instead frames personal circumstances or experiences as the result of individual choices – e.g. you were raped because you wore a short skirt or were out late at night.

According to those who study sexual violence, postfeminism's insistence that individuals can avoid rape in certain circumstances undermines intersectional feminist efforts to eradicate sexual violence by hiding its structural nature and its role in upholding patriarchal norms (McNicol 2012).

Yet in spite of current postfeminist sensibilities which discourage collective, political action, and blame the individual for structural issues like rape, and despite the fact that many Second Wave feminists never stopped campaigning, a new generation of feminists have started agitating for change – they are known as the Third Wave.[1]

Third wave feminism

Although postfeminism is often used interchangeably with Third Wave feminism (for a discussion, see Genz & Brabon 2009), and has been thought to have been used more widely used in the US than in say Europe or the UK (Hollows & Moseley 2007), Third Wave feminism is increasingly being understood as the next 'wave' of feminist resistance (after the First and Second). Emerging in the 1990s, scholars understand that Third Wave feminism is not the same as postfeminism, which assumes feminism's work has been achieved, but instead is made up of feminist activists who operate in a postfeminist context, as described above (Baumgardner & Richards 2000). Like Second Wave feminists before them, Third Wave activists continue to pursue many of their predecessors' struggles, but do so in different ways (Heywood & Drake 1997). As a result, Third Wave feminism has also been used (often rather unhelpfully) to indicate a generational shift which has caused tension between feminists, and has been used as a means of de-legitimizing Second Wave feminist activities (Henry 2004; Mendes 2012). On the other hand, unlike the Second Wave, which attracted criticism, particularly from black feminists, the Third Wave has been informed by postmodern critiques of identity and the individual, and often incorporates intersectional analyses from black feminist and post-colonial theory and does not necessarily regard gender as the key, or only, area of oppression (Genz & Brabon 2009; Reed 1997). As a result, Third Wave feminist activism is extremely diverse (Maddison 2013a), and unlike the Second Wave, which had clearly identifiable goals, organizations and even leaders (Henry 2004), the Third Wave doesn't have an easily identifiable presence but, is instead made up of 'hubs that are unique to this generation' (Baumgardner & Richards 2000, p. 79). While these 'hubs' are increasingly found online, they do of course take form in offline spaces, as we saw with SlutWalk.

Another key characteristic of the Third Wave is its engagement with digital, do-it-yourself media (Keller 2013; Zobl & Drueke 2012). Although Third Wavers are interested in 'politics,' they pay particular attention to cultural activism, which scholars argue has long been ignored as activist practice (Harris 2008a; Keller 2013; Piepmeier 2009; Young 1997). This cultural activism includes textual and cultural production such as culture jamming, zine-making or blogging, where the aim is to raise feminist consciousness rather than forming large-scale social justice movements, or bringing about legislative or government change (Henry 2004; p. 43; Piepmeier 2009). As we will come to see through this book, the proliferation of SlutWalk Facebook groups, Twitter accounts, and other local events indicates the various ways Third Wave activists engage in discursive politics and activism by disrupting hegemonic discourses on rape and rape culture.

Third wave engagement with media and popular culture

Unlike the Second Wave, which was frequently critiqued for being too 'academic,' the Third Wave has been credited for shifting the feminist agenda to a greater analysis of mass media and popular culture (Heywood & Drake 1997; Mowles 2008). Particularly relevant to this project then are the ways in which Third Wave feminists have engaged with digital media (mostly blogs) to challenge rape culture, promote women's equality, and intervene more generally in patriarchal hegemonic discourses (see Keller 2013; Mowles 2008; Rentschler 2014; Shaw, F. 2011, 2012a, 2013). While SlutWalk has no doubt been successful in bringing discussions about rape culture back into the mainstream, it is neither the first, nor the only initiative to do so. For example, in 2005, a group of New York residents founded the organization Hollaback! after experiencing and witnessing many instances of street harassment. Citizens are encouraged to use smartphone technologies and web applications to document their experiences of harassment, and even name and shame harassers through capturing images/video of offensive behaviour. The organization's purpose is not just to shame perpetrators, but also to highlight the pervasiveness of harassment in women's everyday lives, identify harassment 'hot spots,' and spark public conversations about this issue (Hollaback! 2014). Operating in 79 cities in 26 countries, Hollaback! is just one of many similar Third Wave initiatives of this type. In Egypt, the site Harassmap was founded in 2010, and aims to end the social acceptability of sexual harassment and assault of women in public spaces by allowing women to anonymously report and map instances of harassment (Harassmap 2013). And in 2012, the British feminist Laura Bates established *The Everyday Sexism Project* where individuals email or tweet their experiences of sexism, which are posted on its website. Bates established the project as a response to frequent claims that sexism was no longer a problem because gender equality has been achieved (The Everyday Sexism Project 2014).

Third wave bloggers

While these initiatives are likely to be easily identifiable as types of feminist activism, others argue that activism is also taking place in perhaps less obvious forms. For example, Keller (2013, forthcoming) argued that networks of feminist bloggers are participating in feminist activism when they blog about a range of issues, including rape culture. As one of her study participants wrote: 'It was through blogging that I realized changing policies isn't the only way to define activism – I think activism is also about changing hearts and minds, which is what I do (or try to do) when I blog' (Keller 2013, p. 6). This project, like others, challenges the frequent dismissal of blogs – labelled the equivalent of modern diary-writing – as a site of feminine narrative and cultural production (Karlsson 2007). Instead, along with others, I argue that blogs should be recognized as sites of (potential) feminist activism, as they help to raise consciousness about a range of inequalities and systems of oppression, and counter them through discursive interventions (Keller 2013; Shaw 2012b).

The proliferation of Third Wave feminist activism and blogging is becoming increasingly difficult to ignore. For example, a number of Third Wave feminist blogs such as *Feministing, The F-Word, The Vagenda, Hoyden Around Town, Feminist Current* and *The F-Bomb* have become incredibly successful, drawing in thousands of hits per week. Some of these blogs have even translated into successful books including *Feministing* founder Jessica Valenti's *Full Frontal Feminism* (2007), *The F-Word* founder Catherine Redfern's *Reclaiming the F-Word* (with Kristin Aune 2010), *The Vagenda* creators Rhiannon Lucy Cosslett and Holly Baxter's book by the same name (2014). Newspapers are not only covering SlutWalk marches, but report on feminist Twitter campaigns such as #FBRape and #Yesallwomen – the former of which pressured Facebook to tighten its policy on removing misogynistic content, and the latter resulted in widespread discussion about the pervasive nature of sexual assault, harassment and misogyny after the 2014 Isla-Vista shootings in California. Although these interventions deal with serious issues, as feminists have done for decades, they are often creative, playful, 'fun,' carnivalesque, and make use of sarcasm, irony and ridicule to identify and critique oppressive ideologies. And because the news media are a key site of disseminating and upholding a range of oppressive ideologies, they are a target for many Third Wave feminist critiques. These critiques only make sense, however, when we first review the highly damaging ways that sexual violence has historically been represented in mainstream news media.

Representations of violence against women

As a key feminist issue, representations of rape and sexual violence in the media have long been the subject of academic inquiry for feminists. As noted by Kitzinger (2009), the media is a key space in which rape is defined, and as a result, shapes the public's perceptions on what rape is, who commits it, and why. Furthermore, Kitzinger argued that, 'Coverage can decontextualize abuse, encourage racism, promote stereotypes of women (as virgins or whores), blame victims and excuse assailants' (Kitzinger 2009, p. 76). Although other scholars have examined representations of sexual violence in fictional arenas such as literature, television, film and gaming (see Berridge 2015; Cuklanz 2000; Moorti 2002; Projansky 2001), this chapter will focus on literature surrounding sexual violence in the news media.

Sexual violence in the news

Since the late 1800s, scholars have noted how sexual violence and exploitation around women and children 'makes good copy' (Kitzinger 2009, p. 75) – from news of Jack the Ripper in the 1880s in the UK, to the Scarborough Rapist in the 1980s in Canada, to the recent gang rape and murder of a New Delhi student on a moving bus in 2012 – these are the types of stories which prompt outrage, fear, sadness and anger – emotional draws which are used to shift papers and make money (Soothill & Walby 1991; Worthington 2010). Although high-profile sexual assaults and murders have long been included in mainstream newspapers, rape on its own was largely ignored before the 1970s, when feminist activists put it on the public agenda, challenging the belief that rape was rare or exceptional (Kitzinger 2009, p. 77; see also Soothill & Walby 1991). It was also during the 1970s that the news media, particularly in the UK, became increasingly sexualized, and newspapers were interested in the lurid details involving sexual assault (Carter 1998). As a result of these changes, there has been an abundance of research into how the mainstream news media all around the globe reports rape and sexual assault (see Alat 2006; Benedict 1992; Bonnes 2013; Carter 1998; Durham 2013;

McManus & Dorfman 2005; Meyer 2010; Meyers 1997, 2006; Soothill & Walby 1991; Worthington 2008). Common areas of focus in these studies include representations of victims and perpetrators, the causes of rape, and the development and perpetuation of rape myths.

Representing rape victims

When reviewing the literature on representations of sexual assault across the globe, one key trope is that, regardless of the type of assault (domestic abuse, rape, sexual harassment), the news media blame victims for their assault. Scholars have found this to be particularly true if the victims are women of colour, knew their assailant, drank alcohol, dressed provocatively, were not virgins, or worked in the sex industry (Benedict 1992; Bonnes 2013; Cuklanz 1996; Meyer 2010; Meyers 2006; Soothill & Walby 1991; Worthington 2008). The news media help assign blame or innocence through a (lack of) detailed description of victims – their names, ages, occupations, appearance and marital status (Alat 2006; Clark 1992). The news media also assign blame through their description of the victim's behaviour on the night of the assault. For example, Meyer's (2010) study found that binge drinking was seen as a provocation for rape, and any victim was thereby 'asking for it' by drinking excessively (p. 23). Similarly, research into the rape trial of South Africa's former Deputy, and current President, Jacob Zuma also found that the victim's attire (a traditional kanga) was seen by her attacker as a sign of consent for the sexual encounter that took place (Worthington 2010).

In many cases, the news media blame victims for being unable to thwart their attacker (Carter 1998), creating the impression that women who are raped simply did not try hard enough to get away. In other cases, victims are blamed for not following common 'rape prevention' tips, which include ensuring your drink is never left alone (in case it's spiked), having a buddy system during nights out, not walking home alone at night or if drunk, and so forth. These narratives are based on the premise, perpetuated by the media, that rape is a crime committed by strangers, rather than someone the victim already knows (Carter 1998; Soothill & Walby 1991). Instead, everyday acts of violence which take place between spouses, partners, families, friends and acquaintances are ignored in favour of unusual or gruesome cases which, in reality, are much rarer (Carter 1998).

Representing rapists: a few bad apples or just your average guy?

One key feminist goal since the 1970s has been to re-conceptualize rape from a crime of passion and sex, to one of power, violence and control (Benedict 1992). In doing so, it challenges the notion that sexual assault is a crime committed by a few 'bad apples,' and instead recognizes the way it has historically been used as a tool to maintain (male) dominance and (female) oppression. Although there is evidence that feminist understandings are becoming increasingly common (see Durham 2013), research continues to show that rape is still explained as men's inability to control their lust (Alat 2006; Bonnes 2013). Such constructions are rooted in hegemonic ideologies in which men are 'naturally' sexual, and driven by primitive urges which have been ingrained for centuries (Hasinoff 2009). Because such views are rooted in biology, they are particularly difficult to challenge. And because some men are constructed as more inherently sexual than others (poor black men, for example), we see their over-representation in news stories concerning attempted or successful rapes (Benedict 1992; Rapp et al. 2010).

For example, while Benedict (1992) found that instances of rape were more likely to make the news if the perpetrator was black (and the victim was white), it is not only in North America or the Western world where race plays a role in the cultural imagining of who commits rape. In South Africa, Bonnes (2013) highlighted how rape is often associated with poor, black men, and is often seen as a legacy of apartheid (see also Maitse 1998). Similarly, Gwynne (2013) noted how only 'foreigners' are constructed as committing rape in Singapore, while its native citizens are seen as law-abiding individuals. Scholars such as Moffett (2006) have argued that narratives which understand rape as primarily a 'race' issue are problematic because they further ingrained racism, and make educational efforts to prevent rape nearly impossible.

Another problem with media representations of alleged rapists is that they tend to personalize the perpetrators, constructing them as nice people, a good friend, or an outstanding member of the community (Bonnes 2013). In doing so, the media fuels the belief that 'real' rapists are all monsters and psychopaths, and cannot also be 'nice' or ordinary men who may very well do good for their communities. As a result, when it comes to trials, it becomes difficult for juries to reconcile the fact that 'nice' men can also be guilty of rape, and juries become sceptical and prone to believe the victim must be lying (Bonnes 2013; Kitzinger 2009). The belief that women commonly lie about rape is one of the most pervasive rape myths in circulation.

Rape myths

In reviewing the literature on news of sexual assault, it becomes clear that the media perpetuate a number of 'rape myths' which are embedded in news discourses. These rape myths include the following beliefs:

> [W]omen enjoy rape (say no when they mean yes); women provoke rape (by the way they dress, by going out alone, by accepting lifts); only certain – unrespectable – women are raped; women make false accusations of rape (for revenge or to protect their reputation); rape is committed by maniacs (ill, sick, stressed, out of control); rapists are in the grip of impulsive, uncontrollable sexual urges; most rapists are strangers. (Coppock et al. 1995 cited in McNicol 2012, p. viii)

The prevalence of rape myths in the news media normalizes preferred ways of understanding rape for the reader, specifically that male sexual violence is a typical, if not inevitable part of everyday life (Carter 1998; Meyers 2006). This socializes women into both fearing and accepting male sexual and physical violence (Berrington & Jones 2002). Furthermore, rape myths provide the impetus to raise the following questions: Was it a 'legitimate' or 'proper' rape, where the victim a) did not know her attacker, and b) experienced violence and/or weapons used against her in the assault? Did the woman 'provoke' the man through her attire, dress or behaviour? Is there evidence that the woman is in fact 'crying rape,' perhaps in an attempt to seek revenge on a man, or to save face or her reputation? The identification of these rape myths in news coverage of sexual assault all around the globe has led to calls for change in journalistic practices (see Carter 1998).

Calling for change: improving journalistic practices

The prevalence of patriarchal, classist and racist ideologies in the global news media, expressed through rape myths, flags up a serious need not only to challenge journalistic practices in the reporting of sexual violence, but to improve public education on the nature of rape more generally (see Byerly 1994; McKinney 2006). This includes defining rape as an act of violence that often leads to trauma for the survivor, educating the public on the nature of rape (including de-bunking the myth that stranger rape is the most prevalent form of sexual assault), and refraining from reporting graphic details about the assault (McKinney 2006). While representations of rape are undoubtedly shaped by dominant social attitudes, scholars argue they are also framed by internal media dynamics including institutional racism and sexism, as well as news values which prize sensationalism and focus on specific events rather than issues (Carter 1998; Kitzinger 2009; Worthington 2010). Clearly then, while calling for journalists to move beyond old ways of reporting rape is laudable, more needs to be done to address the systemic sexist and racist nature of the institutions themselves. Recently at least, there appears to be a renewed focus on the organizational nature of news media outlets, and questions are once again being raised about the gendered and racial makeup of news organizations, as well as their policies for ensuring diversity and equality (see Byerly 2013; Joseph 2005; North 2009; Poindexter et al. 2008).

While there has been an abundance of research on news of sexual assault, I want to spend the next section reviewing literature on the ways feminism has been represented in popular culture, before examining specific research on representations of anti-rape movements, such as Reclaim/Take Back the Night, or more recently, SlutWalk.

Representing feminism

Not long after the Second Wave women's movement emerged in many parts of the world, feminist scholars became interested in its representations in the mainstream news media (see Ashley & Olson 1998; Barker-Plummer 2000; Bradley 2003; Costain et al. 1997; Douglas 1994; Freeman 2001; Goddu 1999; Mendes 2011a, 2015; Morris 1973a; Pingree & Hawkins 1978; Sheridan et al. 2007; Tuchman 1978; van Zoonen 1992). This was largely due to the recognition that the news media was a key source of information on social movements (Barker-Plummer 2000; Gitlin 2003; Rhode 1995; van Zoonen 1992). Not only do the news media indicate that activism is occurring, but their coverage provides an interpretive framework for how the movement is understood (Hall et al. 1978). Journalists not only tend to reproduce the social order in their coverage, but they are also quick to identify abnormal behaviour as inherently newsworthy, and suggest appropriate responses as a result (Ericson et al. 1987; Wardle 2004). Feminists in particular have risked being cast as 'deviant,' as they demanded equal access to the public sphere and challenged a range of patriarchal ideologies about (middle-class, white) women which construct them as passive, asexual, heterosexual, maternal, unskilled, irrational and so forth (Mendes 2011a).

Because feminism challenges patriarchal ideologies, scholars have noted how feminists are constructed as deviant, shrill, radical, man-hating lesbians, with feminism being turned into a dirty word (see Bradley 2003;

Douglas 1994; Freeman 2001; Goddu 1999; Lind & Salo 2002; Pingree & Hawkins 1978). Others, however, have found that the media at times supported feminism and feminist goals, so long as they did not fundamentally challenge patriarchal ideologies and conventional notions of femininity (see Dean 2010; Freeman 2001; Mendes 2011a; van Zoonen 1992).

Given the news media's love for declaring feminism 'dead,' it is perhaps unsurprising to note that scholars have paid particular attention to women's activism in a postfeminist era (for exceptions see Dean 2010; Douglas 2010; Hinds & Stacey 2001; Jaworska & Krishnamurthy 2012; Kolesova 2013; Lind & Salo, 2002; McNicol 2012; Mendes 2012; Whelehan 2000; Walter 2010). These studies have found that feminism is constructed as a deeply individualized and personalized ideology, with little discussion of collective feminist activism (Mendes 2012). Furthermore, just as the media honed in on so-called 'catfights' between radical and liberal feminists in the Second Wave (Douglas 1994; Mendes 2011a; van Zoonen 1992), contemporary media has focused on generational conflict between Second and Third Wave feminists, labelling the former as 'old-school' and 'retro' and the latter as 'modern,' 'fun' and 'sexy' (Mendes 2012, p. 562). Although there are some real theoretical differences between these feminist waves, scholars have argued that coverage labelling the Second Wave feminism as redundant contributes to an overall backlash towards feminism and its push for radical change (Mendes 2012).

In recent years, along with SlutWalk, feminism has attracted mainstream media attention. Inspired by the riot grrrl movement, the Russian punk group Pussy Riot attracted international headlines for their guerrilla performance and subsequent trial after they criticized President Vladimir Putin through song in a Moscow church. The Ukrainian feminist group Femen has also attracted international coverage for their controversial activities, including topless protests. As detailed in the introduction and earlier in this chapter, feminists are also attracting media attention through their various online campaigns. And while some research has already begun on these new sites of feminist activism (see Carr 2013; Darmon 2014; Keller 2013; Kolesova 2013; McNicol 2012; Mendes et al. 2014; Rentschler 2014; Shaw, F. 2011, 2012a, 2012b, 2013), I anticipate more will emerge in coming years.

Representing anti-rape movements

Despite the emergence of anti-rape movements around the world in the 1970s and 80s, there is an almost complete lack of research examining their representations in the media (for exceptions, see Jacquet 2010).

Instead, most work on anti-rape activism has been to document the histories of the movement (Bevacqua 2001, 2008; Matthews 2005; Mayne 2003; McNickle Rose 1977; Ward 1995), its impact on public policy (Corrigan 2013; Gornick & Meyer 1998), its political messages (Prominski 2012) and the experiences of its participants (Chateauvert 2013; White 2001), or to address controversies within the movement, such as claims of racism and lack of diversity (Mackay 2014; Matthews 1989).

Although just a burgeoning movement, academic articles on SlutWalk have already began to emerge (see Borah & Nandi 2012; Carr 2013; Dow & Wood 2014; Gwynne 2013; Kapur 2012; Maddison 2013a; McCormack & Prostran 2012; McNicol 2012, 2015; Mendes 2015; O'Keefe 2011; Ringrose & Renold 2012).[2] These studies include those exploring the merits of SlutWalk and its emancipatory potential (O'Keefe 2011); the ways Slutwalk was adapted to suit the cultural and political climate of non-Western cultures (Carr 2013; Gwynne 2013); the ways teenagers engaged with Slutwalk's politics (Ringrose & Renold 2012); SlutWalk as a key site of debate and discourse within contemporary feminist activism (Dow & Wood 2014; Maddison 2013a; Mendes 2015); and those sharing first-hand accounts of attending Slutwalk (McCormack & Prostran 2012). As with other types of anti-rape activism, some also examine how it has been represented in the media (for exceptions, see Carr 2013; Darmon 2014; McNicol 2012, 2015; Mendes 2015). For the most part, however, these studies have focused on representations in a single nation (for exceptions, see Carr 2013; Mendes 2015) – a gap this research seeks to fill.

McNicol (2012), for example, argued that the Canadian news media largely regarded SlutWalk as a serious political movement, devoting a surprising amount of attention to it. However, she postulated that overall, the news media presented a 'watered-down version of feminism,' which failed to contextualize the root cause and impact of sexual violence (McNicol 2012, p. ii). In her analysis of SlutWalk in mainstream British news media, Darmon (2014) similarly argued that the movement's political underpinnings were ignored in favour of a focus on the personal. And in my own research, I found that the label 'feminism' was rarely attached to the movement, raising questions of whether it was purposefully erased or ignored (Mendes 2015). When exploring how the news media addressed slut-shaming and victim-blaming – key issues highlighted by the movement, McNicol argued they were constructed as problems emerging from 'individual ignorance' about sexual violence, rather than from a 'rape culture that normalizes misogyny and men's violence against women' (2012, p. 55). Consequently, although McNicol concluded that coverage of SlutWalk marked a 'huge improvement' on reporting of sexual violence, it continued to construct sexual violence as an 'inevitable part of women's lives' (2012, p. 69), and thus failed to dismantle or challenge rape-culture. This is something I will address in my own research.

Social media

There is no denying that social media are increasingly important tools for information, communication and leisure for many people all around the world (Shirky 2011). According to boyd and Ellison (2007), social media (also known as social networking sites or SNS) are defined as web-based services that are used to create public or semi-public profiles, build networks with other users, and view and traverse other users' profiles and networks. And while scholars are interested in many aspects of social media, such as its use among youths (boyd forthcoming), or to form networked publics (boyd 2008, 2010; Keller 2013), relevant to this research are those who have examined it in relation to social activism and protest (for recent examples, see Castells 2007, 2012; Gerbaudo 2012; Juris 2012; Shaw 2012b; Shirky 2011). As scholars note, despite being used mostly for entertainment purposes (Gerbaudo 2012), social media have become coordinating tools for nearly all political movements around the world (Castells 2012; Shirky 2011), and are the contemporary equivalent of the newspaper, leaflet and poster for many movements (Gerbaudo 2012). According to Lim (2013), there is 'nothing intrinsic in social media that automatically makes it promote social change or advance democracy,' but in the right conditions, 'social and cultural participation in social media spheres may translate into civic or political engagement' (p. 3). And while the range of SNS used in modern protest are as diverse as the individual activists using them (Gerbaudo 2012), outlets such as Facebook, Twitter, Tumblr and other microblogging sites have been particularly important for SlutWalk and will be discussed below.

Facebook

Founded in 2004 by Harvard student Mark Zuckerburg, Facebook is an online social media platform in which individuals (aged 13 and above) create a personal profile and connect to others through their friends list. One of the world's most popular social networks, it is estimated that in the first quarter of 2014, an average of 802 million people used the site every day, while 1.28 billion accessed it at least once a month (Facebook 2014a). Although the site is continually changing, at the time of this writing, individuals can use Facebook to post status updates, photos, videos, and links to external sites, send private messages to other users, add comments, share or 'like' others' posts. In addition to their individual page, which hosts a timeline, 'about' section, list of friends and photos, Facebook also allows the creation of 'events' to which individuals are invited and asked to indicate if they are attending or not (they can also select maybe). Although most SlutWalks use these events pages to promote their marches, they also use them for prep days (where individuals make signs for the walk), meet and greets, film screenings (of feminist films), self-defence seminars, panel discussions and fundraising events (such as poker nights and bingo).

Facebook also allows individuals to create group pages where users can post updates, poll the group and start group chats. Group pages offer three security levels: secret groups (only members can see that the group exists, who is in it and what is posted); closed groups (anyone can see that the group exists and who is in it, but not what members post); open groups (anyone can see that the group exists, who is in it and what is posted) (Facebook 2014b). SlutWalk's main presence on Facebook is via open group pages, which anyone can see. However, they also have a number of secret groups which organizers around the world use to share ideas, planning tips and advice (Castieau 2012; Delgado 2014a; Jarvis 2012).

Facebook is particularly important for SlutWalk because this was the platform that sparked the movement. Not only was it the space where co-founder Heather Jarvis first read the article about Michael Sanguinetti's slut-shaming comments, but it is where she shared the article on her Facebook page and connected with Sonya Barnett. The two then then created a SlutWalk Toronto Facebook page, website and Twitter account to publicize the first march (Jarvis 2012). As Jarvis stated, having an online presence was crucial because it is where people have well-established connections and communities. She added that operating online was the only viable route for the movement because they lacked office space, money and status as an official organization. Since the first march, Facebook has continued to be an important tool used to promote marches, discuss issues such as rape culture, and to share ideas, plan events, and even debate and discuss issues within the movement (Delgado 2014a; Jarvis 2012). For example, SlutWalk Seattle organizer Laura Delgado explained that in addition to sharing planning tips, the secret SlutWalk groups had been used to challenge whorephobic practices in other satellite groups. For example, SlutWalk Phoenix organizers were criticized for shaming sex workers and were eventually kicked out of one secret group. Delgado (2014a) insisted, however, that any of these groups would be welcomed back if they changed their practices. What is particularly interesting about these secret SlutWalk groups, is that there are a number of different groups, none of which are controlled by SlutWalk Toronto, indicating the grass-roots and decentralized nature of the movement.[3]

Twitter

Launched in 2006, Twitter is a popular social networking and micro-blogging site, which allows users to post 140 character updates or 'tweets' to a network. In 2014, Twitter reported that it had 255 million monthly active users and that 500 million tweets were sent daily (Twitter 2014). Unlike Facebook, where users can set privacy settings so that only friends can see their profiles, all tweets are publicly available, although only registered users can post them, and users can choose to 'follow' certain individuals whose tweets are collated in reverse chronological order on one's Twitter home page. Unlike blogs or social media platforms such as Facebook, there are no options to comment on a tweet (boyd et al. 2010). However, it is common to reply to a tweet by including the Twitter user's handle (or name), which begins with an '@' sign.

With Twitter, there are also various ways to post messages, depending on the desired outcome. Users can attempt to draw attention to certain topics/events by prefacing them with a hashtag (e.g. #SlutWalk). These hashtags are searchable via the Twitter website, and hashtags which become widely used can 'trend,' drawing more attention to the topic. In addition to hashtags, users can draw attention to individuals by using their username, prefaced with an '@' sign (e.g. @SlutWalk). This is known as @replies, and is commonly used to identify people, address tweets to particular users, attribute quotes and get their attention (Honeycutt & Herring 2009 cited in Marwick & boyd 2011, p. 143). When Twitter users want to share a tweet, they have the option of re-tweeting it via a button on their Twitter account page, which is the Twitter equivalent of forwarding an email (boyd et al. 2010). According to boyd et al. (2010) there are a number of reasons for re-tweeting, including:

> To amplify or spread tweets to new audiences; To entertain or inform a specific audience, or as an act of curation; To comment on some-one's tweet by retweeting and adding new content, often to begin a

conversation; To make one's presence as a listener visible; To publicly agree with someone; To validate others' thoughts; As an act of friendship, loyalty, or homage by drawing attention, sometimes via a retweet request; To recognize or refer to less popular people or less visible content; For self-gain, either to gain followers or reciprocity from more visible participants; To save tweets for future personal access. (p. 6)

While re-tweeting is a common practice, so too is sharing links to other sites (boyd et al. 2010). In their analysis of over 720,000 tweets, boyd et al. (2010) found that 22 percent contained a URL (p. 4). This indicates that Twitter is not only used to provide brief 'news' updates, but direct people to external sites to which they can click through to get further information.

Twitter is frequently discussed in social movement research as an effective method of 'e-mobilization' (Earl & Kimport 2011 cited in Penney & Dadas 2014, p. 80), providing protesters with information on where and when to meet. Although Twitter has been used as a tool to debate issues within various social movements, many activists agree it is not the best platform for in-depth discussions (Lim 2013; Penney & Dadas 2014). Twitter, it then seems, is used in conjunction with a range of other social media platforms, creating what Penney & Dadas (2014) refer to as one tool in a larger 'digital ecosystem,' which allows activists to communicate with one another and bypass the media in publicizing their concerns. In their analysis of Twitter in the Occupy Movement, they identified seven key functions that Twitter served including:

[F]acilitating face-to-face protests via advertisements and donation solicitations; live reporting from face-to-face protests; forwarding news via links and retweets; expressing personal opinions regarding the movement; engaging in discussion about the movement; making personal connections with fellow activists; and facilitating online-based actions. (p. 79)

Researchers have also commented on Twitter's function as a tactical device during protest, which is used to share real time information (e.g. giving people directions on what to do, how to avoid police crowd-control operations, etc.) (Gerbaudo 2012; Penney & Dadas 2014). To my knowledge, however, such crucial, 'real time' information has been less important for SlutWalk, which has not been met with police resistance or crowd-control measures.

Tumblr, WordPress and blogging

A web log, or a blog, is a 'webpage with periodic, reverse chronologically ordered content, posted by an individual or group' (Mowles 2008, p. 30). Many (but not all) blogs are frequently updated, are personal in nature, and encourage interaction via a comment section, blogroll (a hyperlinked list of blogs), and embedded links to other websites or blogs (Keller 2013). While there are many platforms in which one can create a blog, Tumblr is one of the more popular sites, hosting 190 million blogs in 13 languages (Tumblr 2014). WordPress is also extremely popular and claims to be the largest self-hosted blogging tool in the world, 'seen by tens of millions of people every day' (WordPress n.d.). Tumblr and WordPress have been singled out here because they host most of the feminist blogs included in this research.

Although scholars have focused heavily on the role that Twitter and Facebook have played in social movements, less attention has been paid to the role of blogging. Gerbaudo (2012), for example, discussed how the Tumblr blog 'We are the 99%,' functioned as a symbolic rallying point and emotional conduit for the Occupy Movement (p. 14). The blog asked individuals to photograph themselves holding a sign with a message detailing how they have been victims of the economic crisis. Tumblr (and Facebook) hosted a similar feminist campaign 'I need feminism because ...' whereby individuals photographed themselves with a sign indicating why feminism is still necessary and relevant. These forms of activism are important because they provide women the opportunity to 'talk back' to a culture in which their voices are generally undervalued and marginalized (see Keller 2011). Furthermore, they allow for a greater variety of voices to enter into public discourse (Harp et al. 2014).

Although blogs have largely been overlooked by (mainly male) social movement scholars, feminist media researchers have identified them as important spaces for the formation of networks, communities and counterpublics which seek to disrupt hegemonic ideologies about issues such as feminism, sexual assault and rape culture (Keller 2013; Mowles 2008; Rentschler 2014; Shaw, F. 2011, 2012a, 2012b, 2012c). While blogs can be linked to other social media platforms such as Facebook and Twitter, blogging is not inherently about promoting or maintaining social ties. Yet despite this, feminist bloggers have managed to develop communities through blogrolls, re-blogging a post (much like re-tweeting), inviting contributions from other female bloggers, participating on comment boards, and providing links to other feminist blogs in their own posts (Harp et al. 2014; Keller forthcoming). In this way, a range of individual feminist blogs are able to function as a collective community (Keller 2013; Shaw 2012b). As such, scholars such as Keller (2011) argue that feminist blogging should not been dismissed as merely a 'passing trend,' but recognized as a 'significant practice for the future of feminism' (p. 443).

Social movements in a modern era

From the Spanish Indignados to Occupy Wall Street, from the Arab Spring to the Global Justice movement, all around the world, millions of people each year are mobilizing to pursue social, cultural, political and economic change. While most of the movements we hear about through the mainstream media have hundreds to thousands of supporters and might consist of an organized chain of command, others are much smaller and may only involve a handful of people, with little to no resources or formal structure. Similarly, although people continue to aggregate in public spaces through mass demonstrations, marches and protests, much activity takes place online. Given the diverse nature of people's participation, this section will outline how 'activism' is a contentious concept in both mainstream culture and scholarly literature (Keller 2013; Piepmeier 2009; Taft 2011). Even within social movement theory itself, there is debate about the extent to which 'new' social movements – or those based around cultural issues and identity – are in fact new. Frank and Fuentes (1987), for example, argue that individuals have protested many similar cultural and personal injustices for centuries (more rights for women, gays, people of colour; better distribution of wealth, etc).

Yet, as scholars debate and theorize differences between social movements, what has become clear is that the world has experienced rapid technological changes over the past 20 years, which have resulted in a fundamental shift in the ways social movements function (Wolfson 2012, p. 150). Namely, this shift revolves around the growing importance of new media technologies, the internet and social networking sites to build, organize, network, choreograph physical assembly and collective identities (see Atkinson 2009; Castells 2007, 2009, 2012; Diani & McAdam 2003; Downing 2000; Gerbaudo 2012; Juris 2008; Staggenborg 2008). A central concept in this shift is the idea of the network – one of the key markers of difference between 'old' and 'new' movements. Whereas 'old' social movements were characterized by rigid hierarchies, 'new' social movements are thought to have much less (if any) formal hierarchies or identifiable leaders, and operate on consensual decision making processes (Juris 2008).[4] According to

Diani (2003), new social movements can be described as 'a network of informal interactions between a plurality of individuals, groups and/or organizations, engaged in a political or cultural conflict on the basis of a shared collective identity' (cited in Marmura 2008, p. 249). Because these networked social movements operate online, they have greater capacity to spread their message, recruit new members, organize events, raise funds, lobby policy makers, and more (Marmura 2008). Although networks certainly existed before the internet, new technologies are enabling these connections to form faster, in more dispersed geographical locations, more equitably and efficiently, and often cheaper than ever before (Castells 2007; Juris 2012; Puente 2011).

Despite this, Gerbaudo (2012) warns that these new, networked social movements are neither entirely spontaneously as many suggest, or operate free from hierarchy, as every movement has leaders and followers and requires organization (p. 19; see also Freeman 1972). Instead, he prefers to conceptualize social media as the tools used to help movements *choreograph assembly*. This involves directing people towards specific events, providing participants with suggestions and instructions on how to act, and constructing an 'emotional narration' which underpins their physical gathering (p. 12). Gerbaudo identified these choreographers as 'soft leaders' and although are frequently invisible, play an important role in harnessing and directing participants' emotions (2012, p. 159). Furthermore, Gerbaudo argued that social media not only acts as a means of assembling bodies, but as an emotional conduit which builds a sense of togetherness, even when participants are geographically fragmented. Although I agree that Gerbaudo's research presents useful development in social movement theory, I find it concerning that the physical aggregation of bodies on the streets is inherently seen as more valuable than the discussion and political theorization which takes place online. In response, scholars have developed theories which understand the importance of the virtual sphere. These include networked publics and counterpublics.

Networked publics and counterpublics

In order to understand the concept of networked publics or counterpublics, one first must be familiar with Jurgen Habermas' (1989) famous essay on the structural transformation of the public sphere, which outlined the importance of public spaces in which individuals come together to talk, debate and form opinions. Habermas discussed the public sphere as a crucial part of a healthy democracy, in which everyone was welcome to come together as equals and discuss issues of public concern. Although Habermas's theory was criticized by many, one of the most well-known is that by feminist academic Nancy Fraser (1990). Where Habermas talked about the public sphere as a space open to all individuals who were free to discuss a range of social, economic and political issues and reach consensus, Fraser (1990) pointed out that in fact many groups, such as women or the working class, were excluded from these publics and resultantly formed their own *subaltern counterpublics*. These counterpublics are not only places where marginalized groups withdraw and regroup, but spaces where they plan agitation and protest activities directed at wider publics (p. 68). Consequently, a key function of counterpublics is wider social transformation (see also Warner 2002). Both these concepts, the public sphere and counterpublics are important for this book, as well as the way scholars have adapted them in light of technological developments.

For example, new media scholar danah boyd combined the concepts of networks and publics to theorize the concept of 'networked publics' (boyd 2008, 2010), which she defined as publics that have been restructured by network technologies. Like other types of publics, boyd (2010) argued that networked publics provide a space for people to gather for social, cultural, and civic purposes, and connect individuals with a world beyond their close friends and family. Accordingly, social media sites are networked publics because of the ways in which they connect many people and provide space for interactions and information (2010, p. 45). And while this concept is undoubtedly useful for mainstream groups to come together to interact with one another and discuss issues, like Habermas' theory of the public sphere, it does not fully address the ways that marginalized groups create their own subaltern *networked counterpublics* in virtual spaces. For example, feminist media scholar Jessalynn M. Keller (2013), has discussed the ways feminists have used social media platforms and blogs to form their own *networked counterpublics* which emerge 'around particular discursive feminist identities and issues, coming together, dissolving, and reconvening in a fluid manner' (p. 160). This concept will be particularly useful in Chapters 5 and 6, which focus on SlutWalk's use of feminist and social media to transform discourse on sexual assault and rape culture.

Online to offline activism

When reviewing the literature on contemporary social movements, one of the key areas of focus has been on how online tools facilitate offline activism (see Atkinson 2009; Castells 2012; Gerbaudo 2012; Harlow 2011; Juris 2012; Lim 2013; Madianou 2013; Marmura 2008; Penney &

Dadas 2014; Wolfson 2012). The assumption being that offline activity is the space where the 'real' activism takes place, while ignoring the discursive activities which are aimed at bringing about radical change to dominant ideologies (Young 1997). There is also evidence that this view is not only held by academics, but by many contemporary activists as well. For example, Gerbaudo (2012) relayed how Egypt's Mubarak government in the 2011 uprisings attempted to discredit the movement by ridiculing activists as 'Facebook people' and armchair revolutionaries who would not make the jump from 'screens to streets' (p. 160). The Spanish Indignados also apparently chanted 'We are not on Facebook, we are on the streets' (p. 160). While I do not argue against the importance of physical gatherings for many contemporary social movements, I would caution against making broad statements about the inferiority of online activism, particularly because scholars such as Keller (2013) have noted that offline activism is not always possible for certain groups. This could be due to age (too old or young), location (not living in a city in which the demonstrations take place, or live in a rural area without access to a vehicle or public transportation), ability, or class (lack of funds needed to travel). In her research on girl feminist bloggers, Keller (2013) noted that many young women would have liked to attend protests such as SlutWalk, but lived too far away and lacked the financial resources to attend. Because not everyone who wants to participate in offline activism can, they often turn their attention online, which become increasingly important sites of activism.

As Zobl and Drueke (2012) have noted, feminists have long recognized the importance of self-managed, alternative media in movements for social justice. As new technologies emerged, women have continued to use them for the production and distribution of feminist media. Although much of this activity includes the production of zines, newsletters and magazines, with the rise of social media, a number of other, usually feminist researchers, are also interested in how feminist media are used to conduct virtual activism (see Chattopadhyay 2011; Harp et al. 2014; Keller 2013, forthcoming; Mowles 2008; Puente 2011; Rapp et al. 2010; Rentschler 2014; Shaw, F. 2011, 2012a, 2012b, 2013). While social media platforms such as Twitter, Facebook or YouTube certainly play an important role in movements, scholars have noted the ways they do not 'encourage long conversations' (Lim 2013, p. 16). Similarly, Penney and Dadas (2014) noted how activists in the Occupy Wall Street movement admitted that Twitter's brevity (140 characters) meant that it was not the best platform to debate the movement or related political issues. As a result, the focus of this research is on blogs. As Mowles

(2008) explained, 'the clear majority' of scholarship on blogging highlights its ability to 'alter political discourse and inform mainstream media sources,' thus highlighting the most 'salient aspect of their activist potential' (p. 44; see also Juris 2012).

That online (feminist) activism has been overlooked is unsurprising. According to Jessica Taft (2011), feminists have long campaigned for expanded conceptions of activism in order to better understand the contributions of a variety of women, including those of colour, the working class, and non-Western women. For example, Rapp et al. (2010) explained how black women used the internet to ensure their voices were heard in anti-rape protests. This was because they were well aware of the ways the mainstream media reproduced discourses of oppression that they wanted to avoid.

There is no doubt that women have been, and continue to be, excluded from the traditional public sphere (Fraser 1990). Even in the so called 'developed' Western world, where women's presence in the public sphere is generally accepted, they continue to be intimidated by men through street harassment and sexual assault, which leaves many feeling unsafe and vulnerable. At the other extreme, attempts were made to physically exclude women from public protest during the 2011 Egyptian revolution. Women protesting in Tahrir Square were routinely harassed, groped and assaulted in efforts to dissuade them from protesting, and to reinforce the idea that their place is at home (see 'Rape and sexual assault: the hidden side of Egypt's protests' 2013; Trew 2013).[5] Although offline participation may at times be required or preferable, feminist scholars have shown how the internet allows individuals to respond to political events in (safe) alternative spaces, with alternative perspectives, providing counter-hegemonic critiques, and share information about issues usually ignored by the mainstream media (Rentschler 2014; Shaw 2012a). Similarly, Piano (2002) argued that the internet provides 'feminist pockets or zones in cyberspace' through which feminist activism can take place (cited in Keller 2013, p. 31). And Rentschler (2014) stated that the internet often serves as a key source of feminist education. Because of women's exclusion from the public sphere, it is important to recognize that social networking sites are not only the spaces in which political protests are organized and planned, but the *locations* of political protest themselves (Shaw 2012a, p. 68). For scholars like Frances Shaw, then, the internet's revolutionary potential lies in its opportunities for discursive activism and politics, which she argues have not been adequately explored (for exceptions, see Downing 2008; Maddison 2013b; Shaw, F. 2011, 2012a, 2012b, 2013).

Discursive politics and activism

Scholars such as Shaw (2012a), contend that too much social movement theorization concerns itself with how new media and the internet are used to organize offline protest (see Gerbaudo 2012), rather than analysing them as *sites of activism*. The problem with this is that the 'real' forms of resistance and activism are seen to happen offline, while online forms of activism are ignored or seen as less important (Shaw 2012a). This view of what constitutes 'legitimate' activism is particularly problematic for feminists, whose tactics have not historically been recognized as 'political,' nor do they often lead to policy or regime change (Young 1997, p. 167). Yet, as Stacey Young (1997) argued, in the fight to transform power relations and social structures, discursive politics are just as important as other types of politics (such as electoral politics), because they aim to fundamentally change the way people think. Consequently, many feminists advocate the importance of sharing personal experiences about common problems and developing new discourses for them (e.g. rape is about power, not sex), as a necessary first step in enacting social change (Maddison 2013b; Young 1997). Known as consciousness raising (CR), this activist practice has been used by feminists since the 1970s and has been fundamental to the development of counterhegemonic discourses about women and their place in the world (Maddison 2013b; Shaw, F. 2011; Young 1997). Because SlutWalk aims to challenge hegemonic discourses about the nature of rape, what causes it, and who is to blame, it requires 'discursive activism' – or 'political speech ... that intervenes in hegemonic discourses, and that works at the level of language to change political cultures' (Shaw, F. 2011), as much, if not more so, than protests in the street.

Drawing on the importance of discursive politics, in her research on the Australian feminist blogging community, Frances Shaw (2011) demonstrated the ways that many bloggers take part in discursive activism. As a legacy of consciousness raising, feminists have long participated in linguistic and discursive interventions through newsletters, zines, poetry, speak-outs, meetings, film and theatre, which feminists argue constitute legitimate forms of political activism, along with lobbying, protests and marches (Berrington & Jones 2002; Maddison 2013b; Piepmeier 2009; Shaw, F. 2011, 2012a, 2012b; Young 1997). Despite this, such activity has historically been undervalued (Maddison 2013b; Shaw 2012b; Young 1997), and perceived as 'less noteworthy than men's by the nature of their often domestic and personal spheres of reference' (Gregg 2006, p. 85). This is despite the fact that such activities *can* and *do* challenge dominant ideologies, and that 'rhetorical struggle' is seen as crucial to *politics* – however defined (Williams 1995).

For example, Young (1997) wrote about how language acts, including published writings, played a crucial role in both individual and collective social change in the Second Wave women's movement. More recently, Meenakshi Gigi Durham (2013) documented the ways in which (feminist) bloggers, columnists and op-ed writers forced *The New York Times* to apologize for its coverage of the gang rape of an 11-year-old girl in Texas. Bloggers in particular were quick to condemn the story's use of patriarchal and victim-blaming tropes that made it seem 'the girl had it coming' (Knox 2011 cited in Durham 2013, p. 1). Shaw (2012b) also detailed the ways feminist bloggers in Australia intervened in a radio contest to highlight the ways the history of rock music excluded and erased women. Similarly, Jessica Mowles (2008) showed how the US feminist blog *Feministing* has reshaped conventional political discourse, particularly around gender roles and the hypersexualization of women. Mowles quoted the 'about' section of *Feministing*'s blog, which describes the site as 'a platform for us [young women] to comment, analyse, and *influence*' (2008, p. 33, italics original).

While the aggregation of bodies on the streets via SlutWalk protests is certainly an important (and newsworthy) signal that society is seeking to challenge rape culture, hegemonic ideologies can only be challenged through discursive interventions. This requires talking, listening and debate, all of which the internet, at least theoretically, provides. Because the development of feminist discourse has been regarded as having a 'profound effect on women's expectations for their own lives' (Maddison 2013b, p. 31), this research will analyze the extent to which feminists engaged with discursive politics and activism challenge mainstream and hegemonic discourses surrounding sexual assault and rape culture, noting the extent to which such discourses have been embraced by the mainstream news media. Before that, however, I will provide an overview of the study's methods and methodology.

Methodology

Now that I have outlined relevant literature for this study, it is time to discuss my methodology and specific methods used to carry out this research. As someone who has attended a SlutWalk march, and is deeply interested in the media's potential for dismantling rape culture, it is perhaps unsurprising that this research was undertaken using a feminist cultural studies perspective. Inherent in this approach is the analysis of

power structures and the ideologies used to uphold them. Cultural studies scholars are also interested in resistance to these structures (see D'Acci
2005), as witnessed by those who participated in SlutWalk marches, or
discussions about the movement in mainstream news, feminist media,
and social media. Influenced by feminist poststructural theorists such
as Judith Butler (1990), who argue that gender is performative and constituted through discursive means, this research is interested in how the
mass media (re)produces and circulates gender through representation.
In particular, the book examines gender through discourses surrounding sexual assault and rape culture, asking: to what extent do the mainstream news media adopt hegemonic or feminist discourses on sexual
assault in coverage of SlutWalk? How do these discourses compare to
those found in feminist media? To what extent have feminists used
blogging and social media to engage in discursive activism, and form
networked counterpublics on rape culture and sexual assault? Informed
by my feminist cultural studies perspective, this research employs a
variety of methods including frame analysis, qualitative content analysis and critical discourse analysis (CDA) of mainstream news, feminist
media and social media posts. It also employs ethnographic methods
including in-depth interviews with 22 SlutWalk organizers and close
observations of social media sites (netnography), from eight nations
around the world (Australia, Canada, India, South Africa, Singapore,
the UK and the US).

Qualitative content analysis

Content analysis is a widely used method in (feminist) media studies
and is particularly suitable for analysing large amounts of data (Deacon
et al. 1999; Krippendorff 2004). It has also been used effectively in transnational examinations of data (Krippendorff 2004; Mendes 2011a).
Because all content has been subjected to the same explicitly defined
criteria, content analysis ensures a degree of reliability in establishing media patterns and representations (Deacon et al. 1999). Content
analysis can be quantitative or qualitative in nature. Quantitative content analysis generally involves statistical analyses of the data using
complex models and measures. Qualitative content analysis, however,
still involves coding data, tabulating it as simple frequencies, but this
data does not undergo rigorous statistical analysis (Bhattacherjee 2012).
Instead, the focus of tabulation is on qualitative aspects of the data such
as themes, frames, discourses, story tone and so forth. Even when taking this approach however, qualitative content analysis is only capable
of establishing patterns in data, such as identifying what is visible or

absent. It is incapable of analysing systems of representations in text or speech, which is why some scholars (Mendes 2011a; Moore, S.E.H. 2011) have used it in combination with other methods such as critical discourse analysis (CDA). Sarah E. Moore (2011), for example, used qualitative content analysis to establish changing meanings of date rape over a 14-year-period, while Mendes (2011a) used it to identify numerous features of news coverage of feminism, such as genre and source use, which were then explored more qualitatively.

While quantitative content analysis can be used to supply complex statistical algorithms and data, qualitative content analysis was selected for this study for its ability to provide a broad overview of coverage. Because my main area of interest is how SlutWalk and modern feminism were ideologically constructed in the news media, qualitative content analysis was used to provide simple frequency analyses to support my qualitative analysis, and identify trends I might have otherwise missed. My main area of interest is consequently how issues of power, domination and inequality are constructed, sustained and sometimes challenged through the mainstream news and feminist media – a task which I used both frame analysis and CDA to accomplish (see also van Dijk 2008).

Frame analysis

The way a story constructs – or frames – an event is a widely used concept for academics in a variety of fields, and has been particularly fruitful for scholars examining social movements (see Ashley & Olson 1998; Barnett 2005; Baylor 1996; Benford & Snow 2000; Costain et al. 1997; Couldry 1999; Creedon 1993; Lind & Salo 2002; Mendes 2011a; Rohlinger 2002; Strutt 1994). These scholars recognize that any representation of reality, including those presented by mainstream news and feminist media, involves framing (Kitzinger 2009), which is therefore understood as unavoidable (Gitlin 2003). Journalists and bloggers 'frame' reality when deciding which topics to cover, who to interview, what to ask, what angle to take and how to order the information (Kitzinger 2009, p. 137). By selecting 'relevant' facts, assigning them meaning, and ordering them in an 'appropriate' way (Benford & Snow 2000; Kitzinger 2009, p.134; Reese 2001), journalists and bloggers help construct the public's understanding of the world around them. Unlike a discourse analysis, which focuses on individual ideologies and values, frame analysis takes into account the whole picture. As a result, in order to find out, broadly speaking, how the movement was represented, I conducted a frame analysis in both my mainstream news and feminist media samples. Questions asked include: What is SlutWalk seen to be about? What are the key feminist or anti-feminist discourses used when discussing rape or rape culture? Whose voices are present or absent? What are the problems or solutions to the issues at hand? Is the movement supported? I use these frames to help organize my discussion of the various discourses that then emerged to make up these overarching narratives.

Critical discourse analysis (CDA)

According to Teun van Dijk (2008), CDA is a method which is particularly useful for analysing the ways in which social power, domination and inequality are created and sustained through conversation, speech and texts, including the news media. CDA has been a particularly popular method for scholars interested in exploring gender issues, as it aims to unpack how discourse creates and sustains gender inequality, patriarchy and other gender-based discrimination in general (Jaworska & Krishnamurthy 2012; Lazar 2005; Mendes 2011a; Shaw 2012b; van Dijk 2008). CDA has also been widely used in studies examining representations of sexual assault or rape culture (see Alat 2006; Bonnes 2013; Harp et al. 2014; Jamel 2014; McNicol 2012; Meyer 2010; Moffett 2006; Worthington 2010), making it a good fit for this study. Although CDA pays 'close attention to language and its usage' (Meyers 1997, p. 13), it does not analyze merely what is *said*, but what is *implied* and *ignored* (see also Fairclough 1995). As a result, it is a method which requires close and careful reading through the lines. For example, Harp et al. (2014) utilized discourse analysis to analyze news coverage of the sexual assault of CBS reporter Lara Logan during the Egyptian revolution. Their study highlighted how texts explicitly stated Logan was not responsible for her assault while implicitly reinforcing rape narratives that blamed the victim (e.g. commenting on her appearance which suggests that only young attractive women are raped, and that rape is triggered by lust and sexual urges rather than power) as SlutWalk seeks to disrupt hegemonic discourses on rape and sexual assault, my analysis will pay attention to both these implicit and explicit meanings.

Finally, while some forms of discourse analysis pay close attention to meta-levels of analysis such as specific grammatical or lexical choices, I applied CDA to identify key ideological themes (discourse) in order to shed light on the social, political and cultural contexts in which they were produced.

Ethnographic approach

As a well-known method for cultural studies scholars, I selected ethnographic methods such as semi-structured interviews because of the ways they allow research participants to speak about their own experiences, thus providing rich data for the study. In this particular case, I interviewed 22 SlutWalk organizers from around the world, who were involved in the movement between 2011 and 2014. Participants were asked about topics such as the value they placed on social media, their experiences with the movement, trolling and harassment, and organizational tactics, in a way that gave 'space for their own understandings and interpretations' (Taft 2011, p. 193). Semi-structured interviews have also been a preferred method for the growing body of research on girls (see Currie et al. 2009; Driscoll 2002; Harris 2004a, 2004b; Keller 2013; Piepmeier 2009; Scharff 2012; Taft 2011; Zaslow 2009). Although not all interview participants can be defined as 'girls'[6] (indeed four of my participants were male), many SlutWalk organizers were young, and attending secondary school or university during the periods in which they organized marches. Feminist researchers have used semi-structured interviews as a means of privileging, defending and promoting the voices of research participants (Mitchell & Reid-Walsh 2004), many of whom are traditionally marginalized due to age, gender, class, sexuality, occupation, race and so forth (Keller 2013).

Although I strived to conduct all interviews via Skype or telephone, due to busy schedules and dispersed geographical locations, seven interviews were conducted via email or Facebook.[7] The other 14 were carried out by phone or Skype, and interviews ranged from 20 to 80 minutes long. Interviews were conducted between 2012 and 2014. In several cases, I emailed follow-up questions, sometimes days, while at other times months later, when needing clarification on issues. In one case (SlutWalk Vancouver), an interview was carried out with two organizers simultaneously. The criteria for inclusion in the project was participants' involvement in organising at least one SlutWalk march.[8] Research participants were identified and contacted through various SlutWalk Facebook pages or websites. I also made use of snowball sampling, through which organizers put me in touch with other organizers, and I successfully recruited three participants this way. All research participants were recruited with informed consent and were offered anonymity. None took it, but in two cases participants shared only their first names.

Online ethnographic methods – or netnography (Kozinets 2010) – can also include close observation of (online) communities. As Hine (2000) suggested, online ethnography does not necessarily require the ethnographer to physically travel to a field site. Other scholars also point to the ways in which social media ethnography is 'messy' (Postill & Pink 2012, p. 128), with narratives oscillating between on and offline practices. According to Postill and Pink (2012), social media ethnography involves various 'routines' including catching up, sharing and following, which they view as 'entangled' processes. For example, I began this research by first identifying various SlutWalk Facebook pages and Twitter accounts, and then 'liking' or 'following' them so that their activities would pop up on my social media homepage. According to Postill and Pink, following or liking is an important act because it 'opens you directly to the sharing of others' (2012, p. 130), and thus allows you to see how others interact with these accounts. Every day, I spent time 'catching up' with what the administrators posted. Often, I shared, liked or commented on these posts via my own social media accounts. In part, this was because I was trying to make contact with SlutWalk organizers, and these routines made it apparent that I was interested in, and supportive of their activism. By definition, ethnography requires researchers to immerse themselves in the cultures they are studying (Deacon et al. 1999), and I attempted to follow this logic in my own research of online SlutWalk communities.

Mainstream news timeline, search terms and publication selection

Although I could have analyzed representations of SlutWalk in popular culture more generally, I specifically focused on the news media because of its crucial role in maintaining and (re)producing hegemonic ideologies (Dow 1996; Meyers 2006). Furthermore, because I was interested in including research from around the world, I further narrowed down my selection to print and online news media to help maintain a manageable sample size. Like many other contemporary social movements (for example Occupy Wall Street), there is a public perception that SlutWalk is 'over' (Midgley 2013), despite the fact that walks continue to be organized in major cities all around the world. Because of this perception, I deliberately expanded the time frame beyond SlutWalk's first anniversary to explore the extent to which the movement still generated copy in news and feminist media. Material was collected between 17 February 2011, the date of which the SlutWalk Toronto Facebook page was created, and 31 December 2013, providing me with nearly three years-worth of data. Furthermore, because much early coverage focused on the global spread of SlutWalk, and because I have experience conducting cross-national research on representations of feminist activism (Mendes 2011a, 2012), I decided to include a range of other English-speaking nations which hosted the movement. Using the Nexis database, I selected eight nations for which I had access to major English language publications. These were: Australia, Canada, India, New Zealand, Singapore, South Africa, the UK and the US. Although there are a number of significant political, social, economic and legislative differences between these nations, with different histories and experiences of feminist activism, rape and sexual assault is a *universal* problem. As such, I thought it would be interesting to see the extent to which mainstream news and feminist media engage with this issue, and feminist efforts to combat it.

While I was originally satisfied with the 27 publications I had selected via the Nexis database, I soon became aware that it excluded key publications in some of my eight nations, prompting me to expand my dataset. For example, the key Australian newspaper *The Sydney Morning Herald* was not available through Nexis, and given that Nexis only had access to one Singaporean newspaper, I decided to add a second, *The New Paper*. In order to include these other key publications, I conducted searches via the newspapers' online archives. Once I decided to go beyond publications available on Nexis, I also made an effort to include publications of varying moral and political tones from each of my eight nations. I was also careful about including a mixture of 'high' and 'low' brow publications, which are sometimes labelled 'broadsheet' and 'tabloid' (see Conboy 2006; Sparks 2000). This inclusion of publications ranging from those covering more 'serious' issues, such as politics and the economy, to those covering more 'entertainment-based' issues, such as celebrity, gossip, human interest and scandal, was undertaken to ensure my sample included variations in the possible ways SlutWalk might be addressed.

Because several of my nations have public service broadcasters that are key sources of news and information, I decided to include their online news provision where relevant. This included Canada's *CBC*, Britain's *BBC*, Australia's *ABC*, New Zealand's *TVNZ*, and South Africa's *SABC*. Finally, because of the popularity of some online-only news sites, I decided to include the *Huffington Post*, which has separate websites for its Canadian, British and American editions. In total, then, I had 35 news outlets in my sample.[9] However, even when I thought my sample was complete, I discovered that some of my newspapers had also published online-only articles not included in my original Nexis search. I was therefore forced to cross-check the Nexis sample with an online search through each newspaper's website, adding any missing articles in my sample. In total then, I collected 304 news texts from 35 news sites, and developed a coding schedule which sought answers to questions around genre, story length, author gender, news peg, frame, source use, use of feminist and patriarchal discourses on rape, mention of social media and feminism, and overall story tone.

Despite the fact that I selected articles and publications from eight nations, I considered the entire group of 304 texts as a single sample and did not carry out rigorous cross-national analysis as I had done with previous work (Mendes 2011a). This is because, rather than seeking a balance in terms of number of publications or articles per nation, I was more interested in general representations of the movement over time and space. As a result, I make no claims that my study provides a comprehensive picture of how SlutWalk was globally represented. Instead, I argue that this study provides a snapshot into results from one global case study. Further research is needed to supplement my findings, particularly on SlutWalk in non-English-speaking nations, which I lack the linguistic skills to tackle.

Feminist media timeline, search terms and publication selection

Before I embarked on this project, I became increasingly aware of the rising popularity of a number of feminist blogs, such as *Feministing* in the US, *The F-Word* in the UK, *Hoyden Around Town* in Australia, and *Feminist Current* in Canada. Concurrently, I became aware of research highlighting the increased importance of blogs as sources of both information and inspiration in mainstream news (see Fenton 2010; Perlmutter 2008; Thorsen 2009). Within academic literature, I began to read studies demonstrating the ways feminist blogs were helping to cultivate feminist identities and discourses which challenged mainstream hegemonic ideologies (see Keller 2013; Rentschler 2014; Shaw, F. 2011). As a result, I became interested in how SlutWalk was represented in *feminist media*, defined as 'any media project produced by a self-identifying feminist and/ or women's media project which seeks to promote social change' (Zobl & Drueke 2012). Although most of the feminist media included in this sample can be constituted as a 'blog,' some, such as *Ms.*, *Rookie* and *Bitch*, identify themselves as online feminist magazines. As a result of their reach and potential to promote social change, I decided to include these as well. However, for the sake of ease, I will often refer to all texts in this sample as 'blogs' or 'posts' as there is not often a lot of difference in style or tone.

Given that feminist bloggers put a lot of effort into cultivating online feminist communities (see Keller 2013; Shaw, F. 2011), snowball sampling was selected as an appropriate way of collecting material for my feminist media sample. Following in the footsteps of other research on feminist media (Shaw, F. 2011), I based my initial selection on my pre-existing knowledge of feminist blogs, which I regularly read, and searched these for posts on SlutWalk. Next, I went through their blogrolls and searched these for further posts on SlutWalk. Finally, I made a rule that I would follow all embedded links about SlutWalk and include these texts in my sample. As with my mainstream news sample, I included key feminist media from each of my eight nations, although I was not bent on achieving numeric parity between them. When I was really stuck on finding feminist media in places such as South Africa, Singapore, India and New Zealand, I conducted searches via Google Blog, WordPress and Tumblr, and asked my research participants in these nations if they could recommend any feminist media sites. My only real criteria for selection was that the individual author or site identified as a feminist (this was often evident in the blog or post title), that that the blog/article was related to SlutWalk, and that it was published between 7 February 2011 and 31 December 2013. In total, I gathered 390 posts from 96 feminist blogs/websites.[10]

Because I soon realized that the style, format and content of my feminist media sample differed from that of my mainstream news articles, I developed a different coding schedule which provided more space to interrogate the use of feminist critiques of rape culture, as well as feminist critiques of SlutWalk. I was also interested in the texts' use of hyperlinks, and use of visual images – the latter of which I could not consistently quantify in my analysis of mainstream news, as Nexis excludes images. Because scholars have identified blogs as a key site of critiquing mainstream media and promoting feminist counterdiscourses (Durham 2013; Keller 2013; Shaw 2012b), I was also interested in the extent to which feminist media coverage of SlutWalk engaged in these critiques, utilized rape statistics, or drew attention to the feminist blogging community's coverage of the movement. Furthermore, because there was much greater variation in the ways the feminist blogs were written, my coding frame was much more detailed and posed more questions than the one I developed for my mainstream news texts. This difference will necessarily be reflected in my analysis, where I often have more quantitative results to support my discussion of my feminist media sample.

Although I often present results from my mainstream news and feminist media sample in similar spaces, I want to make clear that this study is not seeking to make direct comparisons between them, but instead highlights aspects of coverage which seemed relevant. At times, then, my analysis focuses evenly on results from both samples, where in other instances I focus on results from one sample where relevant. In either case, I will make it clear which sample is being analysed.

Overview

This chapter presented a summation of key academic literature relevant to this study, including conceptions of modern feminism, definitions of violence against women and common rape myths, representations of violence against women and feminist activism. It also explored modern social movements and emergent concepts such as networks and the importance and utility of social media. I also introduced two key concepts for this study, discursive politics/activism and networked counterpublics, which will become important in later chapters. The chapter finished with a discussion about my methodology, providing an overview of my feminist cultural studies position, as well as the specific methods used, including frame analysis, qualitative content analysis, CDA, semi-structured interviews and close observation of SlutWalk social media accounts. Now that I have outlined how I carried out this study, it is time to explore the results.

3
Situating SlutWalk

In 2011, amidst a range of other global protests such as the Spanish Indignados, the Occupy Movement, and the Arab Spring, news began to emerge about a string of SlutWalk marches, held initially in Canada, and then spreading to the US, UK, Australia, Europe, South and Central Americas and Asia. Although the next two chapters will focus on representations of what SlutWalk *is*, this chapter begins by examining *where* and *when* it was represented as taking place, as well as the style in which it was covered. For example, were only local SlutWalks discussed, or was part of the movement's appeal its international spread? During what phase of SlutWalk's cycle was the movement reported – in its planning stages, the march itself, or in its aftermath? Was the movement reported via traditional 'hard' news formats, or were 'softer' genres such as columns and features more common? And in what ways might these formats have impacted upon people's engagement with, and understanding of the movement?

While these questions have traditionally been asked of the news media, as a key site through which people have come to understand social change, changing morals and policies (Rhode 1995), I will also apply them to feminist media given the important role online feminist communities increasingly play in young women's lives (Harris 2008b; Keller 2013; Mowles 2008; Shaw 2012b). In fact, a key theme running through this book is the crucial role feminist media played for the movement. While the mainstream news media has in the past been most people's only source of information on social movements (Barker-Plummer 2000; Gitlin 2003; Rhode 1995; van Zoonen 1992), thereby providing a framework for how to interpret these movements (Hall et al. 1978), this is no longer necessarily the case, as the internet has opened up new spaces for alternative and counterhegemonic discourses (Mowles 2008; Rentschler 2014; Shaw 2012b). And where the news media have historically been important spaces for providing background information and context on a movement's aims and objectives, thus potentially encouraging participation (Weiner 2011), the internet more generally, and social media platforms specifically, are also increasingly taking over these roles (see Gerbaudo 2012; Marmura 2008; Penney & Dadas 2014). As we will come to see in this chapter, despite content, structural and organizational differences between mainstream news and feminist media, there were a surprising number of similarities in how each addressed the movement in its run-up and aftermath. That said, it is important to note that this chapter is not attempting to produce a direct comparison between my mainstream news and feminist media samples, but is instead interested in highlighting important aspects of coverage.

The chapter then moves on to examine variations in (representations of) the movement across the eight nations that organized SlutWalks (Australia, Canada, India, Singapore, South Africa, the UK and the US). In order to make sense of these representations, the chapter must engage with variations in the movement itself over time and space. As a result, the chapter highlights the interface between how the movement developed, and how it was represented. For example, a common critique levelled at SlutWalks that took place outside North America was that their message was too 'Western' and thus did not translate to other nations with very different histories, cultures and contexts of feminist activism. But were all non-Western nations the target of such criticism? And were bloggers/journalists from any particular nation more likely to respond to such critiques? Did the movement adapt its message in light of these concerns, and if so, how? As a result, this chapter not only analyzes representations of the movement, but thinks more broadly about what impact coverage had in shaping the movement itself.

Slutwalk's temporal and geographic locations

When do SlutWalks take place?

For many years, scholars have been interested in the lifecycle of social movements, or how they form, develop and decline (see Blumer 1969; Della Porta & Diani 2006; Taylor 1989). While the purpose of this study is not to provide a lifecycle of the movement per se, it presents a picture of its lifecycle within the mainstream news and feminist media. At what point did SlutWalk become newsworthy or a 'hot topic,' and at what point did its visibility, although not necessarily the movement itself, fade away? Perhaps unsurprisingly, 2011 was the year in which both mainstream news and feminist media were most likely to talk about SlutWalk (see Figure 3.1). With 284 feminist media posts (73 percent of total) and 249 mainstream news articles (82 percent of total) published, the movement was most commonly discussed in its inaugural year. Although there was a significant decrease in coverage in 2012, the feminist media were more likely to continue discussing the movement than the mainstream media (87 posts vs. 38 articles respectively). However, by 2013, neither my feminist media nor my mainstream news sample regularly covered the movement or many of the annual marches that were still taking place (19 posts and 17 articles respectively). Instead, these articles/posts tended to talk about things such as the movement's legacy, therefore assuming SlutWalk was over, or dead. Well-known British feminist Finn Mackay noted a similar trend when she helped revitalize the London Reclaim the Night march in 2004. Although the marches attracted mainstream media coverage in their first year, the media lost interest in subsequent years, despite the organisers sending out regular press releases to major media outlets, and attracting thousands to their annual marches (Mackay 2012).

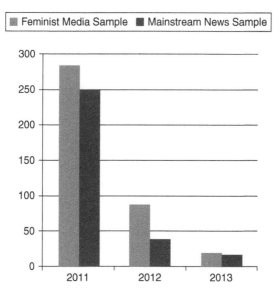

Figure 3.1 Articles/posts published on SlutWalk in mainstream news and feminist Media, 2011–2013

The dwindling of coverage of SlutWalk, as with Reclaim the Night, indicates the extent to which SlutWalk was initially seen as a 'novelty' (Gray 2014a), particularly amongst the mainstream news, which requires something 'new' to take place in order to label in newsworthy. Recognizing this, organizers attempted to 'hook' the movement onto current events in order to demonstrate their relevance. For example, in the case of Reclaim the Night, Finn Mackay explained how the movement found its 'own little soundbites,' and used current statistics about conviction rates, the closure of local rape crisis centres, or controversy over public figures' comments about rape (Mackay 2012). Similarly, SlutWalk Melbourne 2012 and 2013 organizer Amy Gray explained the way the media 'just weren't interested' in the movement after the first year, despite coming up with 'lots and lots of different angles to generate mainstream media interest' (Gray 2014a).

The mainstream media's seeming disinterest in movements that are no longer 'novel' is a problem for movements feminism, which strives for social, cultural, legal and political changes that are difficult to make in a short period of time. Although this is not a new issue (see Mendes 2011a), this media 'fatigue' is something activists involved in other causes or conflicts (such as the environmental and anti-globalization movements) have experienced (see Cottle 2009). And while this issue of media fatigue has been applied to the mainstream news, the decline of feminist posts about SlutWalk, despite the movement's continuation, suggests that media 'fatigue' might apply not only to the mainstream news, but to other, alternative practices as well, such as blogging. More research into this topic, particularly with regards to the extent to which feminist issues mirror, follow, or set mainstream media trends, could provide more insight into my findings. Yet it is also worth noting that some of the overall decline in coverage was linked to changing priorities for activists, some of whom became more interested in community, rather than media, outreach and engagement as the movement developed (see Delgado 2014a; Haugen 2014; Jarvis 2012; MacDonald, C. 2014). This issue of mainstream media vs. community outreach will be explored in more depth in Chapter 6.

Coverage of movement phases

One aspect of coverage I was most interested in was in which phase of the movement was most likely to generate mainstream news or feminist media attention – the run up to the protest, event or march, the march itself, or accounts of future planning and what comes next. Was it the *concept* of SlutWalk which made it newsworthy, or did it only warrant attention *as a result* of the physical aggregation of bodies in the streets? These questions are also important because people only have the opportunity to participate in activism if they know it is going to take place. Given that blogs and the news media frequently, although not always, *react* to events (Herring et al. 2007; Shoemaker & Reese 1996), it was perhaps unsurprising that results from the qualitative content analysis revealed that the majority of articles/posts focused on local marches which had in fact already happened (37 and 38 percent of total articles respectively). Typical news headlines include: '150 join Ottawa's SlutWalk to protest "victim-blaming" attitudes' (Chen 2012), 'SlutWalk march takes place in Bristol' (2011) and '"SlutWalk" hits Saskatoon' (Hamilton 2011). Typical feminist media headlines include: 'SlutWalk London June 2011: An eyewitness account' (Shaw, M. 2011), 'SlutWalk London 2011: Full photo report!' (blatantblithe 2011), '"Hey Rapists, Go Fuck Yourselves": SlutWalk arrives in NYC' (Seltzer & Kelley 2011), and 'Walking off the anger: SlutWalk Christchurch 2012' (Fitzwater 2012). And while these texts undoubtedly provided the movement with a sense of credibility and legitimacy, in many cases, their timing meant that it was too late for potential supporters to get involved, at least in that particular city, or during that particular year.

When the news or feminist blogs focused on marches that had already taken place, there were a number of similarities in coverage. For example, accounts in both samples frequently focused on aspects of the march such as the general atmosphere, how many and who attended. A typical report from the *Globe and Mail* reported: 'The demonstration, which started at Queen's Park and ended in front of police headquarters, featured much outrage, lots of skin, and all walks of life, including activists, Goths, native protesters, artists and a good smattering of men' (McArthur 2011). Similarly, one blogger's account of SlutWalk Ottawa noted: 'The crowd was diverse in age, background, gender identity, ethnicity, etc. And despite what you might have read or seen about the celebratory nature of SlutWalk, it was a rather sombre event. People were angry, not laughing. As they should be – sexual assault isn't funny' (Feminist Catalyst 2011).

For the news media at least, these are aspects of coverage which have historically been used as means of (de)legitimizing movements (Gitlin 2003). In my previous research on representations of the Second Wave feminist movement in the mainstream news (Mendes 2011a), one common way of legitimizing the movement was to report on the diversity of participants, which was not only used to help create a sense of collectivism, but also to counter claims that the movement was a 'fringe' cause, supported mainly by 'radicals' (read 'unfeminine' women). A similar feature of coverage was found not only in mainstream coverage of SlutWalk, but also amongst feminist posts. As a result, although scholars have focused on the ways that the mainstream news is becoming increasingly personalized, feminized and, some would argue, 'dumbed down' (Franklin 1997, 2008a) through greater inclusion of columns and 'softer' news genres (McNair 2008), this research suggests that the bloggers do indeed at times draw from mainstream news conventions as well.

Undoubtedly because of the movement's provocative name, mainstream news and feminist media accounts paid particular attention to what participants wore, either as a way of providing titillation, or demonstrating the range of people the movement attracted. For example, one article in the *Washington Post* noted how: 'Many in the Auckland crowd were wrapped up in scarves and coats because of the cold, but some donned fishnet tights and low-cut tops to get their point across' (Robinson 2011, p. 7). Similarly, a post on the blog *AlterNet* commented that participants were 'clad in everything from lingerie to hijabs to an oft-photographed Hester Prynne outfit. Illustrating that you really can wear whatever you want to SlutWalk, there was also a healthy representation of jeans and T-shirts at the event' (Seltzer & Kelley 2011). This focus on appearance, attire and even attractiveness has long been a common feature of news coverage on feminist activism (Mendes 2011a), but seems notably prominent in news of SlutWalk. And although it might be easy to dismiss coverage on fashion and appearance as 'frivolous,' scholars have argued that it has long in fact been a feminist issue, and a route into political discussions of patriarchy, capitalism or other systems of oppression (see Blackman & Perry 2000; Budgeon & Currie 1995; Groeneveld 2009; Mendes 2012, 2015; Parkins 2008). As will be discussed in Chapter 5, feminist bloggers intervened in mainstream coverage which visually represented protesters as (mainly) white, young and 'sexy.' Appearance, fashion and feminism are therefore important (feminist) issues, which will be addressed in more depth later in the book.

Forthcoming events

While most mainstream news articles and feminist media posts focused predominantly on marches which had already taken place, a smaller proportion, but still significant number focused on forthcoming marches, with a total of 66 stories in both the mainstream news (22 percent of total) and feminist media (17 percent of total). News headlines included: 'SlutWalks to rally against shaming of rape victims,' (2011), and 'Kiwis plan to join "SlutWalk" crusade' (2011), while feminist media headlines included: 'SlutWalk: This weekend' (Spankhead 2012b), and 'SlutWalk Singapore: Happening this December' (AWARE 2011). Headlines for both mainstream news and feminist media ranged from the more factual, which focused on date and location, such as 'New Delhi "SlutWalk" on June 25' (Asian Window 2011), to those which indicated support or opposition for the movement 'Perth "sluts" prepare to walk despite lack of support' (Clarke 2011), 'Why I'm marching in the Slutwalk: Time for New York's women to speak out against rape' (Meyer 2011) and 'Why I won't be at SlutWalk' (Ndlovu 2011).

Regarding the mainstream news, the fact that over one fifth of all articles were published in the run up to the event is a significant indication of the movement's perceived newsworthiness. It also suggests that SlutWalk's attempts to garner media attention *prior* to marches were largely successful. While many pre-march articles were columns (18 articles or 27 percent) or features (12 articles or 18 percent), frequently explaining why the author would or would not attend or support SlutWalk, the vast majority (35 articles or 53 percent) were in fact 'hard' news stories – or those which are seen to be important and take place in the 'public' sphere, and whose publication cannot be delayed (Tuchman 1978). The majority of these stories promoted the march, and included interviews with organizers, thus providing some context for the movement's origin, reach or goals. For example, one typical article from Tasmania's *Hobart Mercury* read:

A GROUP of Hobart activists hope to change perceptions of sexual assault through tomorrow's SlutWalk street rally.

'We want to enlighten people to the myths about sexual assault,' said Monica Poziemski, one of the rally's organizers ...

SlutWalk began in Toronto, after a representative of the Toronto Police said: 'Women should avoid dressing like sluts in order not to be victimized.'

Ms Poziemski said SlutWalk Hobart aimed to condemn victim-blaming and sexual violence, to empower survivors of sexual assault and to involve the community to keep people safe.

'We are walking to spread the word that our clothes are not our consent and that sexual assault is never justified and victims are never at fault,' she said.

Walkers should gather at Franklin Square at 12.30pm for the 1pm march to Parliament House lawns. (Hope 2011, p. 15)

Because its controversial name ran the risk of alienating some potential supporters who found it too risky to call themselves 'sluts,' articles such as this provided much needed context and background to the movement, which could be used to encourage their participation. Furthermore, these articles helpfully included information crucial to those who might want to take part, such as where the participants should meet, the march route, and social media platforms or websites where readers could find out more information. In fact, one commonly reported statistic in the mainstream media was how many people indicated via Facebook that they planned to attend. This information was used to help bolster the movement's newsworthiness and validate the event. For example, one article from South Africa's *Cape Times* reported: 'THOUSANDS of people are expected to attend Cape Town's SlutWalk later this month, as part of a countrywide anti-rape campaign ... So far, about 3400 people have indicated via Facebook that they will attend the march' (Nicholson 2011, p. 6). Another article from Australia's *Herald Sun* stated that: 'More than 2400 people have signed up through Facebook to attend the Melbourne march' (O'Brien 2011, p. 5). The sheer number of people SlutWalk attracted (either to the march itself or to its social media sites), is also one likely reason for its newsworthiness, as scholars have noted that the more people an event affects, the more likely it is to attract media attention (see Galtung & Ruge 1965; Harcup & O'Neill 2001). Other social movement scholars have also focused on the ways that the mainstream media reported on the number of people who stated they were attending protests via social media (Gerbaudo 2012), which was used as a way of legitimizing them.

The global nature of the march

SlutWalk's global reach also proved newsworthy, as international marches were the focus in a fifth of all mainstream news articles (61 articles or 22 percent of total), but only a fraction (25 articles or six percent of total) of feminist posts. This is perhaps because the highly intimate nature of blogging means people tend to blog about personal and local experiences and issues (Simmons 2008). As a result, the few instances of international coverage of SlutWalk tended to come from my sample of online feminist 'magazines' such as *Bust, Jezebel* and *Feministing*, which have broader national and international readerships. Recognizing their geographically dispersed readership, one piece in *Bust* titled '"SlutWalks" go worldwide' (2011) highlighted the global nature of the march as a way of encouraging participation. The piece directed readers to a hyperlinked website, indicating they should click through:

'If you want to get involved, volunteer, participate or find out if a slut-walk [sic] will be in your city.' *Feministing* addressed the global nature of the movement as a means of 'adding more vibrancy to the conversation about Slutwalks [sic] across nation and race' (Miriam 2011). Not only did *Jezebel* provide a visual compilation of SlutWalks across the globe in their post titled 'A Glimpse at SlutWalks Across the Globe' (Jefferson 2011), but requested of readers: 'Capture any great SlutWalk moments on your own camera? Leave 'em in the comments.' Through soliciting contributions from its readers, the feminist blogosphere encouraged and contributed to online community building while advocating aware-ness around particular issues (Keller 2013; Shaw 2012b).

Within mainstream news media, common headlines include the *Toronto Star's* 'SlutWalk protest in New Delhi a first for Asia' (2011), the *BBC's* 'India "SlutWalk" sex harassment protest in Delhi' (2011) and the *CBC's* 'Toronto "SlutWalk" spreads to US' (Cuervo 2011). Although international SlutWalk events were the focus of 61 articles, what wasn't quantified in the content analysis, but noted through a qualitative read-ing, was that the march's global nature was mentioned in a significant proportion of news articles, providing the movement with international credibility. Furthermore, such articles helped create a sense of collective activism – a shift away from the (neo)liberal feminist rhetoric of indi-vidual freedom and choices which has dominated much of the (Western) news media in recent years (see Mendes 2012). Typical examples include: 'SLUTWALK, an international movement rapidly gaining momentum worldwide after being started earlier this year to object to a suggestion that women could avoid sexual assault by not "dressing like a slut", is coming to South Africa' (Mposo 2011, p. 5), and 'WOMEN pro-testing for the right to wear what they like and behave how they choose without facing sexual harassment are set to hold "SlutWalks" across Australia as the movement goes global' ('SlutWalk sweeps Australia' 2011). The global nature of the march was also evident in headlines such as: 'SlutWalk goes global' (2011, p. A2), 'SlutWalk sparks world-wide movement' (Church 2011, p. A6), and 'New Delhi "SlutWalk" brings global sexual violence protest phenomenon to India' (2011). That SlutWalk was seen as a global phenomenon once again provided it with credibility and a certain amount of newsworthiness, important for burgeoning social movements, but historically rare for feminist activism (see Mendes 2011a).

Although there are significant differences between mainstream and feminist media coverage of SlutWalk, as we will come to see throughout the next few chapters, both shared certain features, such as prioritizing past, rather than forthcoming marches, and including descriptions of the general atmosphere, number of participants, and their attire. And while there has been much scholarly attention paid to the ways in which the mainstream news has experienced tabloidization (see Franklin 1997, 2008b), my research provides evidence that the crossover happens both ways, with bloggers adopting traditional 'hard' news conventions at times. Where the news media were more likely to cover the global nature of the march, feminist media were more likely to focus on those events taking place in their local communities – signalling the extent to which blogs are a manifestation of how the personal is indeed the political.

Genre

According to Tuchman et al. (1978): 'The ability to define events as news is raw political power' (p. 186). Yet, despite this, there are clear hierarchies within the news, which is not all equally valued. As a testament to this, the news is often classified into 'hard' and 'soft' news stories. Whereas 'hard' news refers to stories about politics, the economy, social change or other events that take place in the 'public' world, 'soft' news includes stories set in or affecting the private sphere, and connotes non-pressing, light or unimportant events or issues (Mendes 2011a; Tuchman et al. 1978). Because women have long been excluded from the public sphere and areas around which 'hard' news has been based, 'soft' news has traditionally been seen to be news for, by and affecting women, and has therefore been viewed as less important.

According to scholars, genre is an important feature of coverage to analyze because it impacts both where a story sits in a particular publication, and the topics covered, tone, style, headline and use of journalistic conventions in its narrative (Cottle 2003; van Zoonen 1992; Mendes 2011a). Genre is particularly important to analyze when studying 'women's issues' (such as rape and sexual violence) because such issues have historically been associated with the private sphere, and are not necessarily worthy of making it into the 'hard' news sections of the newspaper (Mendes 2011a; Tuchman 1978). While some of the posts found in my online feminist media sample were written as traditional 'hard' news stories, typically revolving around politics, the economy, social change or other 'public' events, the vast majority were personalized commentary or blog pieces. As a result, this section will focus on an analysis of genre in my mainstream news media sample.

When analysing the results from the qualitative content analysis, 124 articles (41 percent of total) were classified as 'hard' news, followed by 80 columns/blogs (26 percent of total), 65 features (21 percent of total), and 29 letters to the editor (ten percent of total). Given that 'hard' news stories have historically been valued more highly than 'soft' news stories focusing on scandal, entertainment and 'personal issues,' the large number of such articles could be interpreted as a success. This is particularly true given the steep decline of 'hard' news of feminist demonstrations, sit-ins, protests, marches, debates, boycotts and more from the Second Wave to the Third Wave (Mendes 2012). However, such conclusions would discount the ways in which 'softer' genres such as blogs, columns, features and letters to the editor are often the spaces where the personal *becomes* political. These genres, which are not bound by traditional journalistic conventions of objectivity and impartiality, provide authors with the freedom to develop and nurture feminist discourses, consciousness (Harp et al. 2014; Keller 2013; Mendes 2012; Shaw, F. 2011) and emotional affect, which has played a key role in mobilizing citizens to engage in activism (see Gerbaudo 2012; Peipmeier 2009).

For example, columns and features in this sample were frequently longer than news articles,[1] providing the author with more space to address the context behind SlutWalk and rape culture. Although several 'hard' news articles noted the controversy around using the word 'slut' in the march's title, few were able to explore this historic meaning of the term, how it is used to regulate women's sexuality, how it is particularly problematic for women of colour and what (if anything) can be done to challenge it. Such discussions were, however, much more plentiful in the 'softer' genres. The following discussion about 'sluts' was found in a column in Australia's *Sydney Morning Herald*:

> But what exactly is a 'slut?' A woman who enjoys sex? A woman who has sex? A woman who has multiple sexual partners? A woman who may be a virgin but shows her cleavage? 'Slut' is an arbitrary insult, aimed not only at those women unfortunate enough to be so called, but all women, who fear it may one day be used against them if they don't conform to expectations on how women should dress and behave ...
>
> The organizers of SlutWalk are not simply trying to reclaim a word – they are trying to redefine it completely ...
>
> The truth is sluts don't exist. Like the witches of yesteryear, burned at the stake for defying societal norms, they are a fictional creature of a patriarchal society that subordinates women by demanding they adhere to different rules. To acknowledge the existence of sluts, a quintessentially gendered term, is to legitimize the divisive language of patriarchy. (Hamad 2011)

Despite the fact that 'hard' news articles are still undoubtedly important to analyze given their place in the more traditionally valued 'masculine' sphere of news, some of the most ideologically rich and challenging sentiments are in fact found in the 'softer' news genres such as columns, which I have previously argued are important spaces of feminist critique and articulation (see Mendes 2012).

While the first part of this chapter has focused on where and when SlutWalk was represented as taking place, as well as which genres were used in the mainstream news media, the following section will focus on regional, national and international variations (in representations) of SlutWalk.

Regional, national and international variations in (representations of) SlutWalk

Given the multiplicity of nations involved in this study, one of the more interesting aspects of this research is the regional, national and international variations in representations of the movement itself. However, these variations only make sense if one understands the ways the movement *itself* varied over time and space. For example, one of the most striking things about SlutWalk is that it is difficult to define. This is in part because the movement's message changed depending on the year and location of the march. Operating in different political, cultural and economic climates, local organizers adapted the movement in order to resonate with the local culture, issues, events and needs. While some might argue that the movement's lack of a unified vision, goal or message is problematic, I argue that such diversity is normal, healthy, and accurately reflects the fact that feminism has never been, nor will ever be, a monolithic movement (see also Dow & Wood 2014). At no point in history has there ever been a singular *feminism*. Instead, women's activism is comprised of multiple *feminisms* which 'seek justice and equality' through various means (Hepola 2012, p, 10).

Just as some of these regional and national variations evolved over time, others were evident from the get go. One of the most obvious differences was the use of parallel or translated names. For example in Israel, the march was translated into the Hebrew 'Mitzad Sharmutot,' while in Brazil the march was renamed 'Marcha das Vadias.' In France it was called 'Marches des Salopes,' while in Panama, Argentina, Columbia, and Peru, it was renamed 'La Marcha de las Putas' (Heather 2011). While these changes were made primarily due to linguistic differences, a range of other changes were also introduced in several cities due to cultural or political factors.

The cases of SlutWalk Singapore, Delhi, Bhopal, Bangalore and Kolkata come to mind here, where organizers were cognizant that the march was unlikely to achieve widespread support if a Western template was simply lifted and reproduced. This is likely because in places like India, Western feminism evokes images of hostile women, intent on leaving their husbands and neglecting their children, and is therefore seen as culturally incompatible to local values (Mitra 2013). In conservative Singapore, where rape and sexual assault are not recognized as a problem (Ward 1995), and where it is assumed that gender equality has already been achieved (Gwynne 2013), the movement worked hard to de-emphasize the focus on 'slut,' and discouraged participants from wearing 'slutty' clothing which they knew would draw negative public and state attention. Avoiding displays which provoke controversy is important in a place like Singapore, whose government is likely to reject permission to protest if there is a fear it will disrupt public order (see da Cunha 2002; Gwynne 2013). While other cities held marches, these are banned in Singapore and all public protests, or gatherings, must take place at Speaker's Corner in Hong Lim Park. Further restrictions are in place so that only citizens and permanent residents (but not foreigners) are able to participate, ensuring that this was truly a 'home grown' movement, and not one imported from the West.

Operating within these conditions, where it was unclear in the run-up to the march if a permit to protest would be granted, SlutWalk Singapore organizer Vanessa Ho went out of her way in the mainstream news media to stress the difference between Singapore's march and those taking place in the Western world: 'Our event is just a gathering, where we will make known support services that are available for victims of sexual violence. It is not a protest like SlutWalks in other countries' ('SlutWalk event given police go-ahead' 2011). In a personal interview I conducted with Ho (2012), she stressed that while the annual gathering was important, there was also a need for smaller, 'quieter' events in Singapore because of cultural differences and state control: 'SlutWalk is very public and is definitely subject to scrutiny and opposition, which can make it really unsafe. As a result, we felt that we need to have quieter, more private events to talk about these issues.' These events have included SlutScreen (which features documentaries on rape culture), numerous Consent Workshops which seek to unpack what consent means, SlutTalk, which invites various organizations to discuss rape culture, and SlutWalk Retrospective and Open Mic, which invites artists to share their work, asks participants to share their views on the movement, and seeks to recruit volunteers for future events. As indicated by Ho, many of these events were indeed 'quiet' and 'private,' with the participation limited to ten people in the case of the Consent Workshops (Consent Workshop #1 2012).

Organizers in India were also aware of the need to make cultural changes, with some such as SlutWalk Delhi, Bhopal and Hyderabad using a parallel name 'Besharmi Morcha' (shameless woman), and SlutWalk Bangalore using 'Gejje Hejje,'[2] with the recognition that 'slut,' an English word, was not commonly used or understood. In an interview I conducted with SlutWalk Bangalore organizer Dhillan Chandramowli (2014), he noted these parallel names were only adopted after great debate, and were a deliberate response to claims that India 'wasn't ready' for a SlutWalk. Co-organizer Aqseer Sodhi (2014) also told me that rather than ditching the name 'SlutWalk' altogether, they deliberately kept it for branding purposes. This was not only because the controversial name drew attention to the cause, but because they wanted their event to 'link to a wider global movement, and have a say, and to say we are part of it' (Sodhi 2014).

As a global movement then, it is clear that many international organizers drew from the well-known strategy 'Think Globally Act Locally,' also known as 'glocalization' (see Robertson 1995). While 'glocalization' has been criticized as yet another tool of imperialist capitalism, Roland Robertson (1995) argued than in our increasingly globalized world, glocalization highlights the interconnectedness of cultures. In the case of SlutWalk, it takes the global issue of rape culture, and adapts it using local language and concepts. For example, although street assault is a problem all around the world, organizers in India were keen on challenging the widely recognized problem of 'eve-teasing,' or the sexual harassment and molestation of women in public spaces. SlutWalk Bangalore's (2011) Facebook page emphasized how the movement sought to disprove the view that women should be held responsible for being assaulted or *abused* (e.g. eve-teasing and street harassment). This was reiterated in a *BBC* report about the march in Delhi, which noted that: 'The protest is to challenge the notion that the way a woman looks can excuse sexual abuse or taunting – "Eve teasing" as it is known in India' ('India "slutwalk" sex harassment protest in Delhi' 2011). The CBC covered Delhi's SlutWalk with a similar focus:

> The event in New Delhi condemned the notion widely held in this traditional society that a woman's appearance can explain or excuse

rape and sexual harassment. In India, public sexual taunting or even groping of women – locally known as 'Eve teasing' – is common. ('India's "Slutwalk" brings tamer, smaller crowd' 2011)

In order to connect to this broader movement then, it became necessary for local satellite groups to adapt the movement message to suit local issues and values. This is certainly one of the advantages of the grass-roots nature of the movement – with no directives ordered from above, satellite groups could still contribute to the wider movement about rape, violence and harassment against women, while ensuring that it addressed local needs and made cultural sense (see also Carr 2013).

Representations of SlutWalk as irrelevant, dangerous and 'Western'

Although the growth of SlutWalk into an international movement was generally praised by Western mainstream news media ('New Delhi "Slutwalk" brings global sexual violence protest phenomenon to India' 2011; Roy 2011; 'SlutWalk goes global' 2011; Tarrant 2011b; Valenti 2011), questions were raised by journalists, pundits and feminists in or from nations such as Singapore, India, Australia, New Zealand and South Africa about the movement's cultural relevance. For example, one Indian columnist for Canada's *Globe and Mail* argued that transposing the idea of SlutWalk to India was 'ludicrous' given the very different trajectories of feminist activism between the two nations (Dhillon 2011). Others voiced criticisms that organizers in India were merely 'aping the West,' which only served to trivialize a serious subject (Bhardwaj 2011). Similar criticisms were found amongst feminist media. Writing on the feminist blog *Just Femme*, Indian blogger Rashmi Vallabhajosyula (2011) noted that 'The NGO/student organisations that work on slutwalk [sic] are taking a concept that is rooted in a completely different context and using it in the Indian milieu.' She went on to ask:

> Why should we have a slut walk [sic] just because a set of other countries have them? A sort of pseudo-feministic keeping up with the Joneses? Do we not have enough home grown women's issues that we should be working on? Is it not possible for us to start with basic inequities that face us as a society? Simple sustainable steps to make out public spaces would go a long way in helping. (Vallabhajosyula 2011)

Other critiques centred on how the movement, born in Canada – a nation with relatively liberal sexual values – did not adapt its message when being transposed to more conservative nations such as South Africa (Ndlovu 2011). As a result, not only was SlutWalk generally viewed as *misguided*, but in some cases it was actually seen as *dangerous* for participants:

> If in so-called liberal countries like America and Canada, people are still saying that women invite trouble by dressing provocatively, how on earth can you even think of transposing the same premise and smack it down in the middle of India, where we've only just started kissing in Bollywood, where we are still hauled up on the road in the middle of the night if we are with a boy? ('SlutWalk' 2011)

In fact, SlutWalk Bangalore was cancelled the night before the march when the police revoked its permit after political parties and religious groups threatened to 'thrash' any women who protested in revealing clothing (Chandramowli 2014). Turning up the next day to let protesters know the march had been cancelled, the organizers were arrested by the police for 'flouting the law' (Chandramowli 2014), demonstrating the extent to which the state felt the movement was dangerous, controversial and incompatible with Indian values.

SlutWalk does translate to other nations

Although most of the *critiques* in both mainstream news and feminist media about SlutWalk being culturally irrelevant centred on the Indian context, the majority of the *responses* about how it was indeed relevant emerged from South Africa, often laden with exasperation. These centred on the retort that sexual assault, rape myths and victim-blaming are universal problems which South African women also encountered. For example, in her post on the *Mail & Guardian* blog, SlutWalk Cape Town organizer Umeshree Govender conveyed her annoyance at the barrage of questions about the movement's relevance in South Africa by writing:

> [D]o I really need to ask what relevance a protest against the prevailing culture of victim-blaming has in South Africa? Do I really need to re-hash our president's [Jacob Zuma] rape trial? Do I really have to mention that a woman is raped every 17 seconds in South Africa (that doesn't even include the rape of men, children and babies)? Do I really need to quote statistics on corrective rape? Or refer to the well-publicized harassment of women who 'dare' to wear a mini-skirt in a taxi rank?
>
> Didn't think so. (Govender 2011)

This frustration in having to justify why SlutWalk was relevant was also evident in SlutWalk Singapore's website, where blogger Kristen Han responded to claims that 'We don't need SlutWalk, we're fine, we don't have this problem' by asking:

> Really? Is there no rape in Singapore at all? Do people not judge others according to the way they choose to express their sexuality? It is not just about the law or the Women's Charter: it is about social mindsets and how we as a community perceive or reject others. (Han 2011)

As a result, many responses centred not only on how SlutWalk *is* in fact relevant, but also on how, as SlutWalk Grahamstown organizer Michelle Solomon stated, it is 'desperately needed.' She went on to list a number of reasons, including:

> We needed Slutwalk [sic] when Jacob Zuma argued during his rape trial that he had been obliged to have sexual intercourse with his accuser because she was sexually aroused. And when Zuma went on to argue that his accuser had given him sexual signals when she wore a knee length skirt and no underwear under her *kanga* (or sarong), and thus he believed she signalled her consent, we needed Slutwalk [sic] again. The use of this deplorable and baseless rape myth, both by government officials and at taxi ranks, resulted in 'My Short Skirt' marches around South Africa – marches which, like Slutwalk Grahamstown, aim to combat rape and rape myths. (Solomon 2011, underlined text to indicate hyperlinks in original)

Although most of the claims that SlutWalk *was* culturally relevant came from women outside North America, defences about its relevance emerged there too. In her speech to the National Sexual Assault Conference in Chicago in 2012, SlutWalk Toronto organizer Colleen Westendorff praised the movement's ability to incorporate local issues. For example, she pointed out how organizers focused on femicide in Mexico, corrective rape for lesbians in South Africa, dowry traditions and eve-teasing in India, street harassment in Israel and homophobia in Honduras. She concluded that: 'SlutWalks have somehow been able to hold on to the simple message against victim-blaming and slut-shaming, but embrace the complexity of violence in people's lives' (Colleen 2012).

What is interesting to note is that while most critiques of the movement seemed to centre on the idea that the march is about promoting female promiscuity and reclaiming the word 'slut,' discourses that defended it focused on how SlutWalk combats rape culture, victim-blaming and shaming. At times this distinction was made explicit, such as in Singapore's *The New Paper*, which wrote:

> Yes, Singapore women are striding forth and getting into the global anti-slut shaming movement on Dec 4.
>   But the Singapore version is doing it their way. This means you don't have to dress like a slut to take part in SlutWalk Singapore. (Lim, J. 2011)

In most cases, however, SlutWalk's cultural relevance was made implicit through the use of language. One article in the *New Zealand Herald* acknowledged controversy over the word 'slut' but stated: 'Whatever the response to the word, SlutWalks are an opportunity to bring together all of those who stand against sexual violence and who challenge the notion that how a women dresses will cause a man to rape her' ('SlutWalks to rally against shaming of rape victims' 2011). And an account from the *Times of India* discussed how participants in New Delhi made the point that: 'Women have been gawked at, groped at, labelled and objectified enough; they aren't taking it anymore' (Mahajan & Chowdhury 2011). This passage, for example, does not clearly state that SlutWalk is culturally relevant in India, but through pointing out the ubiquity of sexual harassment for Indian women in their everyday lives, it suggests the movement is a necessary vehicle through which women can direct their anger and state that 'they aren't taking it anymore.' Another article in the *Huffington Post* documented the march in Cape Town, which brought 'an international campaign against the notion that a woman's appearance can excuse attacks to a country where rape is seen as a national crisis' (Van Zuydam 2011). By identifying rape as a 'national crisis' the article confirms SlutWalk's relevance. According to Harp et al. (2014), an article's implicit meaning is often just as important to examine as what is explicitly stated. When taking this into consideration, it becomes clear that across my eight nations, although articles explicitly stating that SlutWalk is culturally irrelevant stand out, likely because they jar with my own views, the majority assume it *is* relevant by highlighting the pervasive nature of rape, sexual assault and harassment in their own culture.

SlutWalk, privilege and intersectionality

While rape is a crime predominantly committed by men against women, some women are more likely to be assaulted than others (for example, immigrants, women of colour, the disabled and lesbians). As a result, I expected to find discussion about the ways various systems of oppression other than patriarchy fuelled sexual assault in places such as South Africa and India, which have histories of colonialism, imperialism and apartheid. In post-apartheid South Africa, for example, scholars have noted that the news media has largely constructed rape in racialized and classed terms – namely as a problem committed by poor black men in response to the political and social alienation they suffered under the apartheid regime (Moffett 2006). However, despite the particular racialization of rape in South Africa, there was little discussion of intersectionality in either the mainstream news or feminist media. Instead, a number of articles, such as the following, focused on how rape *transcended* issues of class, race and ability:

> What this [movement] tells us is that South African women from different social classes and cultures have collectively had enough of sexual assault, rape and the patriarchal controlling attitudes towards them. (Schutte 2011, p. 9)

Similarly, Desiree Moodie, writing in the *Huffington Post*, argued that 'sexual violence is one issue that affects us all. It strikes freely and willingly. It cuts across every boundary you can imagine. It pays no mind whatsoever to race, age, or class' (Moodie 2011). While articles such as these rightly point out that *all* women are at risk of sexual violence, they do ignore the reality that *some* women, particularly those who are members of socially marginalized groups, are not only more likely to experience sexual assault over others (Amnesty International 2007; Andersen & Taylor 2008; Holzman 1994), but are also more likely to be seen as culpable for their assault (Rozee 1999, p. 100). Consequently, the interplay of various identities not only makes one more or less susceptible to sexual assault, but impacts the public's (and often the victims') perception of the assault in relation to rape myths (e.g. black and Latina women are inherently sexual and therefore *cannot* be raped). So, while the construction that *all* women are joining together to protest rape culture certainly builds a sense of collectivism and solidarity amongst SlutWalkers – something which has been a central feminist tenet for decades (Bryson 2003) – it glosses over issues of power and subordination which fuel sexual assault and rape myths.

Although intersectional critiques of sexual assault were generally missing from my mainstream news and feminist media sample, a number of critiques emerged from women of colour in North America, and deserve detailed attention below.

Critiques from women of colour

By the end of 2011, after dealing with debates about SlutWalk's cultural (ir)relevancy in non-Western nations, a range of critiques, predominantly from women of colour in North America, gained widespread attention, most notably amongst the (Black) feminist blogging community. Women of colour and other marginalized groups raised legitimate questions around issues of privilege and exclusion within the movement. They key problem for many feminists, it seemed, was that the movement lacked an intersectional understanding of sexual assault – or the ways that various forms of oppression interlock with, and fuel one another, to make some women more vulnerable to abuse than others (Crenshaw 1989). Although women of colour had expressed concerns over the movement from its inception, the publication of 'An Open Letter From Black Women to the SlutWalk,' endorsed by numerous black women's organizations, really brought these issues to the fore, and forced SlutWalk Toronto and other satellite groups to re-think some of its branding, tactics (namely, the desire to re-appropriate the word 'slut'), and think more carefully about the ways race, class, ethnicity, sexuality and ability impact women's experiences of sexual assault and the justice system:

> For us [black women], the trivialization of rape and the absence of justice are viciously intertwined with narratives of sexual surveillance, legal access and availability to our personhood. It is tied to institutionalized ideology about our bodies as sexualized objects of property, as spectacles of sexuality and deviant sexual desire. It is tied to notions about our clothed or unclothed bodies as unable to be raped whether on the auction block, in the fields or on living room television screens … Although we vehemently support a woman's right to wear whatever she wants anytime, anywhere, within the context of a 'SlutWalk' we don't have the privilege to walk through the streets of New York City, Detroit, DC, Atlanta, Chicago, Miami, L.A. etc., either half-naked or fully clothed self-identifying as 'sluts' and think that this will make women safer in our communities an hour later, a month later, or a year later … The personal is political. For us, the problem of trivialized rape and the absence of justice are intertwined with race, gender, sexuality, poverty, immigration and community. (Black Women's Blueprint 2011)

Not long after this letter emerged, a photograph of a white protester at SlutWalk NYC holding a sign saying 'Woman is the Nigger of the

World,' went 'viral' and ignited outrage, predominantly amongst the Black feminist community. In her post titled 'SlutWalk and the Legacy of White Feminism,' blogger Maggie not only discussed how the sign 'shocked' SlutWalk supporters, but it served 'as a symbol of the deeper inequalities and exclusion that exist within mainstream feminism' (Maggie 2011). In what followed, critiques, mainly by women of colour, centred on the following two issues which will be discussed below: 1) 'Slut' is a word used primarily against white women as a means to shame those who (are thought to have) deviated from morally conservative norms about chaste sexuality; 2) 'Slut' is not a word women of colour have the privilege or desire to reclaim.

'Slut' is a word used against white women

Although SlutWalk co-founders Heather Jarvis and Sonya Barnett were always aware that the use of the word 'slut' in their event was going to be controversial, Jarvis insisted their intention was to 'sling back' this pejorative word initially used by PC Michael Sanguinetti when he addressed York students on campus safety (Jarvis 2012). Although perhaps assuming that 'slut' was a term used against all women, women of colour began to speak out about the fallacy of this assumption. As feminist Andrea Plaid wrote on the blogging site *Alternet*:

> Even though I have jokingly called myself a slut (as in 'I'm a handbag slut'), as an African American woman I was rather uncomfortable with the protest's racial dynamics, at least how it was shaping up in the US and Canada. I felt the word 'slut' didn't speak to me; I found the word 'ho' more damaging. (Plaid 2011)

Similarly, as the black feminist group the Crunk Feminist Collective noted:

> [T]he term [slut] very much reflects white women's specific struggles around sexuality and abuse. Although plenty of Black women have been called 'slut,' I believe Black women's histories are different, in that Black female sexuality has always been understood from without to be deviant, hyper, and excessive. (Crunktastic 2011a)

Despite the fact that a few mainstream news outlets picked up on problematic notion of 'slut' from the perspective of women of colour ('Are "slutwalk" protests the future of feminism' 2011; 'SlutWalk NYC causes stir in black community' 2011), the bulk of discussions about the movement and intersectionality took place via feminist media circles, with certain posts, such as the Open Letter, becoming widely discussed, quoted and linked to, fostering the connections between online feminist communities (Keller 2013). What is particularly problematic is that, although critiques from women of colour were published in 'mainstream' feminist blogs such as *Rabble.ca* (Walia 2011), most appeared in publications aimed at and written by women (and men) of colour (see for example AF3IRM 2011; Aguilar 2011; Blogando 2011; Crunktastic 2011a, 2011b), while white feminist bloggers generally ignored these issues of intersectionality (for exceptions see Murphy 2012f; Sarkeesian 2011). Although my sample is certainly not representative of all feminist bloggers, the fact that critiques about intersectionality and the different ways women of colour have experienced sexual assault and its aftermath seem to have been located in blogs by people of colour is problematic. It suggests that white feminists today are either unaware of or uninterested in the need for intersectional analysis of oppression, and that there indeed continue to be serious issues of power and privilege which SlutWalk (and feminism more generally) needs to address in order for the movement move forward and become more inclusive. This includes reaching out to the most marginalized and vulnerable members of society and acknowledging our own privileges, prejudices and differing experiences with systems of oppression.

'Slut' cannot be reclaimed

Once it became established that 'slut' was not a word used against *all* women to control their sexuality, the discussion turned to the various ways women of colour *could not* reclaim it. As the anti-imperialist, transnational feminist women's organization AF3IRM noted: 'As women and descendants of women from Latin America, Asia, and Africa, we cannot truly "reclaim" the word "Slut". It was never ours to begin with' (AF3IRM 2011). Instead, the group noted that this label was 'forced upon us by colonizers, who transformed our women into commodities and for the entertainment of US soldiers occupying our countries for corporate America' (2011). As such, they reaffirmed the ways 'there is power and privilege' in reclaiming a word like 'slut' (Petro 2011). This was outlined in detail by the Black Women's Blueprint 'Open Letter':

> As Black women, we do not have the privilege or the space to call ourselves 'slut' without validating the already historically entrenched ideology and recurring messages about what and who the Black woman is. We don't have the privilege to play on destructive

representations burned in our collective minds, on our bodies and souls for generations. (Black Women's Blueprint 2011)

As the blogger Crunktastic wrote, merely to organize an event around the reclamation of the word 'slut' 'is and of itself an act of white privilege' (Crunktastic 2011b). And while white women were seen as privileged enough to have the freedom to embrace the word 'slut,' another blogger detailed how as a woman of colour, her children did not have the same choices:

> White feminists can teach their own little girls to find empowerment through their crotches – my brown little girl cannot afford to be that carefree and cavalier with her life choices. Slutlife is the hard, lonely vocation of rich, educated, privileged white women who <u>will fuck The World</u>, contract social diseases and still, somehow find a husband. No black woman ever got far being a slut. (Izrael 2011, underlined text to indicate hyperlinks in original)

Women of colour also pointed out white women's privilege in taking for granted the fact that they can turn to the police for protection, or the judicial system to get justice, pointing out that for many communities of colour, 'inviting them [the police] into our spaces in order to somehow feel safer rarely crosses our minds' (To the Curb 2011). For some communities this is because they have been subject to decades of police brutality, and are disproportionately incarcerated (Moorti 2002), while for others, their status as illegal immigrants means they would face deportation if they attempted to contact the authorities to report an assault (To the Curb 2011).

The Second Wave feminist movement has long been the subject of a number of well-known (and deserved) critiques from black feminists who have pointed out both the intersectional nature of oppression, and how their experiences have been largely ignored by the white women's movement (see Hill Collins 2000; hooks 2000). hooks (2000), for example, noted how Betty Friedan's *The Feminine Mystique* – the book often credited with sparking the Second Wave, 'ignored the existence of all non-white women and all poor women' (p. 2). Since then, hooks has critiqued feminist discourses, produced mainly by white women who are largely unaware of the racial and class biases they reproduce (p. 3). Rather than assuming sexism provides a common bond amongst women, black feminist and other postmodern theorists have instead focused on how other markers of identity (age, race, class, sexuality, physical abilities, etc.) intersect in people's experiences with oppression, and in how they in turn formulate their identity (see Crenshaw 1989; hooks 2000). In contrast to those white feminists who have concentrated solely on issues of gender inequality (hooks 2000), there is evidence that many feminists involved in SlutWalk took seriously these concerns raised by women of colour, and made changes to the movement as a result.

Changes to SlutWalk in response to critiques from women of colour

In their 'Open Letter from Black Women to the SlutWalk' (2011), the Black Women's Blueprint requested that SlutWalk 'take critical steps to become cognizant of the histories of people of color and engage women of color in ways that respect culture, language and context.' This included 'engaging in a re-branding and re-labeling process' which would enable the building of a truly 'revolutionary movement to end sexual assault, end rape myths and end rape culture' (Black Women's Blueprint 2011). In response, movement co-founder Heather Jarvis posted a reply on the SlutWalk blog, advertising a 'town-hall' style open forum to engage with these criticisms, and to 'establish what SlutWalk Toronto will look like moving forward, and how we can play a role in shaping what the SlutWalk movement becomes' (Heather 2011). Although cognizant that many other satellite groups look to SlutWalk Toronto for guidance, Heather was equally aware that they 'do not control this movement,' or other groups' decision to take these criticisms seriously (Heather 2011). However, Heather stated that they shared the Open Letter with as many other satellite groups as possible, in the hopes that they, too, would engage with these legitimate criticisms.

And it is clear that a number of satellite groups did in fact heed the message. In 2012, organizers in Vancouver held an event titled 'SlutTalk: The (Un)Conference' to discuss rape culture, victim-blaming, sexual stigma and whether or not to change its name in light of criticisms from women of colour (SlutTalk 2012). Using Facebook to poll the community, SlutWalk Vancouver decided to keep the name in the end (Delgado 2014a; Murphy 2012f). Although such practices were taken 'democratically' through a vote, public debate still erupted as some feminists complained that the poll was only advertised on the SlutWalk Vancouver website and not the Facebook page (Beigh 2012), meaning many did not know the poll was taking place. Even when analysing the poll's results, the organizers themselves admitted that, although the majority voted to keep the name, it was nearly a '50/50 split,' and as a result 'in no way do we consider the problems around this name to be resolved or dismissed. The discussion must continue – especially at the march itself. And the question of a name change will remain on the table for any future organizing' (SlutWalk Vancouver 2012).

Although many of the debates about name change emerged in 2011 and 2012, it was clear that these discussions did not go away. In 2013, the CBC ran an article titled 'Winnipeg "SlutWalk" participants mull name change,' noting how the group also debated changing the name, but kept it in the end. In 2014, one of the most visible and active satellite groups, SlutWalk Chicago, did decide on a name change – not for the annual march, which they would continue to call 'SlutWalk,' but for the organizing committee which planned regular events throughout the year, including the march. The name of the new organizing committee, FURIE (Feminist Uprising to Resist Inequality & Exploitation) was announced at the 2014 annual SlutWalk and, as 2013 and 2014 organizer Ashley Broher stated, was one of the most 'contentious issues' the organizing committee had dealt with (Broher 2014). In part, this was because some remained committed to reclaiming the word 'slut,' while for others it was about staying connected to the communities they had engaged with over the past four years (Broher 2014). However, as the organizing committee had become involved in more events than just the annual SlutWalk, they felt it was appropriate to create a new name which reflected the variety of activities they engaged in.

SlutWalk Chicago was not the only organization to approve a name change. After recognizing the movement's issues with privilege and power, SlutWalk Philadelphia rebranded itself as 'The March to End Rape Culture' for the 2013 event (SlutWalk Philadelphia 2013). Organized and hosted by 'SlutWalk Philly and Pussy Division,' the group stated in an open letter that the name change was the result of 'serious discussion on the role that race plays in SlutWalks' (cited in Murtha 2013). The group went on to write:

> For some communities, the word 'slut' is a term they have not been called and cannot relate to in order to reclaim it in any capacity. Systems of oppression have colonized, commodified, or otherwise rewritten their sexualities for centuries, making acts of sexual violence against them a permissible and far too often, expected, occurrence. These are the people who are perhaps the most affected by the victim-blaming SlutWalk stands against, regardless of any 'slutty' dress or behavior, they are considered by some to be 'asking for it' simply by being who they are.

We have decided to put the word 'slut' in the background of the title of the march this year out of a desire to include all those who experience rape culture and want to fight it with us and to bring together as many communities and organizations in Philly and the surrounding areas as possible. We are calling this year's march simply 'A March to End Rape Culture,' as the concept of 'rape culture' has been one that has been identified in many forums and communities to describe the cultural forces which conspire to make it so that sexual violence occurs so often, and with so few of the perpetrators being held accountable for their actions. (cited in Murtha 2013)

It is clear from such posts, then, than some satellite groups have taken criticisms surrounding race and privilege seriously. The SlutWalk Toronto website even lists several cities which re-branded the march, with names such as 'Solidarity Walk,' 'ConsentFest,' 'Walk of No Shame,' and 'STRUTWalk' ('FAQs' n.d.b). However, no further explanation is given for why these names were changed, or if it was in response to criticism from women of colour about power and privilege within the movement.

While some satellite groups at least engaged with the possibility of re-branding the movement, other organizers left it in light of these criticisms, and in at least one case, the movement disbanded as a result.

Abandoning and disbanding SlutWalk satellite groups

In light of the 2011 incident at SlutWalk NYC in which a protester was photographed with a sign saying 'Woman is the Nigger of the World,' SlutWalk NYC disbanded. As organizer Melissa Marturano explained via Facebook messaging:

SlutWalk NYC is no longer an active coalition. We dissolved the coalition because of how 'slut' is an exclusionary and privileged term which does not take into consideration how the bodies and sexualities of women of color were and are legally commodified and controlled by state repression and violence. White women have a much greater privilege to reclaim such terms and our use of the moniker showed a serious lapse in intersectional feminism, no matter how much we tried otherwise. Can that term be used to combat rape culture when there has been no massive paradigm shift? The decision to use the moniker, although very few members of the coalition ever felt comfortable reclaiming it or using it to combat rape culture, was part our coalition's overall misguided praxis which prioritized logistics over politics: we wanted to tap into an international and widely-covered-in-the-media movement and we should have done better to work on our politics. Since the dissolution of the coalition, many of our members are now involved in other groups which are combatting rape culture and which are taking the mistakes we made during SlutWalkNYC very seriously in order to ensure that our activism is doing whatever it can to fight for a world without rape culture for all people and not just the privileged. (Marturano 2013)

Recognizing that there were inherent issues with race and privilege in the movement's name and desire to reclaim the word 'slut,' 2011 SlutWalk Chicago organizer Stephanie Sutton decided to abandon the movement because she did not know how to overcome issues of privilege and racism (Sutton 2014). While this felt like the only option available for Stephanie, others attempted to deal with this issue by de-emphasizing the movement's reclamation of the word 'slut.'

A Shift away from reclaiming the word 'slut'

By 2012, in light of criticism from women of colour, an examination of SlutWalk Facebook groups and websites, and interviews with organizers in mainstream and feminist media demonstrates a shift away from the goal of reclaiming 'slut' amongst satellite groups. Although this goal was never universally adopted, groups which had supported its reclamation in 2011 abandoned this goal in following years. For example, in 2011, both SlutWalk LA and Seattle made it clear through interviews and press releases that they wanted to re-appropriate the word 'slut' (Chloe 2011; Schwyzer 2011). As SlutWalk LA organizer Hugo Schwyzer wrote on his personal blog:

Here's our press release, written by Alixandria Lopez with the rest of our steering committee. 'Note: the decision was made collectively: we *are* working to reclaim the word "slut."' (Schwyzer 2011)

However, in following years, SlutWalk Seattle, for example, highlighted on their website that 'Reappropriating/reclaiming "slut" is not the goal of SlutWalk' ('FAQs' n.d.a). Similarly, SlutWalk LA posted:

We encourage a dialogue about white/heteronormative exclusivity and privilege within feminist movements (including S---Walk), as well as the re-appropriation of the word 'slut' and how it can be problematic. Can we empower ourselves by re-appropriating the word?

Or, by using male-defined terminology, are we continuing to operate within the same paradigm that oppresses us? (SlutWalk LA 2014a)

In the majority of cases, however, satellite groups distanced themselves from the goal of reclaiming the word 'slut' from the beginning. For example, as stated on the SlutWalk Singapore website:

> **One does not need to identify as a 'slut' to be part of SlutWalk –** our ultimate goal is not to reclaim the word, instead we are reclaiming the right to express our sexuality without fear …
>
> Unlike SlutWalks in Western countries, where many protestors turned up in skimpy attire to march, there will be a conscious move to de-emphasize the importance of the word 'slut' for the event here. (Han 2011, bold original)

Similarly, in 2011 SlutWalk Johannesburg noted that although 'reclaiming the word slut might have been the primary focus of the original Toronto SlutWalk,' they instead sought to 'raise awareness around a number of sexual assault issues such as victim-blaming, corrective rape, gender violence, and questioning the acceptance of a "rape culture"' (SlutWalk Johannesburg 2011). In advertising their 2014 march, the SlutWalk Johannesburg Facebook page continued with this message by stating: 'You don't have to identify with or even approve of the word "slut" to support this movement. It is for every human being who believes that NOBODY deserves to be raped' (SlutWalk Johannesburg 2014a).

Perhaps as expected, SlutWalk Toronto in particular was very public about its shifting views on reclaiming 'slut':

> In the original march, reappropriation [of the word slut] was one of the goals, however at no point have SlutWalk organizers required participants to reappropriate the term 'slut' for themselves. After many conversations with folks from different communities that bear disproportionate levels of harm from these words, we now realize that we can better support survivors across diverse communities by keeping our focus on challenging the language. If any folks want to reclaim 'slut' on an individual level, we will support them, but our organizing energies will not be focused on that aspect. ('FAQs' n.d.b)

According to scholars, feminists never have, and likely never will agree on everything. As Redfern and Aune (2010) wrote, no progressive social movement is completely unanimous in its views, and as feminists learn more about the world around them, and other people's experiences of it, their views are likely to change. Just as the SlutWalk movement sought to educate the public about the reality of rape culture, feminists, particularly those of colour, reached out to SlutWalk to educate, and remind them about the intersectional nature of oppression. While it is easy to assume that all Third Wave activism is inherently intersectional, or that we live in a 'post-racial' society in which skin colour does not matter, the critiques from women of colour were an important reminder that ways women experience sexual assault and its aftermath is closely intertwined with race, gender, sexuality, poverty, immigration and community. These critiques were an indication that, in the words of SlutWalk Chicago 2013 and 2014 organizer Ashley Broher, 'Our feminism will be intersectional or it will be bull-shit' (2014).

Concluding thoughts

Rather than examining *how* SlutWalk has been represented, this chapter provided insights into aspects of coverage such as *where* and *when* the movement was seen to take place before moving to focus on variations in coverage of the movement. Overall, my research revealed that SlutWalk was seen as an important and newsworthy event, both in my mainstream news and feminist media samples. That said, most coverage emerged in 2011, dwindled in 2012 and became almost non-existent by 2013. The steep decline in coverage is not unique to SlutWalk; it is something other modern feminist movements have also experienced (Mackay 2012). Because SlutWalk is pursuing long-term cultural change which does not happen overnight, it, like other social movements, faces the challenge of staying relevant and newsworthy for a news culture which values 'novelty' – even when the promise of women's flesh is on display. And while this has long been true for the mainstream news, my research suggests this media 'fatigue' also holds true amongst the feminist blogosphere. As a result, despite the fact that SlutWalks continue to be held in major cities around the world, and to manage extremely active Facebook or Twitter counts, it is extremely problematic that the movement either has become constructed as 'dead' and 'over,' or is ignored and erased. Although other forms of feminist activism, particularly those contributing to the anti-rape movement, continue to attract attention in both mainstream news and feminist media, what will happen to these in a year's time? Will they too be ignored or forgotten? Will the media just move onto the next novel form of feminist protest? Or will they get bored of the current 'feminist zeitgeist' (Valenti 2014c) altogether? While perhaps we have come from an era in which mainstream media coverage is necessary for a movement's survival, is this now the case in an age of 'postmedia,' where citizens can bypass the mainstream news via social media (Castells 2012)? And should feminists seek mainstream, or alternative feminist coverage? These are important questions – questions that this one study alone cannot answer. Instead, there is a need for more research into representations of modern feminist activism which documents how the movement is historicized, recounted and remembered.

While much attention was paid to the marches themselves, it was also addressed, covered and reported on during its run-up. While it is idealistic to think that the news is made up of the most important events and information, gathered and selected by the most creative and talented journalists, research shows that content is strongly shaped by organizational routines, policies and access to resources (Williams 2003). While this isn't to say that journalists have no freedom in deciding what to report, it does suggest that these decisions are constrained by organizational policies and resources (Shoemaker & Reese 1996; Williams 2003). Journalists therefore rely heavily on news about particular events being brought to their attention, such as forthcoming protests and demonstrations.

At the same time as news organizations rely on routine events and stories, the news media is also *reactive* to events which have taken place (Herring et al. 2007; Shoemaker & Reese 1996). While attracting media coverage of events which have already taken place is undoubtedly important in raising the visibility of a social movement, it can often be too late to encourage potential participants to become involved, particularly if it was a one-off or annual event. In order for a social movement to gain popularity and grow, people need to know that it exists, what it is about, and crucially, *how they can become involved*. And this is one of the really important things about SlutWalk's coverage in the mainstream news media – it not only alerted readers to the movement's existence, but also provided them with information on how they could get involved. Readers were commonly directed towards movement Facebook pages, or given specific information about the marches' locations, routes and start times.

By the end of 2011, as the movement expanded across the globe, it became apparent that the international growth of the movement had become news fodder in itself. The news media in Canada, where the movement started, were particularly keen on charting its international development, reporting when the movement reached places such as the US, Australia, India and Singapore. As explained by news theorists, journalists look for *continuity*, or follow-ups on stories that have made the headlines (see Galtung & Ruge 1965). Not only did the global spread of the march provide a sense of international credibility and legitimacy, these articles also helped create a sense of collective activism, which is important given the dominance of neoliberal values of individual choice, freedom and action (see Gill & Scharff 2011; Mendes 2012). Yet while the international nature of the march was a feature in one fifth of all mainstream news articles, it represented a significantly smaller proportion of feminist media posts (six percent), which tended to focus on local activism. This reinforces findings on the highly intimate and personalized nature of blogging, which centres on personal and local experiences and issues (Simmons 2008).

As a global movement, this chapter also highlighted the ways that messages around sexual assault and rape culture were adapted to varying regional, national and international settings. One of the most obvious differences was the use of parallel or translated names in places such as India and South and Central America. Other nations such as Singapore had to adapt the movement's message so as not to attract negative government attention, including distancing itself from the reclamation of the word 'slut,' and the idea that people should attend their event in provocative clothing. Because of these local adaptations, I argue that it becomes very difficult to provide a singular definition of the movements' goals, aims and purpose. Instead, I argue that there are many SlutWalks, each interested in issues around sexual violence and rape culture. And while I recognize that some find this lack of a unified vision as problematic, I argue that such diversity is *healthy* and *normal* for feminist activism, and allows the movement to become relevant in its own particular locality and cultural context. This ability to 'Think Global, Act Local' is important not only for ensuring the visibility of connections between activists around the world, but to combat criticisms that as a 'Western' movement, it was culturally irrelevant in and incompatible with places such as Singapore, India, Australia and South Africa.

Because understanding the ways feminist activism is (seen to be) taking place is an important part understanding the 'storying' of feminism (see Hemmings 2005; Mendes 2011a; 2012), my next chapter focuses specifically on its representations in both the mainstream news and feminist media.

4

Representing the Movement: SlutWalk Challenges Rape Culture

This is the first of two chapters that explore representations of SlutWalk in both my mainstream news and feminist media samples. Both chapters were organized using the results of a frame analysis, derived with the help of a qualitative content analysis. Frames were established after asking questions such as: What is SlutWalk said to be about?; Whose voices were used?; What 'sparked' coverage of SlutWalk (e.g. a forthcoming march, or one which had taken place)?; Which, if any, feminist or oppositional discourses or critiques were used either in relation to the movement or rape culture?; and What is the overall level of support for the movement? Although the qualitative content analysis revealed a number of competing frames, this book focuses on the two most popular ones. Chapter 4 analyzes the means through which SlutWalk was constructed as a movement challenging rape culture, while Chapter 5 analyzes how it was constructed as being opposed and/or misguided, often by feminists themselves.

Using critical discourse analysis (CDA), this chapter analyzes the ways in which most articles and posts about the movement drew upon explicitly feminist, and often radical, discourses. These include the notion that victim-blaming/slut-shaming is wrong; that society should blame the rapists, not the victims; that personal appearance does not cause sexual assault; and that rape is about power, violence and control, rather than sex or passion. Although these discourses were present in both my mainstream news and feminist media sample, I argue that the level of sophistication and depth of these discourses varied widely. For example, these discourses were often deployed superficially in the mainstream news media, with little context, explanation or analysis. Although the inclusion of feminist discourses was a significant and positive development when considering feminism's long history of marginalization and de-radicalization in the mainstream news, I argue that it was not developed enough to truly challenge the hegemonic and entrenched views on sexual assault and rape culture. My feminist media sample on the other hand, as was perhaps to be expected, not only provided much more detailed accounts and explanations of these feminist discourses, but directly challenged hegemonic views on sexual assault by highlighting their flaws and fallacies. As a result, I join other scholars who have questioned the extent to which feminists can rely on such capitalist, patriarchal institutions to foster radical social and cultural change (see Freeman 2001). Instead, I point to the ways in which the feminist blogosphere, like radical feminist magazines, newsletters and zines before it, unhindered by journalistic conventions or restraints, is a more effective means of developing counterhegemonic discourses, and raising consciousness of the reality of rape and sexual assault.

Representing SlutWalk

When speaking about my research to colleagues, friends, family and even strangers, one of the most common questions people ask, particularly if they have never heard of the movement is, 'What is SlutWalk about?' Even though I have spent three years following and researching this movement, it is still a question I have difficulty answering. Although in general I would argue it is an anti-rape movement which focuses on shattering a number of rape myths (causes of rape, victims' culpability) as addressed in Chapter 3, I have also recognized that the movement's message differs from city to city, nation to nation and, sometimes, year to year. For example, as discussed in the previous chapter, while reclaiming the word 'slut' was an important part of the movement for some satellite groups in 2011, this goal was later de-emphasized in light of critiques from women of colour. And while most marches have focused on eradicating rape and sexual assault, the emphasis in places such as India was on sexual harassment or 'eve-teasing'. While I have argued that this diversity in the movement's message is healthy, and necessary for the movement to spread internationally and to reflect local issues, I became interested in analysing how the mainstream news and feminist media defined the movement, asking 'What is SlutWalk about?' This was answered initially through a frame analysis, and more in-depth through a CDA.

Framing

The way a story constructs – or frames – an event is a widely used concept for academics in a variety of fields, but particularly for social movement scholars (see Ashley & Olson 1998; Barnett 2005; Baylor 1996; Benford & Snow 2000; Costain et al. 1997; Couldry 1999; Creedon 1993; Lind & Salo 2002; Mendes 2011a; Rohlinger 2002; Strutt 1994; Worthington 2008). Frame analysis is a particularly useful tool because the construction of particular frames can help reveal ideologies present (or absent) in a text by asking How is a particular issue constructed? Whose voices are present or absent? Which, if any, feminist discourses or critiques were used in relation to either the movement or rape culture? What are the problems or solutions to the issues at hand? What is the overall narrative on the movement? Cumulatively, these helped me to develop a sense of how SlutWalk was framed.

When analysing the results from my qualitative content analysis, a few key similarities and differences emerged. For example, in both my mainstream news and feminist media samples (see Tables 4.1 and 4.2), the most common frame was that of SlutWalk as a movement which challenges rape culture, creates awareness of sexual assault-related issues

Table 4.1   What is SlutWalk? frames used in mainstream news sample, 2011–2013

	Number of articles	Percent
SlutWalk tackles/challenges sexual violence, promotes awareness or empowerment	207	68
SlutWalk is controversial/misguided/opposed	68	23
SlutWalk shows solidarity amongst women/ victims	10	3
Uncertainty over what SlutWalk stands for	4	1
Other	15	5
Total	304	100

Table 4.2   What is SlutWalk? frames used in feminist media sample, 2011–2013

	Number of articles	Percent
SlutWalk tackles/challenges sexual violence, promotes awareness or empowerment	270	69
SlutWalk is controversial/misguided/opposed	92	23
SlutWalk shows divides feminists	14	4
SlutWalk is a successful global movement	15	4
Total	390	100

(e.g. conviction rates, its impact on victims, prevention strategies, etc.), and validates the experiences of sexual assault survivors (207 articles or 68 percent of total in mainstream news media; 270 articles or 69 percent of total in feminist media articles). Given that previous research demonstrates that feminist activism has not always attracted mainstream media support (see Barker-Plummer 2000; Bradley 2003; Douglas 1994; Goddu 1999; Hinds & Stacey 2001; Hollows & Moseley 2006; Lind & Salo 2002; Mendes 2011a; Mills 1997; Molotch 1978; Pingree & Hawkins 1978), these supportive frames are undoubtedly a positive development in the 'storying' of feminism.

The second most common frame was that SlutWalk is a misguided movement, whose efforts are largely opposed (68 articles or 23 percent of total in mainstream news media; 92 articles or 23 percent of total for feminist media). This frame will be the focus of Chapter 5. It is worth noting however, that other frames emerged which were specific to either my mainstream news or feminist media samples. For example, in the mainstream news, another, less frequently used frame was that SlutWalk is a movement that demonstrates women's solidarity, particularly with victims of sexual assault (10 articles or three percent of total). A fourth frame emerged, saying there was uncertainty over what SlutWalk actually stands for (four articles or one percent of total). In my feminist media sample, frames emerged stating that SlutWalk divides feminists (14 articles or four percent of total), and that SlutWalk is a successful global movement (15 articles or four percent of total). Due to space constraints, however, this book will focus only on the two key frames.

SlutWalk challenges rape culture and promotes awareness

It became abundantly clear through my qualitative reading of both mainstream and feminist media articles that SlutWalk was overwhelmingly constructed as a movement that challenges rape culture, and the victim-blaming often associated with it. This frame was evident in news headlines such as: 'Tackling sexual violence' (2011), 'Anti-rape campaign coming to city streets' (Nicholson 2011), 'Fight rape, join first SlutWalk in G'Town' (2011), 'Hundreds march in Toronto SlutWalk to combat sexual violence' (Posadzki 2012), 'Rally to counter sexual assault' (Hope 2011), and 'Steps toward fighting a culture of blame' (Wu 2011). It was also evident in feminist media posts titled: 'Speak out against rape with SlutWalk and Reclaim the Night' (Pearce 2012), 'Sluts don't cause rape, rapists do: Why "SlutWalks" are sweeping the world' (Seltzer & Kelley 2011), and 'SlutWalk: Changing a "don't get raped" culture to a "don't rape" culture' (Kraus 2011). This frame was particularly enabled by the fact that PC Sanguinetti – the man who sparked SlutWalk through his advice to women that they could avoid being 'victimized' if they didn't dress 'like sluts' – was quoted 157 times in mainstream news (52 percent of all articles) and 72 times in feminist media (18 percent of all posts). Sanguinetti's quote was often used as the 'hook' in the first few paragraphs of a news article/blog.

For example, the feminist blog *Feministing* introduced the movement as follows:

> Sonya Barnett and Heather Jarvis are the co-founders of SlutWalk, an incredibly badass protest organized against victim-blaming that was spurred by comments made by a Toronto law enforcement officer who said that women who don't want to be assaulted, raped or otherwise 'victimized' should avoid dressing 'like sluts.' (Adelman 2011, underlined text to indicate hyperlink in original)

Similarly, a news article from Australia's *Canberra Times* opened with:

> More than 60 SlutWalk protest rallies have been organized around the world in response to Toronto police officer Michael Sanguinetti's advice to students at a personal safety talk in January.
> 'I've been told I'm not supposed to say this. However, women should avoid dressing like sluts in order not to be victimized,' he said. (Browne 2011)

Scholars have noted how the use of sources is crucial to the construction of media frames (Benford & Snow 2000; Mendes 2011a). This is because journalists frame events when deciding who to interview, what to ask, what angle to take and how the story will be ordered (Kitzinger 2009, p. 137). These 'primary definers' are important to the story because they 'set the limit for all subsequent discussion by framing what the problem is' (Hall et al. 1978, p. 59) and how to respond to it. That SlutWalk was mostly framed around issues of sexual assault, and not, say, as a movement which fights for women to 'dress like sluts,' (as was the case with some coverage/blogs) was likely aided by the fact that over half of all articles quoted at least one supporter/participant (97 times), organizer (153 times) or banner/placard (145 times) from the event.

These sources were particularly prominent in articles/posts which included the following feminist discourses: personal appearance and clothing do not cause sexual assault; victim-blaming/slut-shaming is wrong; and perpetrators, not victims should be blamed.[1] Although rare in my feminist media sample, I found many instances in my mainstream news sample of discourses stating that women should be free to wear what they want without fear of (being blamed for an) attack. Conversely, my feminist sample included a range of discourses centring on how rape is an act of power, violence and control, rather than passion and sex, and how 'slut' is a word used to control/shame women. As will be discussed below, these discourses were either absent, or presented in a shallow manner in my mainstream news sample.

Victim-blaming/slut-shaming is wrong

When analysing the use of feminist discourses in both samples, the most prominent message was that victim-blaming or slut-shaming was wrong and harmful to women (152 articles or 54 percent of total for news media sample; 125 articles or 32 percent of total for feminist media sample). This discourse was evident in news headlines such as: 'SlutWalks to rally against shaming of rape victims' (2011), 'SlutWalk in Philly and worldwide: Long overdue focus on the blame and shame of women' (Smullens 2011), 'SlutWalk SF says no to victim blaming' (Pinto 2012), '"SlutWalk" fights back against stigma surrounding sexual assault and rape victims' (Mandell 2011), and '150 join Ottawa's SlutWalk to protest "victim-blaming" attitudes' (Chen 2012). It was also found in feminist media headlines which ran from the serious – such as: 'The un-funny, unfair and un-feminist thing about victim blaming' (Chloe 2011), 'It's my fault because I had a drink? How being sexually assaulted introduced me to victim-blaming culture' (Purcell 2011), 'How a victim blaming cop inspired SlutWalk' (Carmon 2011) and 'Protesters unite against damaging stereotypes of sexual assault survivors' (Bonnar 2011) – to a more playful, ironic or sarcastic tone, as evidenced by: 'What did you expect, wearing trackpants like that?' (Ideologically Impure 2012); 'Victim Blaming 101' (Spankhead 2012a); and 'When skirts break the law' (Powell 2011).

Discourses which insist that women are not to blame for their sexual assault are not only very important in alleviating the guilt that many feel (see for example Lisak 1994; Taylor 2014; Weiss 2010) and re-directing blame to perpetrators, but for reflecting one of the most common messages from various SlutWalk satellite groups. For example, one of the movement's taglines, which has been used across a variety of satellite groups, is: 'SlutWalk: The Radical Notion that No One Deserves to be Raped' (see for examples SlutWalk Birmingham 2011; SlutWalk London 2012; SlutWalk Orlando 2012). While this in itself is evidence of the movement's stance against victim-blaming, further explanation is often provided. SlutWalk Toronto, for example, makes it clear that the movement was sparked in response to an 'environment in which it's okay to blame the victim,' and that the movement continued 'because survivors of sexual violence deserve our support, not our scrutiny' (2014). Similarly, SlutWalk Seattle (2014) explained on its Facebook site:

> On January 24th, 2011, a Toronto police officer gave some advice that is all too common: 'Women should avoid dressing like sluts in order not to be victimized.' From an 11-year-old in Texas being blamed for being gang raped to a teenager in Seattle not being able to file rape charges because witnesses 'portrayed the act as consensual,' this line of thought pervades our culture.
>
> The idea that women invite sexual assault by looking like they enjoy sex, or that men's urges become so uncontrollable at the sight of a little extra skin that they can't hold themselves back from raping is ludicrous ... Saying that survivors could have protected themselves by not looking like 'sluts' implies that the survivors are at fault and creates a culture in which the heinous crime of sexual assault is seen as no big deal. (SlutWalk Seattle 2014)

Because this discourse was so prominent in various SlutWalk satellite groups' Facebook pages, Twitter accounts and websites, it is perhaps of little surprise that it was also reflected in mainstream news accounts of the movement, such as the one below from the *Toronto Star*:

> Lenore Lukasik-Foss, the director of the Sexual Assault Centre Hamilton and Area, asked participants to 'unlearn' the lies about sexualized violence.
>
> 'I know you know this but victim-blaming and slut-shaming have got to stop,' she said as the crowd erupted in cheers.
>
> 'They silence women and men survivors of sexualized violence ... The lies we are told about rape help create a community where survivors do not get the help and justice they need and deserve.' ('Slutwalk hits the streets of Hamilton' 2011, p. A8)

Similarly, the *Hobart Mercury* quoted a local organizer saying: 'It doesn't matter who you are, where you're from, or what you're wearing, victims are not to blame for sexual assault' (Hope 2011, p. 15). These discourses were also found in my feminist media sample. In her post on *Rabble.ca*, Harsha Walia (2011) wrote about her conflicting feelings about participating in SlutWalk in light of questions about the exclusion of women of colour from the movement. In the end however, she decided to march 'for the simple reason that "I am committed to ending victim-blaming"' (Walia 2011).

Discursive strategies used to challenge victim-blaming

My research demonstrates that there were a number of discursive strategies used to challenge victim-blaming or slut-shaming attitudes. This included highlighting the ubiquitous nature of rape and sexual assault, noting that 'people get sexually assaulted regardless of what they wear, that most sexual assault occurs between people who know each other, and that dressing "like a slut" is not an invitation to rape' (Carmon 2011). It also included laying out rape myths and then 'busting' them, as seen with a blogger on *come again?* (2011):

> Rape myth:
> If you dress like a slut, you'll get raped. Just by being out in town 'dressed like a slut' (which is what, exactly? high heels? tight skirt? showing cleavage? spangles? a combination of the above?), you set yourself up as a target for rape.
> Myth busted:
> a) This is called victim blaming, and it is bullshit.
> b) It doesn't matter what you wear if a man decides he will rape you.
> c) Most women are raped in places they felt safe by men they thought they could trust. So there is no real correlation between being out on the town (while dressed like a slut) and being a rape survivor. (come again? 2011)

Here, the blogger not only questioned what dressing like a 'slut' actually entailed, but attempted to 'bust' it through directly challenging the notion that such women make themselves a 'target of rape,' calling such views 'bullshit.' Instead of focusing on survivors' clothing, the blogger noted that women get raped because men decide to rape them.

Not all discourses around victim-blaming were challenged or 'busted' in such a straightforward way. Some, such as *The F Bomb's* Evelyn T., challenged victim-blaming through more narrative forms:

> Victim blaming needs to stop. And I mean all types of victim blaming, especially the subtle kinds that are far too abundant for my liking, and easy to miss. Although the SlutWalks have received some controversy for the word 'slut' from non-feminists and feminists alike, I believe the message they are trying to get across

is good: no matter what you wear, or do, nothing can make you to blame for being raped. (T. 2011)

While here the shift from blaming survivors to perpetrators was seen as a worthy goal in and of itself, others recognized the ways that it was necessary to end the legitimization of violence against women. As the feminist blogger Miranda (2011b) explained:

> When we engage victim-blaming attitudes, we make it harder for victims of sexual assault to come forward and report a serious violent crime, we become complicit in the unwillingness of authorities like Constable Sanguinetti to help victims and pursue allegations with the gravity they deserve, and we make the world a safer place for rapists. (See also Miranda 2011a; 'SlutWalk Vancouver' 2011)

Rather than merely stating that victim-blaming or slut shaming is 'wrong' or 'harmful,' such posts are important because they demonstrate the material consequences of such beliefs. For one, they prevent women from coming forward to report crimes committed against them, either because they believe they are to blame, or because they recognize they won't get justice. And second, such beliefs create inertia amongst authorities to take seriously, investigate, charge or prosecute perpetrators.

Although few articles actually explain *why* victims are routinely blamed for their assault, or how it benefits men, I argue they are still potentially liberating, particularly for the women (and men) living with the guilt and shame of their experiences, with no systems of support. For them, the idea that the assault was not their fault *is* radical, with the potential to relieve them of the guilt and culpability they felt over their attack. It is this transformation that is necessary to take one's previously private experiences of something 'designed to isolate and shame us into silence, into a strategy of consciousness raising' (Penny 2013). And as scholars have noted, consciousness-raising has been a crucial element in feminist activism for decades and has material consequences for women's lives (Bevacqua 2001; Bryson 2003; Maddison 2013b; Penny 2013; Shaw, F. 2011). Unfortunately, however, as we will see below, few articles went further, to suggest that society now needs to start re-focusing culpability on the rapists.

Blame the rapists not the victims

Another less used, but still important feminist discourse found in both my mainstream news (17 articles or six percent of total) and feminist media (71 articles or 18 percent of total) sample is the idea that the focus and blame for rape should lie with the perpetrator, not the victim.

Although it was often *implied* that rapists should be blamed for engaging in sexual assault in discourses stating that victim-blaming is wrong, or that victims are not at fault for their assault, I was surprised that so few news articles and, to a lesser extent, blogs, focused *explicitly* on this message. Typical examples include a piece by Shira Tarrant (2011a) for *Ms. Magazine* when she declared: 'We need to change our culture to one that asks not, "What was the victim wearing?" but, "Why is he raping?"' Similarly, blogger Maggie (2012) wrote on *Where Is Your Line?*: 'Let's shift the blame where it belongs: to the perpetrator, not where it usually lingers, with the survivor.' One article posted on the *BBC's* website similarly noted how SlutWalk was 'about putting the blame back where it belongs, on the rapist rather than the victim' ('Slutwalk march takes place in Bristol' 2011).

What was particularly noticeable about the use of the discourse saying rapists, rather than survivors, should be blamed, is the passion behind such utterances. Here, it was common to see the use of italics, capital letters or bold to emphasize the importance of the message. A blog on SlutWalk London's Tumblr site insisted that: 'We believe that rape is **always** the fault of the rapist, never the survivor. And until that attitude is held globally, we will continue to **speak up**' (SlutWalk London 2012, bold original). Humour, sarcasm and irony were also common features used to support this discourse. Although a fierce critic of SlutWalk, blogger Meghan Murphy satirized current tactics used to 'prevent' violence against women and emphasized the need to focus on changing men's behaviour:

> Hey! Here's a newfangled idea! How about we, FOR ONCE, put the onus on the violent men. How about we even go so far as to blame *men* for the violent acts they commit rather than blaming the victim for 'dealing with' violent men in the 'wrong way.' How about, instead of learning how to be nicer to johns, so as to avoid being attacked by them, we teach johns that they won't get away with being violent? What's that? <u>Criminalize the johns</u>? Oh no. That's crazy-talk. All women need is more 'skills.' Skills will stop male violence, right? (Murphy 2012b, underlined text to indicate hyperlink in original)

Bloggers' frustration at how society continues to ignore men's autonomy in perpetuating violence against women is also evident in the following blog.

> And apparently people still haven't gotten the memo that rapists are actually to blame for rape, not drunk women, or being out at 1am or

3am or 6am, and or short skirts. Funny that, because it seems like it would be fairly easy to comprehend. I feel like reiterating the point: rapists are to blame for rape, nothing else ... If that's still to [sic] difficult to accept, think about this: take all those things – a short skirt, alcohol, a poorly-lit street late at night – and add them together. Drunken woman+miniskirt+alleyway =/= rape. You might think that sounds like the perfect equation for rape, but you'd be wrong because there's one crucial element missing: A RAPIST. Without a rapist in the equation – this equation or any equation – there wont [sic] be a rape. It seems like such a simple idea to grasp, and yet we're still swimming against the tide of a victim-blaming rape culture, desperately trying to get people to understand. (Lady News 2011a)

Although it might seem commonsensical, I agree with the bloggers above who highlight the importance of bringing rapists into discussions of sexual assault, rather than implicitly assigning them blame. Feminists have long critiqued the use of language in media reports of sexual assault, noting for example of men are 'absent' from coverage (Clark 1992). As Clark writes: 'Naming is a powerful ideological tool' (p. 209), and by not placing the blame on rapists, where it belongs, perpetrators continue to avoid blame, which is then transferred to someone else (most often the victim). Therefore, while it is important to emphasize the ways that survivors are never at fault for their assault, I argue the discourse needs to go further and *explicitly* lay blame with the rapist.

Personal appearance does not cause sexual assault

Given that the SlutWalk movement emerged in response to the views expressed by Toronto PC Michael Sanguinetti, that women who dress like 'sluts' invite sexual assault, it is unsurprising that a feminist counter-discourse emerged precisely challenging this myth. Discourses stating that personal appearance and clothing do not cause rape were commonly found in both news texts (118 articles or 42 percent of total) and feminist posts (103 articles or 26 percent of total). In fact, given that Sanguinetti was directly quoted in 157 news articles (55 percent of the total), I would argue it is surprising that this discourse was not *more* prevalent in the mainstream news. Since at least the 1970s, when feminists across the world began to theorize rape as a tool used to maintain women's subordination, they began to identify a number of 'rape myths' which are used to legitimate sexual assault by constructing it as natural, normal, and in some circumstances, inevitable (Berrington & Jones 2002; Carter 1998; Meyers 2006). For example, a common myth is that women 'invite' rape by wearing certain clothing which men interpret as a sign of their sexual availability *and* consent. A common and related myth is that women 'provoke' rape by wearing clothing that sexually excites men to the point that they lose control and commit rape. In both cases, women will be blamed for the assault, either for arousing men to the point where they 'lose control,' or sending out 'confusing' signals.

Although I do not believe that there is a single piece of clothing women can wear which is capable of sexually arousing a man to the point where he can no longer control himself and he commits rape, I do recognize that some men might *choose* to rape a woman to control, punish, degrade or humiliate her *as a result* of her clothes, personal appearance, choice of friends/partners/lovers, or other behaviours such as drinking alcohol or staying out late at night. However, it is important to distinguish here that while perpetrators might argue the woman 'provoked' the assault, such cases only further support the argument that rape is a crime of power, violence, control or domination, not lust or sex.

In recognition of the widespread myth that clothes cause rape, SlutWalks around the globe have sought to challenge discourses constructing clothes as a key to – or even contributing cause of rape. This is evidenced by numerous placards at walks including 'My Clothes Are Not My Consent,' 'My Dress is Not An Invitation,' 'This Skirt Doesn't Cause Rape: Rapists Do,' 'It's A Dress Not A Yes' and 'I was raped when I was 4. I didn't know that footsies were slutty' (see Seltzer & Kelley 2011; Tarrant 2011a). Furthermore, the idea that clothes don't cause rape is a key feminist discourse found in both my mainstream news and feminist media samples, although they range from simplistic to more sophisticated analyses. For example, many news articles, which are subject to restrictions in terms of style, length and background information, presented a rather superficial relaying of this discourse, as evident below:

> 'Sexual assault has nothing to do with how you are dressed, where you are, how much you've had to drink, where you are at night, what gender you are, what age you are, your abilities, anything,' said [SlutWalk] Saskatoon organizer Leah Horlick. (Hamilton 2011)

Similarly, one news report from New Zealand's *Sunday Star-Times* explained:

> Auckland organizer Angela Smith, 22, a self-described feminist, says advice on how to dress does nothing to protect people.

'Statistically, how you dress doesn't increase your chances of being raped.'

She and fellow organizer Amato, 27, say they both heard the advice given as conventional wisdom as they were growing up. ('Slutwalk protest targets dress slur' 2011, p. 3)

Even well-known feminists such as Jessica Valenti provided a somewhat simplistic explanation in a *Washington Post* interview:

I tell folks who talk about rape in this way that clothing has absolutely nothing to do with whether or not women get attacked. There is no research showing a link between clothing and sexual assault. I also think it's telling that you very rarely (if ever) hear this argument about clothing directed at male victims of rape. (Rogers 2011)

These superficial discourses were also evident in my feminist media sample. Posting on the feminist blog *Bad Reputation,* Sarah Ross (2011) wrote: 'Personal stories [are] told by all kinds of people, but all pointing to the same conclusion. Rape happens to people regardless of what they are wearing. Rapists, not those who are raped, and certainly not the clothes of those who are raped, are to blame.' Although these articles reproduce one of SlutWalk's key and original discourses, that clothes do not cause rape, I question the extent to which they are capable of challenging the patriarchal ideologies at the root of such 'common sense' understandings of sexual assault, as they lack critical assessment of what actually *does* cause rape.

A slightly more sophisticated challenge to this rape myth, relayed in many articles and blog posts, attempts to dismantle the view that rape is about sex by pointing out how modestly dressed women, the elderly, the 'unattractive' and the young get raped. As *The Guardian* columnist Suzanne Moore asked:

But if rape is understood as a confusion about outfits, then the solution is that we all wear burqas. No woman in a burqa is ever abused, is she? But the thinking behind the get-up is similar. Sexual desire, or nine tenths of it, somehow resides in the female. This does not explain why some men rape babies. Or elderly women. In war, rape is increasing used as a weapon of mass destruction. Dying, mutilated women are raped in front of their children. I hardly think this is to do with 'stripper shoes' and miniskirts. (Moore, S. 2011)

Similarly, writing on SlutWalk Singapore's blog, Anu Selva-Thomson (2011) noted that: 'Rapists don't hang around void decks or car parks assessing women and their clothing before attacking. They don't ponder the merits of zippers versus button-fly and wish women would all just wear Velcro.' Instead, while noting that women in tracksuits and burkas, and nuns, get raped, she asks 'how do we account for provocative clothing as a reason in these cases? We can't' (Selva-Thomson 2011).

While the logic presented in such articles at least provides evidence that rape is not *always* about clothing, it leaves unchallenged the notion that in some cases *it is*, and that while most men can control themselves when they see a scantily clad woman, 'slutty' outfits remain a 'trigger' for others. As a result, discourses such as this solve only part of the problem by rendering certain victims as more 'innocent' than others (see also McNicol 2012). Yet, while I applaud them for promoting feminist beliefs, these articles do nothing to challenge the virgin/vamp dichotomy in which 'sluts,' sex workers, or those who were drunk, flirted with or knew the perpetrator, or were out late at night, are blamed for their assault. So, while a step in the right direction, the use of feminist discourse saying clothes doesn't cause rape is not enough on its own to challenge patriarchal ideologies. Instead, it must be used in combination with discourses constructing rape as an act of power, violence, domination and control (not just sex, lust or passion).

Rape is about violence, power and control

In 1975, American feminist Susan Brownmiller's ground-breaking book *Against Our Will* was one of the first to theorize rape, not as a crime of uncontrolled passion, sex or lust, but one of violence, power, domination and control. For readers unfamiliar with this theory, I understand and remember how radical and even unbelievable it may seem at first. After all, the hegemonic discourse on rape in both popular and political culture is that it is a crime of passion and sex, carried out by 'deviant' strangers, rather than your average father/brother/friend/husband/ boyfriend/acquaintance (see Benedict 1992; Cater 1998; Clark 1992; Soothill & Walby 1991). In this understanding of rape, men become so overcome by their sexual urges that they (often unwittingly) commit rape as a result. While it is easier to contest the idea that clothes are the root cause of rape by identifying how people are raped while wearing all manner of clothing, and pointing out that not every beautiful or provocatively dress woman is raped, it is much harder to convince people that rape is not primarily about sexual desire and gratification.

And while it would be foolish to claim that sex or sexual gratification has nothing to do with rape, researchers who have interviewed convicted rapists argue that it is instead a 'perk' or an 'added bonus' rather than the driving force (Scully & Marolla 1985, p. 254).[2] Instead, rape serves a multitude of purposes, and is a weapon of violence which, depending on the context, can be used to degrade, punish or humiliate victims (or their male relatives or community), assert power and privilege, or maintain dominance and control (see also Groth 2001 [1979]; Scully & Marolla 1985).

Rape in times of conflict

When thinking about what motivates individuals to rape, it would be naïve to assume it always serves the same purpose. For example, during times of war, rape is a weapon that has historically been used to demoralize, humiliate and instil fear in one's enemies, as well as as a means of genocide and ethnic cleansing (Wood 2006). As a result of increased research into sexual violence in conflict, rape has been re-conceptualized from being an inevitable by-product of war, where men, deprived of women's company, rape to fulfil sexual needs, to being recognized as a 'planned and targeted policy' (Buss 2009, p. 146) meant to demoralize and destroy individuals and communities (UN Human Rights 2014). Although scholars note that rape is not used as a weapon in all wars (Wood 2006), the effects can be devastating. For example, after experiencing a 13-year civil war, a 2005–2006 survey of Liberian women found that 92 percent had been subject to sexual violence, including rape. Such staggering statistics cannot be accounted for by men's insatiable lust, but as evidence of the ways rape was systematically carried out during the conflict.

Revenge rape

Although not a new concept (see Black 1983; Scully & Marolla 1985), the use of rape as a tool of revenge or punishment has recently attracted media attention. For example, in July 2014, a 14-year-old girl in Jharkhand, India was raped as a means of 'punishing' her brother, who had in turn been accused of assaulting the perpetrator's wife ('Arrest over "revenge" rape in Jharkhand' 2014). In January that year, a 20-year-old woman in West Bengal was gang raped by order of a village council for falling in love with a man from a different community ('Woman gang raped on orders of a "kangaroo court"' 2014). In the first circumstance, rape was used as a method of revenge and punishment for the victim's family, but in the latter, it was a method to punish her.

Sometimes women are raped in the name of 'collective liability' (Black 1983) in which the victim is held responsible for 'crimes' committed by other members of a particular category (e.g. women). For example, in their research on 114 convicted rapists in the US, Scully & Marolla (1985) noted how several rapists admitted using rape as a means of getting revenge on someone else (normally a partner or girlfriend). Rapists often admitted to visualizing that they were raping their partner in these circumstances.

Date rape

Even in cases such as date rape, which is seemingly motivated by sex, the experience is more about men's *perceived entitlement and access* to women's bodies than it is about sexual gratification. While perhaps initially motivated by sex, the act is transformed to an assertion of power at the point where one person says 'no' but the other proceeds anyways. When the perpetrator decides that the fulfilment of their needs, desires and fantasies becomes more important than the victim's bodily autonomy, it is no longer a case of 'unbridled' sexual desire, but an act of power, domination and control. The prevalence of date rape in many societies can be explained by cultural values, in which men's entitlement to women's bodies is so engrained that rape becomes a suitable method of conquest when women say no (Scully & Marolla 1985). What is truly scary is the ways many men's sense of entitlement in such scenarios runs so deep, they are unable to recognize their actions as 'rape' and instead believe they are merely asserting their right to sexually access women's bodies (Scully & Marolla 1985). As we witnessed in 2014, this sense of entitlement drove 22-year-old Elliot Rodger to murder six people and injure 13 more before killing himself. Just before the attack, Rodger posted a You Tube video in which he expressed his desire to punish women for rejecting him, and sexually active men for having access to women's bodies. As he said: 'I don't know why you girls aren't attracted to me, but I will punish you all for it' (cited in Valenti 2014a).

So, the view that rape, while of course involving sex, is instead driven by the need to punish, control or dominate women (and sometimes male relatives or their community) is truly radical. This understanding of rape challenges the common sense construction of masculinity and male sexuality in which men are innately sexual beings who are biologically wired to seek (subconsciously and aggressively if need be) sex in certain circumstances (e.g. when turned on or 'provoked' by certain modes of behaviour or dress) (Scully & Marolla 1985). In recent years, the construction of rape as a crime of passion and sex has been particularly difficult to challenge, as scholars have identified a resurgence of discourses perpetuating gender essentialism claiming that men and women are driven by 'psychological and physiological urges ingrained in the era of 'cavemen' (see Hasinoff 2009, p. 267). Because these 'urges' are supposedly based on science and biology, discourses stating that men cannot help but rape in certain circumstances are particularly difficult to challenge.[3]

In fact, only 16 mainstream news articles (five percent of total) and 26 feminist media posts (seven percent of total) explicitly talked about the ways rape was a crime not of passion and sex, but of power, violence or control. Therefore, although these discourses were not prominent in either sample, they are worth addressing because they hold the potential for challenging the one rape myth upon which I believe the others are based. After all, if rape is understood as a crime of violence, power, domination, humiliation, entitlement, punishment and control, it is easier to move discussions away from how women 'provoked' rape, to why men rape in the first place. Only then can strategies be implemented, ideally to prevent rape, but realistically, to hold rapists accountable, end victim-blaming and provide more comprehensive support for survivors.

Varying levels of analysis

Similar to discourses that state personal appearance does not cause rape, there were varying levels of depth to discourses constructing rape as a crime of power and control. For example, this discourse was quickly glossed over in Britain's conservative *Mail on Sunday,* when columnist Liz Jones (2011) quoted a 15-year-old participant at SlutWalk London (donning a 'short red dress') who said: 'I dress how I like, but it[rape]'s not about how you dress, it's about power.' No further information or follow up discussion was included before Jones moved the discussion on. Although less common, the simplistic relaying of this discourse was also found in feminist media posts. For example, one entry on the Canadian blogging site *Rabble.ca* noted that PC Sanguinetti's comments:

> [O]utraged the students who know that rape is a crime of violence and power and it has nothing to do with how anyone dresses. Women of all ages, of all shapes, sizes and colours, blondes, redheads, women with grey hair, women tall and short, women with physical or mental disabilities – all can be targeted for rape. (Fraser 2011)

Although the simplistic relaying of this discourse was present in both samples, in general my feminist texts elaborated on this discourse.

Writing on the SlutWalk Singapore blog, writer Laïcité (2011) argued that: 'Rape has more to do with how the perpetrator views women than about sex.' She went on to note that if it were simply a matter of sexual attraction, 'a man would take "no" for an answer.' Yet, instead, she explained:

> But to ignore a victim's sovereignty over her own body suggests that the perpetrator has issues of power and control and is probably unable to respect women as equal human beings with a right to choose their attire and a right to not be touched without consent. What a woman wears is merely a convenient excuse to disguise the desire to dehumanize and possess a victim and to violate her bodily integrity against her will. (Laïcité 2011)

Worth noting is that many of the more nuanced analyses of rape as a tool of violence, power and control were promoted by women of colour, who demonstrated an understanding of how sexual assault has long been used to maintain control over black women's bodies and lives. Referring back to the time of slavery, the Black Women's Blueprint (2011) detailed the ways sexual assault has been used as a 'radical weapon of oppression' particularly against women of colour, whose bodies have historically been viewed as 'sexualized objects of property.' Similarly, writing on the popular blog *Racialicious,* blogger Andrea noted how sexual violence was not just a tool used to maintain the status quo, but a tool for 'ensuring white status quo' (Andrea 2011). These discourses were not solely reproduced by women of colour. White feminist blogger Meghan Murphy also recognized that 'All women are vulnerable to violence at the hands of men, but marginalized women are particularly likely to be victimized and men who are violent against marginalized women are more likely to get away with it' (Murphy 2012a).

Although feminists really began to theorize the ways rape has been an effective tool used to maintain male dominance over women since the 1970s, scholars note that women have been intimidated by the *threat* of male violence for millennia (Brownmiller 1975; Clark 1992). Both Susan Brownmiller (1975) and Kate Clark (1992) have talked about the ways that the (threat of) violence has long been an effective way to keep women submissive and in a state of fear. And although I agree that rape has been used as a means of power and control over women, it does not explain why women have accepted responsibility for their assault. This is where Antonio Gramsci's (1971) concept of hegemony applies. Unlike Karl Marx, who argued that the ruling class maintained control through merely 'brainwashing' sections of society, Gramsci stated that ruling groups maintain power and control through accommodating views from subordinate or marginalized groups. In the case of sexual assault, discourses emerged stating that while rape exists, women can avoid it if they follow certain guidelines or rules (e.g. dress conservatively, don't drink alcohol, remain virginal, do not go out late at night, do not go out on your own, etc). In fact, Jessica Valenti (2007) popularized the term 'rape schedule' to talk about the ways women schedule their lives around the avoidance of rape:

> Because of their constant fear of rape (conscious or not), women do things throughout the day to protect themselves. Whether it's carrying our keys in our hands as we walk home, locking our car doors as soon as we get in, or not walking down certain streets, we take precautions. While taking precautions is certainly not a bad idea, the fact that certain things women do are so ingrained into our daily routines is truly disturbing. It's essentially like living in a prison – all the time. We can't assume that we're safe anywhere: not on the streets, not in our homes. And we're so used to feeling unsafe that we don't even see that there's something seriously fucked up about it. (Valenti 2007, p. 63; see also Herman 1978)

As Valenti pointed out, these ideologies have become so entrenched that women aren't fully aware of the ways we police not only ourselves, but other women, through slut-shaming and victim-blaming. In the meantime, as women busy themselves by organizing their lives around not getting raped, questions revolving around why men rape in the first place are ignored or overlooked. This is truly problematic and indicates the desperate need for widespread consciousness-raising, something I hope this book contributes to.

SlutWalk and postfeminist sentiments of choice and empowerment in the news

For several years, feminist scholars have been aware of and critiqued the ways feminist messages have been influenced and co-opted by neoliberal rhetoric. According to Gill and Scharff (2011), neoliberalism is an ideology governing Western social and cultural values that emerged in the late 1970s and early 1980s when US President Ronald Reagan and UK Prime Minister Margaret Thatcher came to power. The neoliberal values prioritized under these administrations have become dominant in many parts of the world and have influenced other ideologies, including feminism, resulting in what scholars have identified as a 'postfeminist' culture and sensibility (Douglas 2010; Gill 2007; McRobbie 2009; Mendes 2012). Unlike other political theories (such as radical feminism), which stress collective activism and social responsibility, the current postfeminist sensibility has been criticized for promoting individualism and rejecting any notion that structural inequalities exist (Negra 2008). In our postfeminist culture, women's equality is seen as having already been achieved and feminism is thus constructed as dead, irrelevant, redundant or passé (Douglas 2010; Gill 2007; McRobbie 2009; Mendes 2012; Tasker & Negra 2007). Instead, when issues surrounding women's empowerment arise, postfeminist tropes stipulate that it is best achieved through self-gratifying choices (often demonstrated through purchasing power or self-subjectification), rather than collective, political action (Douglas 2010; Gill 2007). At the same time, the consequences or politics of women's 'choices' remain irrelevant or ignored (Mendes 2012).

Because postfeminism has been a central theme of feminist analysis in recent years (see for examples Genz & Brabon 2009; Gill 2007; Gill & Scharff 2011; Gwynne 2013; Gwynne & Muller 2013; Harzewski 2011; McRobbie 2009; Mendes 2012; Negra 2008; Tasker & Negra 2007), I felt it was important to discuss the use of postfeminist discourses in this study. Although only ten mainstream news articles (three percent of total) framed SlutWalk as a movement about women's empowerment, postfeminist discourses of choice and (sexual) empowerment were identified in a number of other mainstream news articles (feminist media posts will be discussed separately below). These articles drew upon both feminist and postfeminist discourses. According to Darmon (2014), who has also examined news of SlutWalk, postfeminist discourses are those which 'strip away the political element of the protest, leaving behind a very stark postfeminist take on the protest, its name and its value' (p. 703). These postfeminist discourses were evident in headlines such as: 'It's all about the clothes' (Vasudev 2011), 'Being a slut, to my mind, was mostly fun – wearing and doing what you liked' (Moore, S. 2011) and 'I plan to wear a sari at the SlutWalk' (Rii 2012). These, and other articles like it, tended to focus on the march's provocative name, women's rights to dress and sleep with whomever they choose, and the empowerment derived from these choices.

While freedom and choice are important foundations for (neo)liberal feminism (Genz & Brabon 2009; Jaggar 1983), such values have been scrutinized by a number of feminist scholars for deflecting attention away from collective political action, towards individual self-management, consumption and (sexual) empowerment (see Gill & Scharff 2011). Instead of disrupting the link between attire and likeliness of sexual assault, such articles promoted the idea that SlutWalk was merely about women's right to dress how they want (see also Darmon 2014). This was evident in the following *BBC* news article:

> One protester told our correspondent: 'Every girl has the right to wear whatever she wants, to do whatever she wants to do with her body. It's our lives, our decisions, unless it's harming you, you have no right to say anything.' ('India "Slutwalk" sex harassment protest in Delhi' 2011)

Similarly, one Muslim woman quoted in the UK's *Observer* noted:

> I chose to wear my hijab, and I find this piece of cloth really liberating because people don't really judge me by what I look like. I absolutely believe a woman has a right to wear whatever she wants. I do not want the police, the state, anybody else, to tell me as a woman what I can and can't wear. (McVeigh 2011, p. 24)

Such articles promote neoliberal rhetoric that states that individual freedoms and choices are justified, so long as they do not harm or interfere with freedoms and choices of others (Jaggar 1983). Furthermore, and more problematically in my opinion, these articles ignore SlutWalk's attempts to collectively challenge rape culture, and instead focus on individuals' right to dress as they please. At no point through my explorations of dozens of SlutWalk Facebook pages or websites have I come across any information that stipulates that this is the movement's main purpose.

Feminist discourses of choice and empowerment, on the other hand, situated SlutWalk within wider feminist political goals of ending slut-shaming and victim-blaming. Examples of feminist discourses which addressed choice and empowerment included: 'Stop Telling Women What to Wear' (Schutte 2011), 'Scantily-clad "SlutWalk" women march on New York after police tell them to "cover up" to avoid rape' (Arthurs 2011), and 'SlutWalk protest targets dress slur' (2011). While these articles often referred to women's clothing and appearance, this was done as a means of repudiating the blame assigned to sexual assault survivors (see also Darmon 2014). For example, as one *Toronto Star* columnist wrote:

> Being a 50ish woman, my days of slut dress are behind me. It was never a fashion choice of mine, but I will go to the wall to defend

a woman's right to dress any way she wants. The point I would like to make is there is no manner of clothing or dress that will protect me from the misogynist social attitude that 'I want it' or 'I asked for it' or 'I deserved it.' I am not, nor is any woman or girl, responsible for the behaviour/violence of men who view me and my sisters as objects. (MacKinnon 2011, p. A18)

Although the beginning of the quote perhaps suggests that columnist is merely interested in defending a woman's right to dress how she wants (a postfeminist trope), the rest of the quote indicates that her choices should be granted, not because choice in itself is inherently important or a sign of liberation, but because in our misogynistic and patriarchal culture, it has no bearing on whether a man chooses to assault or judge her. Even if she were wearing 'non-provocative' clothing, whatever that may be, other excuses would be used to justify why the survivor should be blamed (perhaps she was out late at night, drank alcohol or was not a virgin). Consequently, the discourse found in articles such as this has some radical potential in challenging rape myths because it attempts to re-direct attention away from the victim to the perpetrator, where it belongs.

Postfeminist tropes in feminist media?

Unlike my mainstream news sample, which either constructed SlutWalk as a postfeminist movement or utilized postfeminist discourses in a seemingly supportive or celebratory manner, a number of feminist bloggers critiqued the movement for what they saw as its co-optation by postfeminism, and the absence of more radical feminist theories and understanding of sexual assault, victim-blaming and the nature of patriarchy. For example, *Feminist Current* blogger and founder Meghan Murphy was a fierce critic of what she saw as the vacuous, apolitical and postfeminist nature of movement. She wrote a number of anti-SlutWalk blogs whose titles include: 'Breaking! SlutWalk is about spectacle, individual empowerment, wearing sexy lingerie, says everyone with eyes and brains' (Murphy 2012c), 'The naked protestor (or, how to get the media to pay attention to women)' (Murphy 2012d), 'Grasping at Straws: Comparing SlutWalk an Occupy Wall Street' (Murphy 2011a), and 'Liberal feminists realize that feminism is a movement after all. Confusion ensues' (Murphy 2012e).

These posts highlight what Murphy identified as the problematic co-optation of SlutWalk by postfeminist tropes. In her post titled: 'Breaking! SlutWalk is about spectacle, individual empowerment, wearing sexy lingerie, says everyone with eyes and brains' (Murphy 2012c),

Murphy critiqued an article about SlutWalk LA posted on *Ms. Magazine* (see Barbato 2012) where the author praised the event for its absence of politics in favour of 'individualistic empowerment.' Murphy was also set off by the author's admission that SlutWalk is about 'spectacle,' and responded by asking:

> Are we all getting this? Slutwalk is an apolitical, individualistic spectacle about wearing lingerie and having something called 'slutitude' ... On one hand I'm relieved that Slutwalk [sic] is being upfront about how very lost they are, on the other, I feel like stabbing myself in the eye. (Murphy 2012c)

In another post, Murphy (2011a) explicitly critiqued what she saw as SlutWalk's neoliberal and capitalist nature, arguing that unlike other truly radical and potentially revolutionary movements like Occupy Wall Street, which is unbrandable, SlutWalk 'provided exactly what mainstream culture wants and needs in order to sell a product: women's bodies.' In a long explanation, Murphy went on to detail exactly how SlutWalk has been co-opted by capitalism:

> Slutwalk bought right into to everything that we are being sold, turned it around and told the world that this was the route to liberation. Most of all, it sold a message of individualism – the key to the success of the capitalist system. Capitalism is all about the message of individualism vs. collectivism, man *is* an island under a capitalist system, and we are all to believe that if we work hard enough, *as individuals*, we can be successful. Health care, social safety nets, affordable housing? Those things are all a pain in the ass if you're already wealthy and privileged. Those things don't affect you if you aren't poor or marginalized, so why bother? Other people aren't *your* responsibility if you are a capitalist and if something makes *you* feel good then gosh darn it, you should do it!
>
> Sound familiar? Slutwalk argued, right off the bat, that this was a movement all about individuals and that, if what they were doing, as individuals, was impacting other women negatively, well, too freakin' bad. If you think sex work is great, then it's great, regardless of how it impacts and hurts and exploits other women; women with less privilege than yourself. If you want to call yourself a slut and encourage men to call you a slut (because now that's empowering!), then do it! Even if it throws other women under the bus in the process.

Slutwalk followed the rules. They bought into a patriarchal, neoliberal, capitalist message and tried to sell it back to us as revolutionary. But it wasn't. (Murphy 2011a)

Although Murphy's blogs perhaps provided the most detailed critiques of the ways SlutWalk is (at least perceived) to be about 'me-first power feminism' (see Genz & Brabon 2009, p. 10), she was certainly not a lone voice. Many other feminist bloggers expressed their discomfort about various aspects of the movement, particularly the focus on individual empowerment, which could be derived from anything from reclaiming the word 'slut' (Hart 2012) to walking down the street in 'slutty' clothes (see Ana 2011), or the privilege certain groups have in claiming empowerment from such actions (see Izrael 2011; Petro 2011).

While I argue that these critiques of the ways SlutWalk has been understood as a postfeminist movement are important, a handful of articles managed to address concepts of empowerment, choice and liberation emerging from a feminist position. For example, when interviewed by the New Zealand blog *The Lady Garden,* SlutWalk Aotearoa organizer MJ Brodie was asked what she wanted participants to take away from the march. Brodie responded that she hoped participants would feel 'empowered,' but unlike postfeminist tropes which might suggest this could be achieved through dressing in a certain way, she envisaged this to be achieved through the mass coming together and sharing of stories from survivors:

Ultimately, I want people to come away with a sense of empowerment – it can be a huge thing to talk about your own experiences, to hear about other people's, but I really think that just walking amongst a crowd of survivors and refusing to be shamed or afraid can be an incredible, enriching experience. (Spankhead 2012b)

For Brodie then, SlutWalk wasn't necessarily empowering because it gave individual women permission to wear what they wanted, but because it was an opportunity for women (and men) who had been sexually abused to *come together* to speak out against this crime. This move towards 'anti-victimization' (Cole 2007) in which individuals transform from sexual assault *victims* to *survivors* has been an important mental shift in helping women to reclaim a sense of agency and power over their lives, and to reject the stereotype that women are passive and easily dominated. Discourses of agency, empowerment and survival were specifically identified by one feminist blogger who noted that amongst the variety of speakers at SlutWalk sharing horrific accounts of sexual abuse, 'were triumphant stories, and the way in which these speakers were able to share their experiences and frame them in terms of their own personal empowerment showed that they were not victims of sexual abuse; they were sexual abuse survivors' (Hanson 2012).[4]

Concluding thoughts

When examining the use of frames and discourses in both my mainstream news and feminist media sample, it is abundantly clear that SlutWalk has achieved a level of support which is historically unprecedented for feminist activism (Mendes 2011a, 2012). And while I applaud both my mainstream news and feminist media sample's general support of the movement, and the extent to which they employed feminist discourses challenging rape culture, I remain cautious, particularly with the mainstream news media, about the extent to which they are truly capable of challenging patriarchal rape myths. For example, I hope to have highlighted a key difference between articles/posts which *report* that SlutWalk is a movement which challenges rape culture, and those which go further and *critique, explain* and *analyze* rape culture itself. The former involve (superficial) constructions of SlutWalk as 'part of a broader, and healthy phenomenon, of ending the silence, stigma and shame around the crime of rape' (Editorial 2011, A16). While on first appearance such discourses appear to promote feminist rhetoric on rape, such as the harm caused by victim-blaming, most fail to discuss what causes sexual assault in the first place, or what can be done to end it. In other words, while such articles certainly *support* SlutWalk, their shallow and superficial analysis of rape culture renders them unlikely to challenge its patriarchal and misogynist foundation.

And although my feminist media sample was certainly guilty of reproducing these shallow accounts, they were much more likely to provide detailed critiques and explanations of sexual assault and rape culture. These were the texts which not only asked what fosters and perpetuates rape culture in the first place, but demanded attention be given to destroying it. Because the SlutWalk movement aims to change people's *understanding* of sexual assault and rape culture, much of its battle is being waged at the discursive level. As a result, a change in people's understanding of these issues requires an investment in *discursive politics* – or 'speech which intervenes in hegemonic discourses, and that works at the level of language to change political cultures' (Shaw, F. 2011; see also Maddison 2013b; Young 1997).

After years of researching mainstream news media's representations of feminism, and comparing those representations to the feminist blogosphere, I feel confident in arguing that as inherently capitalist and patriarchal institutions, the mainstream news media are by and large incapable of providing critiques, context and depth necessary to foster widespread cultural change. While they may inspire readers to find out more about SlutWalk, rape culture or the nature of rape, in the words of Barbara Freeman: 'The mainstream news media are not, given their capitalist nature, revolutionary, and feminist messages tend to be eventually subsumed within the status quo' (Freeman 2001, p. 5). Although I am not suggesting is that feminists should 'give up' on, or ignore the mainstream news media, I do believe they should be (as many already are as we will come to see in Chapter 6) focusing their attention towards platforms such as the feminist blogosphere. It is these platforms, unrestricted by journalistic conventions such as objectivity, balance or bias, and which, as mostly non-commercial entities, don't have to worry about alienating advertisers, that can provide radical challenges to oppression.

And it was in the feminist blogosphere that I found posts that stood in stark contrast to the often shallow and pithy discussions of rape culture in the mainstream news. Although I certainly encountered a range of superficial analyses and critiques amongst my feminist media sample, I also came across plenty of detailed, theoretical explanations of sexual assault and rape culture. For example, rather than simply stating 'clothes don't cause rape,' many feminist media posts explained the ways various systems of oppression (capitalism, patriarchy, racism, colonialism) fuel rape. Others talked about the ways in which women's experience of sexual assault and its aftermath differ depending on various identities (age, race, ethnicity, sexuality, ability). These were the types of post which went beyond merely *stating* that rape is not a crime of passion or sex, but which *explained,* sometimes using the authors' personal experiences, the ways in which it is fuelled by power, domination and control. These were the posts that explained the ways in which victim-blaming perpetuated sexual violence, and the ones that debunked rape myths. And while none of the theories presented in these blogs are 'new,' and just as feminists have articulated critical consciousness around sexual assault for decades through consciousness-raising sessions, zines and other alternative publications (see Maddison 2013b; Piepmeier 2009), the feminist blogosphere has provided a new, online space for the formation of *networked counterpublics* (Keller 2013). These are online spaces that feminists use to create and disseminate counterhegemonic discourses, in this case about sexual assault and rape culture. And although many blogs are written by individuals, as we will come to see in the next chapter, they make frequent interlinkages with one another to create networked communities (Keller 2013).

Overall then, while the vast majority of mainstream news articles and feminist media posts supported SlutWalk and framed it as a movement which challenged rape culture and promoted awareness of the devastation of sexual violence and, in some cases, as a sign of women's (sexual) empowerment, other articles were more critical, taking up the frame that SlutWalk was misguided or opposed. These frames, the discourses that comprise them, and the ways they have been contested, will be the focus of the next chapter.

5
Representing the Movement: SlutWalk is Misguided or Opposed

Where Chapter 4 focused on the frames and discourses used to construct SlutWalk as a movement which challenges rape culture and victim blaming, this chapter focuses on the way the movement was framed as misguided and/or opposed. This chapter pays particular attention to feminist critiques of the movement as one which plays to the male gaze, and thus is incapable of challenging patriarchal rape culture. It also focuses on the ways the movement was seen to focus on 'trivial' issues instead of those of 'real' concern. Moving on, the chapter evaluates the utility of these critiques, arguing that a critical examination of the movement's aims, tactics and goals is important, particularly in a postfeminist era in which women's empowerment is said to be best achieved through the overt display of one's sexuality. At the same time, I argue that SlutWalk provides evidence of a departure away from a postfeminist 'sensibility' (Gill 2007), in which feminism has been 'taken into account' only to be depoliticized and rejected. Instead many of the texts recognize the need to challenge rape culture, and the issue of contention revolves around which strategies are the most appropriate or effective. The chapter concludes by de-bunking discourses stating SlutWalkers are naïve in regards to men's 'true' nature, and argues that the main problem with rape prevention tips is not merely that they condone victim blaming, but that they ignore the reality of rape as a crime of domination, violence, entitlement, control and power, rather than sex and passion.

SlutWalk is misguided or opposed

Although vastly outnumbered by articles framing SlutWalk as a movement which challenges rape culture, the second most prominent frame in both my mainstream news and feminist media sample was that SlutWalk is a 'misguided' movement, which is largely opposed

(68 articles or 23 percent of total in mainstream news media; 92 articles or 23 percent of total for feminist media). News headlines which support this frame include: 'The trouble with SlutWalks: They trivialize rape' (Flanagan 2011), 'SlutWalk's priorities misplaced' (Panahi 2012), 'SlutWalk may damage women's rights cause, professor says' (Griffin 2011), and 'SlutWalkers are missing the point' (Adams 2011). Amongst feminist posts, headlines include: 'SlutWalk: A stroll through white supremacy' (To the Curb 2011), 'Endorsing a critique of SlutWalk' (Clay 2011), 'SlutWalk, Slutslurs and Why Feminism Still Has Race Issues' (Peterson 2011) and 'Is SlutWalk the end of feminism?' (Nair 2012).

That less than one quarter of all articles/posts in both samples opposed SlutWalk is a positive development for feminist activism, which has historically been de-legitimized, marginalized and demonized in the mainstream news media (see Ashley & Olson 1998; Barker-Plummer 2000; Bradley 2003; Costain et al. 1997; Douglas 1994; Freeman 2001; Goddu 1999; Mendes 2011a; Morris 1973a; Pingree & Hawkins 1978; Sheridan et al. 2007; Tuchman 1978; van Zoonen 1992). As we will see throughout this chapter, several of these critiques levelled against the movement have helped it evolve, become more inclusive and develop more sophisticated analyses of the interlocking nature of oppression regarding sexual violence. As a result, just as I remained critical about some of the more supportive articles/posts on SlutWalk which lacked an analysis of power, I am not necessarily critical of coverage which opposed it. However, as we will come to see, there remains a qualitative difference between those articles which promoted a backlash against feminism – or the common sense construction that society (and particularly women) was better off before feminism (or that it is now seen as dead and redundant) (see Douglas 2010; Faludi 1992; Mendes 2011b), and those highlighting issues which the movement must engage with if it stands a chance in the fight against sexual assault and rape culture. For example, as discussed in Chapter 3, critiques about the re-appropriation of the word 'slut' raised by women of colour served as an important reminder about the intersectional nature of oppression, and about issues of privilege and power in the women's movement. As we will see throughout this chapter, there were also valid concerns raised about SlutWalk's (misguided?) tactics, and the benefits and drawbacks of building a radical movement around a word as divisive and provocative as 'slut.'

SlutWalk's tactics are misguided

One of the most common oppositional frames and discourse present in the sample was that the SlutWalk movement, its aims or tactics were 'misguided.' And although it might be intuitive to argue that that all opposition to the movement is harmful for feminism, I argue that these oppositional texts presented some important, and legitimate, criticisms that the movement has had to engage with in order to become more inclusive and develop a better understanding of how sexual assault interlocks with various systems of oppression. In all, the three most common reasons the movement was constructed as misguided were: 1) It is neither possible nor desirable to reclaim the word 'slut' (as discussed in Chapter 3); 2) The movement focuses on sexualizing women/ survivors rather than challenging patriarchy; and, 3) The movement detracts attention away from 'real' issues of concern.

Worth noting is that while the majority of these articles/posts suggest that SlutWalk's *tactics* are misguided, they make explicit their support for anti-rape activism *in general*. For example, one *Huffington Post* column began by stating: 'Now before the SlutWalk army gets their undergarments in a twist and adds me to their enemies list, let me state for the record that we are on the same side when it comes to the issues. But when it comes to execution in addressing said issues? Not so much' (Goff 2011). Similarly, Britain's *The Sun* began by supporting SlutWalk's aims:

> I absolutely agree with their [SlutWalk's] conviction that the responsibility for sexual violence always lies 100 percent with the perpetrator. But, how the hell is taking to the streets in bondage gear with SLUT written across your belly going to shift the emphasis onto the perpetrator? All it does is create a sideshow and gives those not-so-right-minded folk an excuse to keep on focusing on the way women look rather than the scumbags who carry out evil acts. (Adams 2011, p. 11)

That bloggers/reporters/columnists take issue with SlutWalk's tactics, rather than its mission (ending rape culture and victim-blaming) is a significant shift from how women's activism has historically been reported. For example, my research on representations of feminism in the 1960s–80s indicated that there was little attention paid to the tactics used in specific demonstrations or campaigns, and instead, opposition was directed towards larger feminist goals (e.g. equal pay, equal rights, abortion, etc.) (Mendes 2011a). That feminist goals within the SlutWalk movement were overwhelmingly supported, but the ways in which they were achieved were disputed, therefore provides evidence of an ideological shift away from a postfeminist 'sensibility' (Gill 2007), in which feminism and feminist goals have been 'incorporate[d], revise[d] and depoliticise[d]' (Stacey 1978, cited in Gill 2007, p. 268). Rather than assuming feminist goals have been achieved, or should be abandoned because they have ushered in a range of new 'problems' for women (see Faludi 1992; McRobbie 2007; Mendes 2011b, 2012; Tasker & Negra 2007), there is consensus that a rape culture exists, that it is problematic, and that something must be done to challenge it. So, departing from the belief that women and men are now equal, these texts recognize sexual assault as a major issue and the dispute now lies around the best ways to eradicate it. For example, a number of articles or posts supported anti-rape activism, but were concerned about the ways in which they felt the movement played to the male gaze.

SlutWalk plays to the male gaze

A common charge against SlutWalk, particularly amongst my feminist media posts was that, rather than challenging rape culture, SlutWalk played to the male gaze and commoditized women's sexuality. As feminist academic Gail Dines argued in a *Sydney Morning Herald* interview:

> 'By dressing in fishnet and push-up bras and brandishing "slut" signs, the organizers are playing into the hands of raunch culture,' she said.
> 'Men want women to be sluts and now they're buying in.' (Griffin 2011)

Feminist Current founder Meghan Murphy also contributed several scathing critiques of the ways SlutWalk sexualized and commoditized women's bodies in the name of women's liberation. While Murphy accepted that SlutWalks have successfully attracted media attention, she pointed out the problematic ways women's access to the public sphere is generally only guaranteed when their bodies are sexualized (Murphy 2012d). As a result, while SlutWalk has caught the media's attention, Murphy argued that no one is actually listening to what they are saying, and as a result, the movement is incapable of enacting social change:

> The reason Slutwalks have become so popular is because of the name and the sexy photo ops. It isn't because anything is changing, it isn't because Slutwalks are revolutionary, and it isn't because the media are just so freakin [sic] excited about female liberation. Women on stripper poles have always been able to capture the gaze of their audience but *never* have these images provided women with equality or humanity. (Murphy 2011b, italics original)

The worries that Murphy expressed above were also shared by *The Times* writer Janice Turner. She commented on how SlutWalks are yet another example of how women must bare their flesh in order to make their activism palatable (and unthreatening) to men:

> [W]omen must make a calculation about how to be heard without being reviled: I may be more successful or more powerful, richer or faster or smarter than you, there may be 50,000 of us marching here, but honestly we're not threatening or ball-breaking. Here, we'll prove it, have a quick ogle at our fun bags. (Turner 2011, p. 25)

At its core, these critiques present legitimate feminist concerns about the ways women living in a neoliberal and postfeminist climate are encouraged to sexually subjectify themselves in order to gain access to, and acceptance in, the public sphere. This sexual subjectification only makes sense in a culture in which women's liberation and equality is seen as a *fait accompli*, and feminism as redundant (see Douglas 2010; McRobbie 2009). As a result, women are told it's now okay to embrace things which were once considered sexist, such as partaking in beauty contests, acting ultra-feminine (Douglas 2010; Mendes 2012) and, in this case, celebrating one's 'inner slut' via the SlutWalk. Rather than being seen as degrading, these actions are now presented as empowering in what feminists would argue is an attempt to make patriarchy 'pleasurable for women' (Douglas 2010, p. 12). And it is precisely these postfeminist constructs that bloggers are rejecting.

For example, Meghan Murphy wrote several scathing blogs about (some) women's willingness to sexually subjectify themselves in their quest to gain power, acceptance, money, and so forth. And it is for these reasons that Murphy argued SlutWalk is incapable of challenging patriarchy, systematic inequality or the roots of rape culture (Murphy 2011c). Because those with power want to maintain it (Gramsci 1971), she argued that if SlutWalk were truly a challenge to patriarchy, 'you can bet most of those men would not be standing on the sidelines, smiling and taking photos. They would be angry' (Murphy 2011b). And while I agree with Murphy that the seeming widespread support of SlutWalk by men could be viewed as a worrying sign that the movement is incapable of challenging patriarchal power, there is ample evidence that SlutWalk *is* in fact making men angry. All of the organizers with whom I discussed trolling – or online harassment – have shared a range of experiences of being harassed, insulted and threatened for their role in the movement (see Brodie 2014; Broher 2014; Delgado 2014a;

Govender 2014; Gray 2014a, 2014b; MacDonald, S. 2014; Sutton 2014; Wraith 2013). And while I agree that sexual violence is a tool used to maintain patriarchal (amongst other) power, it is incorrect to state that men cannot be concerned about sexual violence, that they have no role to play in feminist activism, or that they cannot be feminists.

Men's involvement in SlutWalk

For example, four of the 22 SlutWalk organizers I interviewed were men, and all demonstrated genuine interest in preventing sexual assault, ending rape culture and engaging more men in the movement. For example, when speaking with SlutWalk St. Louis 2012 organizer David Wraith, he understood the need to involve men in the movement. After all, 'it's the men who are doing the bulk of the violence, regardless of the gender of the victim. If we are going to change things, we need more men involved' (Wraith 2013). SlutWalk Cape Town 2011 organizer Stuart MacDonald said he became interested in the movement because he was aware of the ways women had long been oppressed by the 'histories of patriarchy and capitalism and power structures' across societies (MacDonald, S. 2014). When I asked SlutWalk LA 2011 organizer Hugo Schwyzer what he thought the movement was about, he said: 'Wherever women go – and whatever they wear – they should be free from sexual assault and harassment. Respect for women is not contingent on their sexual behaviour or on their dress, but on their humanity' (Schwyzer 2014).

Although these male organizers clearly felt that they were able to contribute to the movement, I am very aware of longstanding debates amongst feminists about whether men should be allowed to participate in, or lead the women's movement (see Bryson 1999; Digby 1998; hooks 1984; Tarrant 2009). These debates also arose in regards to SlutWalk, particularly amongst my feminist media sample, with headlines such as: 'Do men belong in the women's movement?' (Strauss 2012) and 'Why men can't lead the women's movement' (Thorpe 2012). These debates emerged in light of controversy surrounding male feminist and former SlutWalk LA organizer Hugo Schwyzer, who admitted to racially abusing women of colour and sleeping with female students (see Holman 2013). When I asked what role he thought men should play in feminist activism, he responded:

> I think that's for women to decide. If women want to invite men to participate, then they should. Men have a huge role to play in terms of reaching other men, confronting sexist behavior and so forth.

But men can't and shouldn't demand a role. They should wait to be asked. (Schwyzer 2014)

Although there is continued debate surrounding men's involvement in women's activism, in speaking with my organizers it became clear that many, although certainly not all SlutWalk satellite groups had men involved. While in many cases they were main organizers, in others, they were responsible for PR, media relations or other delegated tasks. And the involvement of men was certainly not universally welcomed. Two of my male organizers talked about how many women were surprised to see them involved, or treated them rather frostily at first (MacDonald, S. 2014; Wraith 2013). Clearly the involvement of men in the women's movement is not universally accepted, however, I believe that their involvement is necessary, particularly when it comes to challenging sexual violence and rape culture.

The importance of interrogating feminist critiques of SlutWalk

Given the global dominance of neoliberal and postfeminist ideologies, it is important to interrogate the messages, tactics and politics of modern (feminist) activism (including who can or should play a role). It is worrying that we live in an age in which women are told that equality and liberation have already been achieved (Gill 2007; McRobbie 2009; Mendes 2011b), and that empowerment is best achieved through the sexualized display of one's body rather than collective political action (Douglas 2010; Gill & Scharff 2011; Levy 2005). It is worrying that under neoliberalism and postfeminism, structural inequalities are re-framed as individual problems, which can be overcome if individuals simply try harder, think positive or police their behaviours. Although on the whole, I disagree that SlutWalk is just another example of 'enlightened sexism' in which women subjectify themselves as a sign of their empowerment (Douglas 2010, p. 9), I *do* believe it is necessary and important to critically analyze SlutWalk (and other types of feminist activism) and ensure it does not fall into the trap of making patriarchy 'pleasurable for women' (Douglas 2010, p. 12). After all, no movement is perfect and missteps are inevitable.[1] And while I would not go so far as to say that the name the movement SlutWalk was a misstep, there is no doubt that it is problematic. On the one hand, the name was largely responsible for the generation of widespread attention – both in the mainstream news and feminist media. On the other hand, the name alienated many women of colour, highlighting issues of privilege and power while at the same time creating a disproportionate focus on the visual display of women's bodies, which in turn gave credence to the feminist critiques above.

SlutWalk through a neoliberal lens

I will use this section to analyze the visual representation of SlutWalk in both mainstream news and feminist posts, not because they contributed to the frame that SlutWalk is misguided or opposed, but because they constructed the movement through a postfeminist and neoliberal lens which feminists, commentators and journalists alike *used* to construct the movement as misguided (as seen in the section above). Despite the rapid rise of social media over the past few years, and its potential for spreading information quickly, research indicates that the traditional news media has historically been people's primary source of information about the world (Barker-Plummer 2000; Gitlin 2003; Jones & Saad 2013; McNicol 2012; Media Insight Project 2014; Mitchell et al. 2013). Although social media is undoubtedly playing a role, the news media not only identifies what is significant, but also provides an framework for how to interpret these events (Hall et al. 1978). As a result, the news can be a rich source of information about societal values, ideologies and discourses surrounding certain events. When examining visual representations of SlutWalk, it becomes clear how the movement has been interpreted as promoting postfeminist and neoliberal values of individualism, personal choice and sexual expression.

SlutWalk is comprised of young, thin, white, 'sexy' women

As someone who had been closely following the SlutWalk movement since it started in April 2011, I had become familiar with the typical range of images accompanying news coverage: mainly young, white women in various stages of undress. Some had words such as 'slut' or 'don't touch' written on their exposed flesh, while others carried signs with statements such as: 'It's My Hot Body, I Do What I Want', 'Don't Tell Us How To Dress,' 'My Vagina, My Rules,' and 'Still Not Asking for It.' While some marchers look serious, defiant or even angry (see Figure 5.1), many others are smiling, cheering or jumping (see Figure 5.2). Few mainstream news photos, however, focused on women in jeans, T-shirts, or other 'unprovocative' attire, men, the elderly, the disabled or people of colour (see also McNicol 2012). Yet when I attended my first SlutWalk in London, 2012, I was surprised at not only the diversity of marchers, but how few were 'provocatively' dressed. Yet, those who attended in various states of undress were easy to spot, as they were often surrounded by (mainly male) photographers. Therefore, while it

Figure 5.1 Protesters march through downtown Boston during the SlutWalk in Boston, Massachusetts, Saturday, 7 May 2011

Source: © Josh Reynolds/AP/PA Images

would be incorrect to argue that the media 'misrepresented' SlutWalk, it provided an interpretive framework (Hall et al. 1978) in which the movement, at least visually, was seen to be by, for and about young, thin, white, women who, rather than simply challenging rape culture, were marching to 'celebrate' their sexuality, individual bodily autonomy and right to dress as they please (see also McNicol 2012).

My personal observations were also confirmed by other SlutWalk organizers, who expressed a range of emotions at the ways the news media represented the movement. These ranged from irritation (Brodie 2014), to disappointment (Castieau 2012; Gray 2014b; Pillay-Siokos 2013; Wraith 2013), to disillusionment (Govender 2014), and infuriation (Ho 2012). For example, SlutWalk Aotearoa 2011 and 2012 organizer MJ Brodie said she was 'irritated' by media coverage which emphasized all the 'slutty sluts with these slutty clothes,' when in fact most participants were wearing jeans and hardly showed any skin (Brodie 2014). SlutWalk Newcastle 2011–2013 organizer Lizi Gray stated that although some coverage was nuanced and thorough, she was disappointed by others

Figure 5.2   From left, Isa Stearns of Somerville, Mass., Nadia Friedler of Cambridge, Massachusetts, Louisa Carpenter-Winch, of Cambridge, Massachusetts, and Emma Munson-Blatt, of Cambridge, Massachusetts, chant during the SlutWalk in Boston on Saturday, 7 May 2011

Source: © Josh Reynolds/AP/PA Images

which focused on 'short skirts and sensation stories' and failed to discuss the purpose of the march (Gray, L. 2014). When asked her views on how SlutWalk Singapore was reported, organizer Vanessa Ho stated she was 'infuriated' with 'gut-wrenchingly disgusting' coverage which represented the movement as a 'two dimensional issue by simply flocking to the scantily clad women' (Ho 2012). When thinking about the implications of the media's treatment of the movement, SlutWalk Chicago 2011 organizer Stephanie Sutton concluded that the focus on scantily clad women is 'one of the flaws of SlutWalk in general' (Sutton 2014). And while she went on to defend the movement's celebration of sexuality, sex positivity and openness, she acknowledged that the disproportionate focus on these aspects 'limited the movement in a way.' So, while the promise of sexy photo opportunities was likely a draw for mainstream media attention, organizers were concerned that it also limited the ways the movement was interpreted and understood and was a distraction from the true purpose of the march – to challenge rape culture.

Feminist interventions into mainstream media

SlutWalk organizers were not the only ones who were cognizant of the limited ways the mainstream news media (visually) represented the movement. Results from my content analysis revealed that feminist bloggers were very aware of the ways the mainstream media reported SlutWalk. In fact, 146 posts, or 37 percent of this sample discussed the mainstream news at some point. In some cases, feminists used their blogs to 'call out' the media on what they saw as misrepresentative coverage, and disgraceful tactics. For example, in 'This is What a SlutWalk (Really) Looks Like' (Corinna 2011), the blogger protested that the visual representations of the march in the mainstream media ranged from the 'incorrect to [the] exceptionally dishonest.' The blogger went on to note that: 'as [far as] I can tell, the images that keep getting picked aren't those which are most representative of the protests as a whole, but which are most representative of what a given person either found most provocative or most interesting' (Corinna 2011). Writing on the Canadian website *Rabble.ca* another blogger shared in disgust how a CBC cameraman 'asked two "slutty" young women to dance for his camera' (Kraus 2011). The blogger recounted that after she told the young women they didn't have to dance for the media, 'the CBC cameraman went off hunting elsewhere.'

What became clear after reading these 146 posts is that for the most part, these bloggers were not just *complaining* about coverage, but attempting to make an active *intervention* into how the movement was understood, represented and remembered. At times, the bloggers spoke directly to the mainstream media, imploring them to provide more nuanced coverage. In a speech she delivered at SlutWalk Aotearoa in 2011, organizer MJ Brodie challenged the media to:

> [N]ot be so distracted by the 'slutty' outfits that you forget that this march is about rape and sexual assault. We would beg you to cover this march properly, and fairly – show the range of people, men and women, who are here today, not just close ups of tits and ass. (Brodie 2011)

Writing on the morning of SlutWalk Wellington and Auckland in 2011, another New Zealand blogger wrote that she hoped the media would 'pull up their socks and actually engage in the issues and practice some legitimate journalism!' (Lady News 2011b). Although there is no way of measuring the extent to which the mainstream media were aware of these critiques, nor how they might have altered their coverage as a result, it is clear that feminists are using online spaces to 'talk back' to a patriarchal culture in which women's bodies are sexualized (see Gill 2007) and their voices are marginalized or ignored (hooks 1989, p. 5; Keller 2011; Piepmeier 2009).

Through thinking about, and 'talking back' to the mainstream news media, these feminist bloggers are participating in discursive politics and activism, and in doing so, are developing alternative discourses and understanding of themselves, the SlutWalk movement and the world around them (see Maddison 2013b; Shaw 2012b). According to Piepmeier (2009), these 'micropolitical' interventions 'are so personalized that they are often invisible as activism to scholars who are searching for the kinds of social change efforts that were prevalent in the social justice movements of the earlier twentieth century' (p. 20). Yet, in 'talking back,' feminist bloggers are not only challenging mainstream media accounts of the movement, they are also creating their own 'counter-memories.' Drawing on the work of Michel Foucault (1980), Red Chidgey (2012) argued that: 'Feminist media can become discursive "weapons" … to contest hostile framings [of feminism] and to put forward counter-understandings of what feminism is, what feminism can do, and who a feminist can be' (p. 87). In the section below, I therefore argue that many feminists in my sample used blogs to challenge postfeminist constructions of SlutWalk as a movement about women's freedom to dress as they please. Blogs were also frequently used to challenge the visual whitewashing of the movement – or the ways the movement ignored women of colour (see also McNicol 2012).

Discursive activism and counter-memories

A critical discourse analysis of my feminist media sample provides ample evidence of various ways feminist bloggers sought to disrupt mainstream constructions of SlutWalk and provide alternative accounts, or counter-memories, of the movement, primarily through the use of photos, video and hyperlinks. For example, one blog embedded a short film of SlutWalk NYC 2011 in their post, as well as a quote from the filmmaker who explained why she felt the need to provide an alternative account of the movement:

> For me, one of the truly frustrating things about coverage of SlutWalks all over the world has been the media's focus on the most elaborately undressed and risque marchers, leading people to believe the events are solely about demanding the right to dress like a slut. I hope this video gives people a sense of the range of participants (gender,

orientation, background, race, age) that were there marching, chanting and generally raising some hell. (Seltzer & Kelley 2011)

The embedded trailer to the documentary, just over 30 seconds long, features panned out shots of diverse crowds, close-ups of signs ('I will be post-feminist in the post-patriarchy'), and a clip from a protester who, making reference to PC Michael Sanguinetti's comments that women could avoid being 'victimized' if they didn't dress like 'sluts,' explained what was needed to combat sexual assault and rape culture: 'What we need from police is enforcement, what we need from the larger culture is anti-violence education, not fashion tips' (Trixie Films 2011).

Although some bloggers embedded videos and photos into their posts, the vast majority used hyperlinks instead. In her post titled 'An Open Challenge to mainstream media re SlutWalk Sydney', Australian blogger tigtog (2011) used hyperlinks to the photosharing site Flickr to demonstrate the ways in which the news media flocked to the provocatively dressed, while ignoring those in 'normal' clothes. One image shows a woman in a black corset and feather boa literally surrounded by between 30 to 50 (mostly male) photographers. A second photo shows two women in 'normal' dress standing right beside the media swarm, being ignored. Angered by the media's omission of the broad range of people attending the walks, she asked:

Do any of you publishers and editors have the integrity to instruct your field reporters to gather images and stories of more than just the sexy young things marching in their skimpies tomorrow? Does a single one of you have the guts to forego predictable titillation and let the public know the truth about SlutWalk and the hundreds and hundreds of other women and male and queer allies who will be marching in non-skimpy wear, and why they are there? (tigtog 2011)

Similarly, in her effort to showcase the diversity of participants at SlutWalk London 2011, blogger Lipsticklori (2011) directed viewers to the photojournalism site Demotix in order to 'give you an idea of the dedication and strength of the views of many of those in attendance.' In going through the photos, it becomes clear that yes, SlutWalks certainly did attract white, middle-class, women who turned up in 'skimpy' attire. But it also attracted hordes of men, women and children, of diverse backgrounds, wearing mostly 'everyday' items of clothing.

Although some feminist bloggers embedded professional photos of marches taken by news agencies such as Reuters and AP into their posts, the majority appeared to use photos they took themselves, or borrowed from others who attended the march. In total, 130 posts or 33 percent of my feminist media sample included at least one photo of a SlutWalk event, poster or advertisement.[2] Of the images present, only a minority focused explicitly on provocatively dressed women (11 percent of all photos coded). The majority captured crowds, placards, posters or 'ordinary' women and men (89 percent of all photos coded). Even a cursory examination of the visuals used in my mainstream news and feminist media samples indicates a significant difference in their representations of various marches, with the former focusing on provocatively dressed women as previously discussed, and the latter on large crowds, signs and posters and 'ordinary' women and men. As a result, while I will not try to claim that the feminist media more 'accurately' represented SlutWalk marches, its coverage certainly is more *diverse* – something which I think needs celebrating.

Just as there is no one definition of feminism, there should not be one image of what feminism is, or what a feminist looks like. As evidenced by the range of photos on various photosharing websites, those attending SlutWalk are not in fact only young, white, thin women, but are also old, curvy, (dis)abled, gay, straight and bisexual. They are black, white and brown. They are men, women and transgender. The diversity evident in photos shared by feminist bloggers is a challenge in itself to the visual representation put forward by the mainstream news media. And while convincing the mainstream news to reframe the narrative might indeed be a 'fruitless endeavor' (Echo Zen 2012), the feminist blogosphere has at least provided a counter-memory of what the movement is about and who did, or did not attend. If thinking about this in terms of the 'storying of feminism,' and how the feminist movement has come to be remembered and told, feminist blogs have revealed their potential to expand the number and types of voices heard, people seen and experiences recounted.

Identifying the backlash?

In my previous work on representations of the women's movement from the 1960s to the noughties (Mendes 2011a, 2011b), I argued that while anti-feminist discourses are obviously unhelpful in the fight towards gender equality, there is something particularly insidious about discourses of *backlash* – or those articles which suggest an unfulfilled desire to support the women's movement and its members, because it has 'gone too far,' and its tactics or goals have become irrational.

While appearing to support feminism, these articles imply that the movement has become unreasonable, and sadly must be rejected. And although I argued at the start of this chapter that SlutWalk provides evidence of a move away from these backlash discourses, where feminist goals are widely accepted and it is only the means through which they are achieved which remains controversial, I have written elsewhere (Mendes 2015) of the ways in which a small, but discursively significant, selection of articles sought to repudiate the movement and convince the public of SlutWalk's redundancy. For example, one column in Australia's *Herald Sun* identified SlutWalk as proof of 'the twisted priorities of modern feminism' which focused on 'the trivial while ignoring real issues of consequence' (Panahi 2012, p. 39). Britain's conservative *The Daily Mail* had one headline reading: 'These "SlutWalks" now prove feminism is irrelevant to most women's lives' (Phillips 2011), noting that feminism is now well past its 'sell-by date,' and that 'The great causes which animated it [feminism] have been won.' Such articles contribute towards a backlash by highlighting the supposed disconnect between issues of *real* concern to modern society, and those advocated by (crazy and irrational) feminism (see also Faludi 1992; Mendes 2011b). Luckily, however, these backlash articles that outright reject feminism were few and far between. This does not, however, mean that there was agreement on which (feminist) goals should be pursued. For example, a number of texts appeared to support feminist activism in general, but criticized activists for pursuing the 'wrong' (feminist) goals.

SlutWalk focuses on the 'wrong' goals

Although not measured through the qualitative content analysis, a close reading of texts, particularly in my mainstream media sample, revealed a clear support for feminist activism, but critiques of SlutWalk for focusing on the 'wrong' goals. For example, writing about the SlutWalk movement in the Indian context, columnist Amrit Dhillon opined:

> In a country where 10 million babies have been killed in the womb because they were girls, where women are burned for dowry, murdered in honour killings, where Dalit women fear sexual humiliation by upper-caste men and where young girls are forced into prostitution, who needs the right to dress like a slut? And while we're listing women's sorrows, a recent global survey by TrustLaw found India to be the fourth most dangerous place in the world for women.
> Such a misguided protest only serves to mock the real issues Indian women face. They are still denied so many fundamental rights

that this event, aping the actions of educated Western middle-class females, can be only a frivolous irrelevance. (Dhillon 2011, p. A13)

Here, it was clear that Dhillon was concerned about the quality of women's lives in India, by highlighting many of the dangers they face simply for being born female. And given these dangers, Dhillon appeared perplexed that the public was rallying around what she perceived as the movement's quest to give women more freedom to sexually express themselves through their attire. As a result, unlike backlash discourses that state that feminism is redundant or harmful, Dhillon argued that activism is necessary, but should be redirected to more worthy issues.

A similar critique was found in Australia's *Herald Sun*, where SlutWalk was constructed as irrelevant when compared to pressing *local* issues:

> But why march like a Goldfinger dancer because some Toronto policeman said something stupid to a group of 12 female university students?
>
> I'd like to know where this outrage was when Sheik Taj Din al-Hilali, then mufti of Australia, told hundreds of men in his mosque that if a woman dressed immodestly, she deserved what she got.
>
> 'If you take out uncovered meat and place it outside on the street ... and the cats come and eat it, whose fault is it, the cats or the uncovered meat? The uncovered meat is the problem,' he said.
>
> Nope, no marches then ... Anyway, I would have thought anti-rape campaigners would be more concerned about the prevalence of violent, hardcore porn than what some dumb cop said thousands of kilometres away ... And yet here we have a bunch of do-gooders dressed as if they might have just stepped off the set of a porn movie, marching against rape.
>
> Sorry ladies, but I think you've mucked this one up. (Morrell 2011, p. 35)

While the two excerpts above certainly constructed SlutWalk as misguided, I would not classify these as 'backlash' articles because if anything, they reiterate the continued *need* for feminism. Their main concern was not that feminist activism was taking place, but that it focused on the 'wrong' goals.

When locating SlutWalk into the context of historical feminist activism, it is worth highlighting that feminism has never had a universally agreed-upon list of issues in need of resolving, theory of why those issues existed in the first place, or understanding of how those issues should best be tackled (Jaggar 1983). And although I do not wish to deny that cultural context matters (this last column was from Australia, not Canada where SlutWalk originated), it becomes a tricky matter when individuals hierarchically rank women's oppression, and deem some causes more important than others. While issues such as female genital mutilation (FGM), honour killings and hardcore porn certainly need our attention, does this mean that we should ignore other, 'lesser' forms of violence such as street-harassment and victim-blaming? Is it fair to tell a woman who has been assaulted that her experience of oppression is less important than that of someone else? Or that she does not have the right to challenge a culture in which victims are routinely blamed for their assault, and should instead focus her attention on the 'real' issues? I think not. Instead, what these critiques reveal is a fundamental misunderstanding of what SlutWalk is. It has never been a movement about the right to dress like a porn star. It has, however, been about the right to dress as one pleases without this being used as an excuse for being attacked. Yet, it is clear that, albeit for a minority of commentators, this was a message that was not grasped. And once again, if we only examine visual images of SlutWalk in the mainstream media, it is easy to see how many came to this interpretation of the movement.

So, although the articles above do not support SlutWalk, they are not contributing towards a backlash against feminism, as, at their core, they support the need to improve women's lives. On the other hand, other texts, once again predominantly found within the mainstream news media, delegitimized SlutWalk by framing supporters as overwhelmingly naïve, particularly about men's 'true' and sexual nature. Such articles therefore contributed to the frame of SlutWalk as being misguided while at the same time reproducing common rape myths that the movement ironically aimed to challenge. As a result, I argue these articles do contribute towards a backlash against feminism and feminist discourses.

Naïve SlutWalkers, socio-biology and the reproduction of common rape myths

One of the most common ways of discrediting SlutWalk in the mainstream news media was through constructing its participants as naïve in regards to the 'reality' of men and male sexuality. This was evident in headlines such as 'When naïve girls would be sluts' (Lim, T. 2011). The logic behind this discourse is two-fold. On the one hand, it says that women send out certain signals, such as their sexual availability, through their dress and behaviour, and should therefore not be surprised if 'bad things' happen to them when acting or dressing in a certain way. In fact, not only should women not be surprised at the consequences of their behaviour, the discourse upholds the view that women in fact should be *held responsible* for any sexual violence used against them, because they have sent out the wrong signals, or aroused men's libidos beyond a point of control. This discourse was evident in content such as the following letter to the editor:

> IF these SlutWalk women, pictured in London, believe they can dress as provocatively as they want and expect no reaction, they are worryingly naive. Of course, thousands of men will do nothing but it just takes one who is unstable to put these girls at risk.
>
> I will teach my daughters what happens in the real world, not these silly women's fantasy world. (Skelly 2011, p. 49)

Letters such as this contribute to the victim-blaming ideology by reinforcing the common myth that some women, knowingly or not, 'ask' to be raped. According to the letter above, rape is constructed as a *normal*, *understandable* and even *inevitable* reaction to scantily-clad women. And although the letter writer acknowledges that, while most men can control their sexual urges, 'it just takes one' who cannot, and any woman who doesn't recognize this 'reality' deserves what she gets. After all, she 'provoked' him. What these texts then criticize is not the idea that some men 'can't help' but rape, but that women are naïve about men's 'true' nature – namely that they are inherently sexual beings unable to control their sexual urges once piqued (or 'provoked'). This was evident in a *Calgary Herald* column in which the author Brian Spackman wrote:

> [Wo]men who dress and act provocatively, 'slutty,' and then claim there should never be any negative consequences for their behaviour are blissfully, yet frighteningly, ignorant of male human nature. Actions have consequences. Those who disregard boundaries of decency and respect do so at their own peril. (Spackman 2011, p. A9)

Similar to the letter above, the logic presented in this column draws upon patriarchal ideologies about the nature of 'aggressive' masculinity. It stipulates that while women should have the freedom to dress as they choose, they must recognize that 'actions have consequences' (Spackman 2011). What is worth noting is that while both authors talk about the importance of individuals taking *responsibility* for their actions, it is clear that their judgment is not focused on the attacker – after all, he *can't* help himself – and they focus instead on the responsibility of the *victim*. I want to spend time going over these discourses because I believe they are not only extremely common, but complex and fuelled by patriarchal ideologies which need unpacking. One of the most common discourses, then, is that women 'provoke' or 'trigger' rape.

Women 'provoke' or 'trigger' rape

As scholars have noted, one of the most common rape myths is that women 'provoke' rape through their attire or behaviour, which 'leads men on by suggesting sexual availability' (Meyer 2010, p. 23; see also Benedict 1992; Berrington & Jones 2002; Bonnes 2013; Durham 2013; Groth 2001; McNicol 2012). This discourse only functions if one buys into patriarchal views of masculinity as inherently sexual and aggressive. That these discourses have become hegemonic and 'common sense' is evident in advice given to young women, such as that delivered by Brix Smith-Start, an American singer and television producer who said:

> It's important as a woman, as a girl, when you're growing up, to experiment with different looks. When I dressed as a teenage slut I felt sexy, I felt grown-up, cool, I had hot pants, platforms – I loved it. I was innocent, though, I wasn't prepared for the trigger that would happen in the men. Yes, dress however you want, but be aware it can trigger things in other people which you cannot control. (McVeigh 2011, p. 24)

These discourses are rooted in socio-biological beliefs about gender that are essential to interrogate in order to fully challenge.

As briefly mentioned in Chapter 4, academics have noted how socio-biology, or the logic that men and women are 'naturally' or 'genetically' *different,* has been used to legitimize a range of oppressive ideologies over women (Hasinoff 2009; Macdonald 1995). Discourses drawing on socio-biology maintain gender essentialism by arguing that men are 'driven by psychological and physiological urges ingrained in the era of "cavemen,"' thus providing a 'scientific rationalization for race, gender, and class stratification by constructing a fixed human nature that transcends environment and context' (Hasinoff 2009, p. 271). Since the Second Wave feminist movement, academics have noted that socio-biology has been used to justify a backlash against women's liberation (Faludi 1992; Hasinoff 2009), and any attempts to re-define gender roles are constructed as either inherently doomed, or as harmful to society (see Mendes 2011b).

In the context of rape, socio-biological arguments are the foundation for several rape myths, including the idea that 'rapists are in the grip of impulsive, uncontrollable sexual urges' (Coppock et al. 1995 cited in McNicol 2012, p. viii). These myths materialized in a range of articles claiming that men are 'genetically' wired to be turned on at the site of women's flesh, and therefore cannot be held responsible for sexually assaulting women whose bodies are on display.[3] An example of such discourse is found in one *Calgary Herald* column, which advised:

> Healthy men are *biochemically* driven by their *mating instincts* and can be aroused by various visual and behavioural cues. The porn industry, which dehumanizes and objectifies women, makes billions off this fact ... Sadly, some men have no moral compass and follow only their *animal instincts*. (Spackman 2011, p. A9, italics mine)

This is a perfect example of how the news media at times reproduced rape myths when reporting SlutWalk. By focusing on how men are 'biochemically driven by their mating instincts,' the author absolves them of responsibility for their behaviour. As previously stated, inherent in this discourse is the powerful ideology that men are, first and foremost, sexual beings (in contrast to (white) women, who are constructed as asexual, or at least able to control their sexual urges), and thus are akin to animals. By rousing men's animal instincts, women therefore only have themselves to blame when sexually violated.

Although this article referred to 'animal instincts,' others talked directly about the powerful nature of male hormones, and once again focused on men's (presumed) lack of ability to control their behaviour as a result. While claiming that 'slutty' clothing is 'no excuse for rape,' one article published on *New Zealand TV* argued: 'We need to understand a male has testosterone. They're turned on by the visual. Images are important – that's why the porn industry does so well' ('Slutwalks brave cold to get message across' 2011). However, what the article failed to note is that women also produce testosterone, yet to my knowledge, this has never been used as a reason to explain why some women commit sexual assault.

While most articles promulgated socio-biological discourses through a serious tone, others used more colloquial language. Writing for the UK's *Observer*, Victoria Coren not only confirmed men's inability to resist biological urges, but insisted that living in such a world would be undesirable: 'Oh, give the boys a break. What do you want, to retrain men's biology so thighs and cleavage no longer strike them as sexual?

It's unachievable – which is lucky, because I don't want to live in a clockwork orange' (Coren 2011). Worryingly, Coren's article could be read as supportive for our current rape culture (yes, a few women might be raped, but wouldn't it be a shame if men no longer found women so overwhelmingly sexually attractive?), suggesting that any attempts to alter men's 'true' nature would lead to the *real* chaos – or clockwork orange. Discourses such as this are particularly worrying because rather than critiquing men's behaviour, they construct it not only as inevitable (Carter 1998; Meyers 2006), but as *desirable*. What Coren also ignored is that while some women might appreciate sexual attention from men, this is *not* the same as asking to be sexually assaulted against their will. As several signs at SlutWalk marches noted 'By definition, you can't ask for rape' (SlutWalk Johannesburg 2012).

So, while some articles simply criticized SlutWalk participants for being 'naïve' about the 'real world,' like Michael Sanguinetti's advice which sparked SlutWalk, a number of others focused their attention on providing women with 'advice' on how to avoid rape.

Women must *be careful*, and the problem with individual solutions to rape

One discourse that I regularly encountered, which upon first reading is seemingly logical, but which I criticize for taking an individualistic approach to rape prevention, is that women must *be careful*, and take every possible precaution to avoid rape. As British columnist Janet Street-Porter advised:

> [T]here's a fine line between expressing your individuality through your clothing and starting a chain of events you may not be able to control. We dress to be noticed and admired but do we think through the consequences? ... Of course men are 100 percent responsible for their actions – but why some women dress so provocatively in situations where a lot of drink is being consumed and both sexes might feel more uninhibited is difficult to understand ... Women should be able to go out at night and have fun without worrying about being attacked. I'm not saying they should be fearful, but they *should be mindful*, that what they are wearing, where they are walking and whether they are alone should all be considered. (Street-Porter 2011, italics mine)

Upon first reading, I would argue that this advice seems sensible. After all, while we would all like to live in an ideal world in which crimes (including sexual assault) are non-existent, we will likely never experience such a utopian society. Therefore, given the reality of the world we live in, and the neoliberal ideologies which inform it, of course it seems sensible for everyone to take whatever precautions they can to minimize their risk of crimes such as rape. This includes being aware of the ways drugs and alcohol affect us. And although I am aware of the ways feminists have critiqued rape prevention advice (avoid 'dangerous' places, behaviour and dress) for contributing to a victim-blaming culture (see McNicol 2012), my issue with this advice is two-fold. First, it reinforces the idea that rape prevention is solely *women's responsibility* or concern, and second, such advice ignores the structural nature of rape.

Starting with the first criticism, although the article begins by stating that perpetrators (mostly men) are '100 percent responsible for their actions,' it goes on to argue that women should 'be mindful' of what they are wearing and walking (Street-Porter 2011). As a result, sexual violence prevention is still constructed as best 'address[ed] through the bodies of women, always already victims' (Hall 2004, cited in McNicol 2012, p. viii). Instead, we need more articles focusing on what society as a whole can do to do prevent rape. This includes educating the public about what sexual assault actually is, condemning it when it happens (not just brushing it off as inevitable, or noting that 'boys will be boys'), and punishing rapists properly. And even though articles such as the one above view rape as *impermissible*, the use of personal solutions (women must be careful) detracts from the ways that rape is a political issue requiring *widespread and collective change.*

Yet, the notion that women must be careful is so entrenched and pervasive that there is even a whole industry geared towards helping *women* prevent rape – from self-defence classes, to anti-rape underwear, clothing, condoms, nail-polish and other purchasable devices (see Valenti 2007). It is unsurprising that in our neoliberal society, in which women are told empowerment is only a purchase away (see Douglas 2010), that rape is also seen as something that can be avoided if women consume the right products. And it is the ways in which both men and society as a whole are largely absent from these solutions and discussions which I find particularly worrying. And I am not the only one. As one columnist in the *Sydney Morning Herald* noted: 'Women are still taught to take responsibility for the actions of others in a way that men are not' (Feeney 2011). By directing attention to what women can do to avoid rape and ignoring men's responsibilities, this perpetuates the fallacy that rape is a 'woman's issue,' which women must solve.

My second critique of 'be careful' discourses is not that this advice won't work in some situations – after all, I agree that being careful will prevent *some* assaults (for example, guarding your drink to make sure no one spikes it, having a buddy system in which women watch out for one another on nights out). However, it is not a viable large-scale solution for rape prevention. This is because it ignores the *reality* that 'simply being female' means we are at risk of sexual assault in our current rape culture (Valenti 2014b), with some being more vulnerable than others, depending on factors such as migration status, age, race, skin colour, ethnicity, sexuality, class and so forth. While some might say the solution is to keep women indoors (particularly at night), or dressed modestly, the reality is that rape happens at all hours and is mostly committed by someone the victim knows – a boyfriend, husband, lover, father, brother, friend or acquaintance – and is most likely to take place in familiar and seemingly 'safe' places such as home (see Järvinen et al. 2008; RAINN 2009b; Valenti 2007). Crucially then, advice telling women to *be careful* ignores the way rape is a method used to humiliate, punish, gain power and control over women, rather than simply a way to achieve sexual gratification (see Groth 2001 [1979]; Scully & Marolla 1985). And while I do not doubt that there are some scenarios in which a woman's actions might help her, *the individual*, escape rape (e.g. always protect one's drink), as Jessica Valenti (2014b) argued, 'We should be trying to stop rape, not just individually avoid it.'

Moving away from 'be careful'

I must admit, I have spent a long time reflecting on 'be careful' discourses. And while it is easy to criticize them, it is much more difficult envisioning better advice on how to avoid a crime which, although serving a multitude of purposes, is the result of interlocking systems of oppression. And while I know that telling women to 'be careful' will not stop rape, I am not sure what, if anything, will, until society experiences widespread social change. So taking my cue from SlutWalk and other anti-rape organisations, we need to develop new strategies and discourses which take into account the nature of sexual assault and how it is not fuelled simply by sexual desire, but by power, entitlement, domination and control. We need to educate both men *and* women that no one is entitled to another's body, and that sexual aggression is *not* a normal or healthy part of sexual relationships.

With the rise in pornography and the 'pornification' of society, in which women are frequently represented as sexual objects there to satisfy men's desires (see Dines 2010; Levy 2005), this is no doubt a difficult, but worthy task. But it is a task that might just be starting to take hold. In September 2014, The White House released a public service campaign 'It's On Us' (2014), which, rather than telling women how they could avoid rape, works to create a culture which: (1) recognizes that non-consensual sex is sexual assault; (2) identifies situations in which sexual assault may occur; (3) intervenes in situations where consent has not or cannot be given; and (4) creates an environment in which sexual assault is unacceptable and survivors are supported. University campuses are beginning, at least discursively, to take zero-tolerance approaches to rape culture. In 2014, the University of Calgary's campus bar staff received training on sexual assault prevention (Ho 2014). Although it is too soon to see what impact it will have, these are just two examples of initiatives which mark a watershed moment away from placing sexual assault prevention on women's shoulders, and instead makes it a collective responsibility.

Concluding thoughts

When examining the ways that SlutWalk was opposed in both my mainstream news and feminist media sample, I want to conclude by reiterating my argument that not all criticisms of SlutWalk are necessarily 'bad' for the movement, and may at times be necessary for its development and growth. For example, genuine concerns about women of colour's ability to appropriate or march under the word 'slut'; claims that SlutWalk panders to the male gaze; and fears about an emphasis on individual choices and freedoms, rather than collective action against patriarchal culture, are all constructive criticisms that open up necessary dialogues about the intersectional nature of oppression, patriarchy's hegemonic hold in a 'postfeminist' context, and the possibility of social change in neoliberal societies. Furthermore, if taken into account by movement organizers (as many of these issues have been), such critiques can help sustain the movement, improve its theoretical position on rape culture and increase its relevancy and following. Such critiques after all have been responsible for satellite groups such as SlutWalk Toronto posting a series of blogs on becoming more inclusive and better recognizing privilege. They have also been responsible for the closure of satellite groups (SlutWalk NYC) and individuals' departure from the movement when they felt responsible for, but ultimately unable to resolve these issues (Sutton 2014). As SlutWalk Chicago 2011 organizer

Stephanie Sutton explained, she left the movement after its first year in light of criticisms from women of colour:

> I feel like I heard a lot of criticisms that I needed to hear which made me a better feminist and a better person down the line. And it took me a really long time to understand a lot of criticisms about race, but I am really glad that it was criticized. (Sutton 2014)

Similarly, SlutWalk NYC 2011 organizer Melissa Marturano (2013) explained that the coalition dissolved because of serious issues surrounding exclusion and privilege within the movement.

Other criticisms against the movement, however, were not constructive and instead contributed to an overall backlash towards SlutWalk and feminist collective action. Such articles re-hashed well-worn tropes about feminism's supposed irrelevancy and the futility of changing men's 'true' nature. Such articles not only de-legitimized SlutWalk, but reproduced the very rape myths the movement has been trying to dismantle. These discourses provide an indication of how deep patriarchal ideologies about the nature of rape run, and about the extent to which gender roles are seen as fixed. These findings at least identify areas in need of addressing if we are to challenge patriarchal discourses. At the same time, they raise questions about whether we can ever really expect such ideologies to be challenged within institutions such as the news media, which, around the globe, are patriarchal in nature (see Byerly 2013; Global Media Monitoring Project 2010).

While this chapter provided evidence of backlash discourses, I argue that they were the minority within my overall sample, and were largely limited to the mainstream news media. Instead, I argue that in many cases, even when the movement was framed as being opposed or misguided, the majority of texts still supported an end to sexual assault or rape culture. Although my results are limited to one case study – SlutWalk, they do provide early evidence of the ways society is increasingly accepting feminism and the need for feminist intervention (see also Valenti 2014c).

So, while I am optimistic overall about the ways in which SlutWalk was represented, I want to conclude this chapter by highlighting some key questions and reservations. For example, to what extent has SlutWalk paved the way for other types of feminist activism, even those where women's flesh is not on display, to make it onto the news agenda? Is baring one's flesh a reasonable and sustainable strategy for news copy?

Is this a strategy future feminists should follow? While I believe that the mainstream media's attention to SlutWalk is significant, has it marked a watershed moment in the news media's treatment of feminism? Or is it instead a one-off exception, both in terms of news volume and support? Such questions are an important part of SlutWalk's legacy, and only time and more research will tell what its long-term impact will be.

6
SlutWalk Hierarchies and Organizers' Roles

Engaging with the work of social movement scholar Manuel Castells, this chapter explores theories of horizontal, leaderless and 'postmedia' movements in relation to SlutWalk. Drawing from interviews with 22 organizers from around the world, I demonstrate the ways that SlutWalks differed in their organizational structures, strategies and priorities, which in some cases shifted dramatically over time. Unlike other contemporary social movements which scholars have argued are leaderless and operate through consensus (Castells 2012), this chapter demonstrates that *all* satellite groups had leaders, with some being more visible or prominent than others, raising questions about how SlutWalk, and perhaps feminist activism more generally, fits into broader theories of networks and horizontalism. Furthermore, while some groups adopted policies of collaboration, equitable distribution of labour and consensus, others openly embraced hierarchy, and established procedures for maintaining it. The chapter concludes by exploring the challenges organizers who were new to activism faced, their strategies for overcoming these challenges, and their views on the importance of professional vs. social media skills in an age of 'postmedia' (Castells 2012), in which social movements have the potential to bypass the traditional media to spread their message.

Overall, what struck me the most about results from my interviews is that, despite the plethora of differences which emerged, ranging from entry points into the movement to media strategies and levels of activist experience, all of my participants emphasized the importance of social media platforms. Whether they were used to find out about the movement, get involved, target mainstream news or community groups, share information or publicize events, social media, particularly Facebook, were seen as invaluable. As a result, rather than devoting one section entirely to social media, I have integrated organizers' comments about it throughout the following two chapters.

Getting involved

One of the key questions I asked most of my 22 SlutWalk organizers was how they became involved in the movement. Although social movement scholars have documented the origins of various well-known protests such as the Arab Spring, the Occupy Movement or the Spanish Indignados, these have largely remained focused on specific geographical centres or nations (e.g. Tahrir square, New York City, Spain) (see Castells 2012; Gerbaudo 2012; Juris 2008), and have not examined the ways such protests have spread beyond their geographical origins to other cities around the world. While in cases such as the Occupy Movement, social media *eventually* played a key role in publicizing the activism which had already taken place on the ground, SlutWalk, like the Egyptian uprising and the Spanish Indignados, began as a 'social media event', with a pre-determined date set well in advance (Gerbaudo 2012). And like these campaigns, SlutWalks went 'viral' on social media, *before* any on-the-ground activism ever took place (see also Gerbaudo 2012). This appears to be in stark contrast to the Occupy Movement, which only really gained momentum several weeks after the initial occupation of New York City's Zuccoti Park, when protesters became faced with 'police repression and a threat of eviction' (Gerbaudo 2012, p. 113).

  In thinking about SlutWalk in relation to the importance of social media, it is clear that the movement could not have happened without it. While I presented SlutWalk co-founder Heather Jarvis' account of the movement's genesis in the introduction to this book, it is worth reiterating the role that social media played from the get-go – a theme we will see time and again in this chapter. As Jarvis noted, she first came across PC Michael Sanguinetti's advice that 'women should avoid dressing like sluts in order not to be victimized' in an article from York University's student newspaper *The Excalibur* (Kwan 2011), which she found on Facebook. Therefore, despite popular misconception, SlutWalk was not started by the 12 or so students to whom PC Sanguinetti delivered his advice, but by Toronto residents who became both aware of, and outraged by this event, via social media. A 2011 report by Ogilvy Public Relations Worldwide found that the majority of Americans acknowledged the important role that social media can play for enhancing the visibility of social causes, and this appears to be particularly true for SlutWalk. Of the organizers I asked, many first heard about SlutWalk via social media, most notably Facebook (Brodie 2014; Broher 2014; Delgado 2014a; Gray 2014a; Jarvis 2012; Sodhi 2014).

For example, SlutWalk Melbourne 2012 and 2013 organizer Amy Gray recounted how she first heard about SlutWalk and why she decided to become involved:

> I started hearing about the Ottawa SlutWalk campaign by social media. The more I heard about it, the more I started seeing references to the Australian version that was going to happen in Melbourne. It seemed well organized and to have a lot of media attention and it was taking up a lot of conversation on social media as well. (Gray 2014a)

As the movement gained momentum, with new events being organized in other cities, nations and continents, SlutWalk's currency soared amongst both mainstream news and feminist publications. Given the 'messy' nature of the web (Postill & Pink 2012), several organizers couldn't recall exactly where they first heard about it, but knew it was 'around the internet' (Broher 2014), 'on Facebook and Twitter mostly' (Brodie 2014) or 'online somewhere' (Sutton 2014). As a result, based on the results from interviews with 22 organizers, one could conclude that SlutWalk, like other contemporary social movements, is 'postmedia' (Castells 2012), in the sense that its growth was not contingent on mainstream media coverage, but instead went 'viral' for presenting messages that 'resonated with people's personal experiences' (Castells 2012, p. 122). For instance, SlutWalk Chicago organizers Stephanie Sutton and Ashley Broher both found out about the movement on online feminist spaces, such as feminist blogs, Tumblr accounts and Twitter feeds (Broher 2014; Sutton 2014). Similarly, results from a small, unrepresentative sample taken at SlutWalk London 2012 demonstrated that out of 53 respondents, 25 (47 percent) found out about the march through Facebook, Twitter or around the internet. As we will discuss further in the chapter, friendship circles or other networks also played an important role, with 20 people (38 percent) hearing about the march through friends, families or other societies to whom they belonged (e.g. university feminist groups; the Socialist Workers Party).

In some cases, organizers responded directly to social media posts seeking to recruit organizers. SlutWalk Bangalore 2011 organizer Asqeer Sodhi (2014) explained that she first heard about the movement after (what became her co-founder) Dhillon Chandramowli 'sent out a message to a bunch of people on Facebook' which led to a planning meeting for the event. As Dhillan confirmed, SlutWalk Bangalore 'started over a status update' (Chandramowli 2014). For SlutWalk Seattle 2013 and 2014 organizer Laura Delgado, she found out about SlutWalk on Facebook when it 'popped up as a page I might like' (Delgado 2014a). When she went to their website and Facebook page for more information, she found posts about planning meetings, and has been involved ever since.

In a few cases, organizers first heard about SlutWalk through the mainstream media. For example SlutWalk Newcastle 2011–2013 organizer Lizi Gray stated that she first read about SlutWalk Toronto in *The Guardian* (Gray, L. 2014). Similarly, SlutWalk Bangalore 2011 organizer Dhillan Chandramowli (2014) said he heard about the movement from the news. SlutWalk Cape Town 2011 organizer Umeshree Govender (2014) found out about the movement after her friend, and soon to be co-organizer, Stuart MacDonald, showed her a link to a *CBC* article about the movement. Therefore, although research suggests that despite the rise of social media, most people continue to get information from traditional media sources such as television, radio and newspapers (see Barker-Plummer 2000; Gitlin 2003; Jones & Saad 2013; McNicol 2012; Media Insight Project 2014; Mitchell et al. 2013; Rhode 1995; Ogilvy Public Relations Worldwide 2011; van Zoonen 1992), my small, unrepresentative sample suggests that, for SlutWalk at least, whose participants are often plugged into online feminist communities, this might not be the case. As further evidence of this, of the 53 surveys completed at SlutWalk London 2012, only six people (11 percent) had heard about the movement from the national or local media.

Although I cannot claim that these findings are representative of all SlutWalk organizers or participants, they do indicate the need for further research how news of (feminist) activism is spread, and what prompts people to join the cause – either as organizers or as protestors. Is the mainstream news media the best, fastest and most in-depth way to learn about feminist protest and women's issues, or are citizens regularly turning to alternative sites of information, such as the feminist blogging community, feminist Twitter users, or feminist Facebook pages? If so, what role do online communities and 'digital socialities' (Postill & Pink 2012) play in regards to spreading news of feminist activism, information and mobilization? Although further research is needed to answer these questions, one aspect of movement I can comment upon is levels of hierarchy and organizers' roles.

Hierarchical or horizontal movements?

According to social movement scholars, one of the key attributes of many new social movements is their supposedly 'horizontal' and egalitarian nature, enabled by digital communication and social media platforms (see Castells 2007, 2009, 2012; Juris 2008). Manuel Castells (2012), for example, has argued that movements such as the Spanish Indignados were 'leaderless', and lacked spokespeople (p. 129). Instead, all decisions were made through consensus at General Assemblies, which sometimes attracted thousands (Castells 2012, pp. 129–30). More recently however, scholars such as Gerbaudo (2012) have challenged such assertions, claiming that 'hierarchies continue to exist within current social movements', despite the absence of formal leaders or structures (p. 19). According to Gerbaudo then, although they may not gain public recognition for their activism, contemporary social movements still need a few individuals to step up and *choreograph* collective action (2012, p. 4). But, within SlutWalk, how much power did these choreographers have? And how did they divide up the work, or even decide who could become a choreographer? What impact did these decisions have on how satellite groups saw themselves in relation to the wider movement? These questions will all be addressed below.

The importance of networks

By definition, grassroots movements such as SlutWalk are organized at the local level, supported by volunteers, who, although committed to the cause, might have very different views on how to organize and run a movement. With no one being paid for their time, the group can only function if there are enough willing people to do what is necessary to make the march happen. In most cases, then, as SlutWalk Vancouver 2013 and 2014 organizer Caitlin MacDonald (2014) explained, organizing boards become 'literally made up of people who email us and say, yes, I have the capacity to help organize.' Just under half of the organizers I interviewed told me they joined the movement out of their own initiative, i.e. they were not prompted by anyone they knew, but found out about the movement, whose message resonated with them, and decided to become involved. This was the case with SlutWalk Seattle 2013 and 2014 organizer Laura Delgado, who heard about the movement when it popped up as a Facebook page she might like (Delgado 2014a), and SlutWalk Aotearoa 2011 and 2012 organizer MJ Brodie, who contacted SlutWalk Toronto to find out if any marches were being planned in New Zealand. When they said no, she ended up organizing one herself (Brodie 2014).

In the majority of cases, however, individuals found out about the movement, and then joined as a result of pre-existing networks. According to other social movement scholars (see Freeman 1972; Gerbaudo 2012), pre-existing friendship networks have long played an important role in recruiting new members and spreading information about events and issues. SlutWalk St. Louis 2012 organizer David Wraith joined after a fellow community activist became involved in the movement (Wraith 2013), and SlutWalk Cape Town 2011 became a reality after two friends, Umeshree Govender and Stuart MacDonald, read about the movement and decided, seemingly spontaneously, to plan one. Similarly, SlutWalk Bangalore organizers Dhillon Chandramowli and Asqeer Sodhi were already connected via Facebook when Dhillan put out the call for organizers. In the case of SlutWalk Chicago 2013 and 2014 organizer Ashley Broher, pre-existing activist networks played a key role. Ashley explained that many current SlutWalk organizers were heavily involved in the Occupy Movement, and transferred their energy, enthusiasm and experience to SlutWalk (Broher 2014).

The recruitment of leaders via social media

While acknowledging the important role friendship circles play in many social movements, Australian feminist and writer Amy Gray (2014a) stated that we should not discount social media's role in enlarging various networks. While arguing that SlutWalk 'definitely relies on networks', she argued it's more about 'social media than social networking.' Using her own experience as an example, Amy explained how she became involved in SlutWalk Melbourne after leader Karen Pickering literally waved to her at the 2011 march, 'because she recognized me as someone who was vocally supportive of it on Facebook.' Amy joined the organizing committee a few months later, after Karen advertised a planning meeting in which anyone was welcome to join. At the meeting, Amy met a lot of new people who soon *became* friends. As a result, she stated:

> I think the friend network definitely becomes a factor later as you know more people for specific skill requests but most of the recruiting to known or unknown people occurs online. No one gets a personalized invitation. (Gray 2014b)

Instead, Amy believed that friendship networks become increasingly important for recruiting people to attend, rather than plan the march, noting that: 'friends will text each other the day of a march and arrange to meet, etc.' (Gray 2014b).

That social media also played a role in recruitment was evident with SlutWalk Chicago 2011 organizer Stephanie Sutton, who found out about the movement through the feminist blogosphere. She became involved after reading a Tumblr post inviting the public to a planning meeting (Sutton 2014). Similarly, SlutWalk Seattle 2013 and 2014 organizer Laura Delgado saw an advertisement about a planning meeting on their Facebook page and decided to attend (Delgado 2014a). In fact, many SlutWalk groups continue to recruit new members through social media. Laura, for example, explained how SlutWalk Seattle is open to anyone who wants to join: 'It's super grassroots and whoever wants to be involved, can be involved.' Planning events are regularly posted on their Facebook wall.

And in the many hours I have spent trawling through SlutWalk Facebook pages, I have come across dozens of open invitations for members of the public to become involved on the planning committees. So, although friendship circles or pre-existing networks can be very important, my research indicates that social media is an effective way of recruiting people who might otherwise not have known about the movement or found information on how to take part. In these cases then, social media is a vital tool used to reach out to members of the public, in much the same way as the newspaper, poster, leaflet and direct mail campaigns of the past (see Gerbaudo 2012, p. 4). Consequently, SlutWalks, like other contemporary social movements, are not inventing new strategies for recruitment, they are simply using different technologies.

Horizontalism vs. Hierarchy

Although this idea of horizontalism – or leaderless, non-hierarchical movements, has been associated with contemporary social movements (see Castells 2000, 2007, 2009, 2012; Juris 2008), some radical social movements such as (radical/socialist) feminism, environmentalism and the student-movement, have adhered to these principles for decades. More recently, this notion of horizontalism has been both advocated and celebrated as the way forward, particularly amongst anti-globalization movements, who 'do not look to one leader, but make space for all to be leaders' (Sitrin 2006, p. 2; see also Juris 2008; Sitrin 2012).

However, not all activist organizations believe that horizontalism is the way forward, and views on this largely come down to political theory. For example, within the women's movement, contemporary liberal feminists have often reproduced organizations with clear hierarchies and centralized power. This is evident with prominent groups such as the National Organization for Women (NOW) and The Feminist Majority Foundation, which, for example, will have a President and board of directors, local chapters and membership fees. These organizations seek to intervene directly within political processes in their attempts to bring about social change. So, for example, NOW has a Political Action Committee (PAC) which endorses and promotes electoral candidates who are committed to advancing women's rights, and the Feminist Majority Foundation lists a number of traditionally 'political' campaigns and actions to promote women's equality.

These tactics are in stark contrast to those adhered to by many radical and socialist feminists, who have historically rejected these hierarchical organizations and advocated collectives instead. Within collectives, egalitarianism, anti-exploitation and group decision-making are prioritized (see Bouchier 1983; Mendes 2011a). Furthermore, rather than attempting to intervene in formal political processes, they often seek to foster change at local or cultural levels. Because radical feminists have also historically shied away from or rejected the mainstream media, instead producing their own accounts of their activities, they are historically not as well documented, particularly by the mainstream news (Mendes 2011a). As a result of these real theoretical differences that exist within feminism, one of the questions I asked most respondents was how the groups organized themselves and assigned roles.

Collectivism

In the majority of cases, organizers told me that they shared the responsibilities equally, with people helping out as best they could, where they could. In these cases, the satellite group was run as a collective, in which all major decisions had to be agreed upon by the group, which worked to develop policies, from what the movement's key message should be, to whether they should change the name, to how they should respond to online trolling. For example, several SlutWalk satellites such as Toronto, Vancouver, Winnipeg and Chicago, have held meetings in which they discussed changing the name. While those on the organization committee were all invited, in the cases of Toronto and Vancouver, members of the public were also asked to feed back on the topic. In other cases, however, such as with SlutWalk Chicago, a decision to change the name of the organizing committee which hosts an annual SlutWalk was taken by the collective, comprised of 14–16 people who meet every other week. Although 2013 and 2014 organizer

Ashley Broher admitted that the issue of the name change was contentious, she stated that, as a 'democratically run collective', they reached a consensus in the end. When asked how the work is divided up, Ashley explained 'We don't have positions, we all organize on all things together' (Broher 2014).

Ashley's experience working with a collective in Chicago is just one example of the ever evolving nature of the movement. Since she was one of several SlutWalk organizers who joined after being involved in the Occupy Movement, which adhered to collective principles, it is perhaps unsurprising that a similar organizational structure was implemented at SlutWalk Chicago. And yet, my interview with SlutWalk Chicago 2011 organizer Stephanie Sutton revealed the extent to which this particular satellite group has evolved. As Stephanie explained, when she was involved in the movement in its inaugural year, each organizer had specific titles and roles (such as 'Guerrilla Outreach Coordinator') (Sutton 2014). SlutWalk Chicago experienced a change not only in structure, but in core message. As Ashley explained, whereas the original march focused on the message that 'clothes don't cause rape', they have attempted to provide a more sophisticated analysis by explaining what *does* cause rape over the years. So, for example, the movement pays particular attention to the how 'lots of systems of oppression [capitalism, patriarchy, neoliberalism] cause rapists' (Broher 2014). This 'deepening of the message' Ashley explained, is a 'sign of a healthy organisation.'

Organizational hierarchy

While SlutWalk Chicago in its current manifestation prioritizes egalitarianism, others have embraced hierarchy and transparent organizational structures. For example, not only do most organizers at SlutWalk Seattle have specific titles (such as Director and Treasurer), but they have established formal procedures for appointing these leaders (formal interviews). Similarly, interested parties must fill in an application if they are interested in becoming a speaker at an event. When thinking about who took responsibility for certain tasks, 2013 and 2014 organizer Laura Delgado stated that the march was mostly planned by the Directors. Their responsibilities include getting necessary permits and organizing a line-up of speakers (Delgado 2014a). This trend towards 'professionalization' and 'organizational building' has been criticized by some social movement scholars who argue that it is simply a way for leaders to pursue personal interests and gain power over their rank (see Piven & Cloward 1977). However, others have highlighted the ways 'combat ready' and viable organizations are more likely to be successful (see Cress & Snow 2000; Gamson 1990). And as several SlutWalk organizers from around the world have told me, having good organizational skills and people to carry out certain tasks is crucial to the smooth running of events (see Gray 2014a; Wraith 2013).

It is clear within SlutWalk, however, that while there are those organizing the movement with formal titles, there are others within the movement whose activities are extremely important, yet largely hidden. For example, although SlutWalk Seattle 2013 and 2014 organizer Laura Delgado does not have 'an exact title', her responsibilities include managing the Facebook page, a key, if not primary means through which the organization connects with the public and *choreographs* activism (Gerbaudo 2012). And while Laura undoubtedly plays a crucial role in 'setting the scene' (Geherbaudo 2012, p. 13) for the movement through deciding what to post, I would describe her as, in Gerbaudo's terms, an 'anti', 'reluctant', or even a 'Facebook' leader (2012, pp. 164–5). Laura's reluctance was evident when I asked if she would consider running for a Director role one day. She replied that she was unsure, in part because, as someone in her early 20s, 'I feel like people want to listen to someone older' – and in part because she 'wanted to help behind the scenes' (Delgado 2014a). One benefit of modern social movements then, is the ability of those who want to help out without taking a visible or public leadership role.

SlutWalk Melbourne is another example of a satellite group with a clear hierarchy. According to 2012 and 2013 organizer Amy Gray, well-known feminist and writer Karen Pickering is the group's clear 'leader':

> Karen Pickering basically is the person who brought the SlutWalk to Melbourne, and she has been the leader ever since, and the one who schedules it every year, the one who draws together a group of organizers, who then draws together a group of volunteers. So, it's very much Karen's operation. (Gray 2014a)[1]

According to Amy then, one of the reasons Karen has been so successful is because she understands the need to recruit 'talented, seasoned activists' who are drawn in to perform specific tasks. As she argued: 'It's not just about getting the message out, it's working out what the tactics are, and working out what skills you need, and getting those people and convincing them and persuading them that they should get involved.' In this way, SlutWalk Melbourne with Karen Pickering at its head is very strategic in deciding who to bring in. However, Karen's strategy has not merely been to draw in volunteers from *pre-existing* networks and connections. Instead, Karen has used social media as a way of expanding the pool of potential volunteers, while specifically targeting certain groups such as sex workers and the Trans community.

So, in the past, while it might have been easy to identify a movement's theoretical position based on their organizational structure, my research raises doubts on the extent to which such generalizations are possible today. For example, the two organizers I interviewed, SlutWalk Melbourne's Amy Gray, and SlutWalk Chicago's Ashley Broher, demonstrated the most nuanced and radical understandings of sexual assault, yet their satellite groups were on complete opposite ends of the spectrum when it came to organizational hierarchy. And even though SlutWalk Chicago adheres to collectivism principles that seem to resonate with those of other contemporary movements such as Occupy and the Spanish Indignados, as Gerbaudo (2012) argued, those on the collective still acted as 'soft' leaders who choreographed the movement. I therefore want to conclude this section by pointing out that I do not judge SlutWalk Melbourne or Seattle for having more rigid or hierarchical structures, and praise SlutWalk Chicago for their collective organizational principles. All three satellite groups have been highly visible and active since 2011, and have worked tirelessly to end and better understand rape culture. And while SlutWalk Chicago might on the surface be more 'horizontal', as stated:

> [F]or all its participatory ideals, the process of mobilization always involves inequalities and asymmetries in which there are people who mobilize and people who are mobilized, people who lead and people who follow, and the categories only ever partly overlap. (2012, p. 165).

That all social movements require 'choreographers', or some sort of organization, structure and direction, is therefore important to keep in mind. A more important question in my mind is to what extent have these choreographers become visible, and how does this visibility help or hinder the movement?

Roles, levels of experience and expertise within the movement

As a grassroots movement, built upon the willingness of individuals to volunteer their time and effort, I was interested in finding out how my research participants learnt what was required to organize a protest. What became clear was that the level of previous knowledge on such matters varied widely from satellite group to satellite group, and that SlutWalk attracted anyone from those who had never previously been involved in any form of political activism, to those with years of experience participating in, and organizing events. My interviews with organizers revealed differences in terms of what, if any, existing skillsets they felt were required to organize successful protests.

Learning as they go

One of the most striking things when thinking back over my 22 interviews with SlutWalk organizers, was the truly 'grassroots' nature of the movement – community driven and run, volunteer based, and for the most part, run collectively. When asked about their role as a SlutWalk organizer, most respondents indicated that they did a little bit of everything –organizing protest permits, route marches, speaker line-ups, fundraising events, publicity, advertising and PR, and managing social media accounts. In several cases, organizers joined the movement with no 'professional' media skills to speak of.

For example, as a graduate student at the University of Cape Town, Umeshree Govender explained how friend and fellow graduate student Stuart MacDonald decided to host their own walk after reading about the movement's global spread. Inspired by their activism, Umeshree declared: 'we should totally do that in Cape Town, and voila, we did' (Govender 2014). Although this statement makes it sound as though organizing a march was smooth sailing, both Umeshree and Stuart admitted they learnt a lot along the way. For example, when I asked how they targeted media outlets, Umeshree explained that they sent out press releases to all the media houses they found on Google. When I asked how they knew how to write a press release, she confessed: 'We were just two students sitting in a bar, and we were like, how do we write a press release? And we Googled "how to write a press release" and sent it out there, and amazingly people showed up' (Govender 2014). SlutWalk Aotearoa 2011 and 2012 organizer MJ Brodie also described how she turned to Google to learn how to write a press release that first year (Brodie 2014). SlutWalk Singapore 2011 and 2012 organizer Vanessa Ho agreed that the organizing team often consulted the internet and friends and 'learnt as we went along' (Ho 2012). Clearly then for some organizers, a prerequisite for organizing a march was not the possession of PR, or other professional media skills. Instead, these organizers were confident that they could learn along the way. While several organizers turned to the internet to learn these new skills, others such as SlutWalk

Victoria 2013 organizer Diondra drew upon the professional expertise of friends, who worked in the newspaper and PR industry (Diondra 2013). For example, she explained the ways they helped her learn how to write a press release. She too admitted that 'For the most part, I am learning everything as I go' (Diondra 2013). So, although there is no doubt that activists in a pre-internet age found alternative means to learn develop 'media skills', my research presents evidence of the ways that modern technology has made these tasks much easier. However, while some aspects of movement planning were easy to learn, others, such as march logistics remained a tricky issue for some.

March logistics

When speaking with march organizers, it turned out that learning how to write a press release was one of the easier tasks they encountered, particularly when compared to sorting out march logistics. In my interviews, I asked SlutWalk Cape Town organizers Umeshree and Stuart about criticism they received for marching through a predominantly white, affluent and 'trendy' area, rather than, say, some of the black townships, in which it was thought such a movement might have had a bigger impact. From a critical perspective, while march logistics are of course important to consider for any protest, assumptions that poor black townships 'need' a SlutWalk more than white, middle-class urban areas implies that sexual assault is a crime committed predominantly by poor, black men, and ignores the ways that white, middle-class men also commit such crimes (see also Bonnes 2013; Maitse 1998; Moffett 2006). But as Umeshree articulated, while she acknowledged that the march route alienated many poor, black women:

> [Fr]om a logistic point of view we were just two students trying to organize a march, and we had to secure permission from the city. There had just been the World Cup [in 2010], and they already had a designated area [for protests], and we thought, this was the easiest thing to do. (Govender 2014)

Stuart also defended the ways that logistics played a key role in keeping the march in the white, middle-class city centre, rather than out in the poor, black townships. As he explained:

> The city centre is easy to get to and set things up, but if you are going to the townships it means you are going on random dirt roads which [white] people might not be too familiar with. So, I would say part of it was about planning. (MacDonald, S. 2014)

Although not overtly expressed, it is clear from Stuart's response that both he and Umeshree assumed the march would attract (white) middle-class marchers. This assumption was also confirmed by Umeshree, who was disappointed at how she felt some people only attended because it was seen as a 'trendy' thing to take part in (Govender 2014). And although the march route in the city centre was partly done out of convenience, there were also safety issues to consider. As Stuart argued:

> [I]f you are organising something like that [a SlutWalk], you also have to recognize that there are safety issues, and with a whole bunch of random people walking through townships, there might be danger to them [because of the historic racial tensions in South Africa] ... It might discourage people, because, in South Africa, a lot of white people don't go to the townships because they think it's ridiculously dangerous and so it would have alienated people if we had tried to do that. (MacDonald, S. 2014)

As a Canadian international student, Stuart was particularly attuned to the racial tensions he witnessed in South Africa. He also recognized the ways that hosting marches in townships, in which patriarchal traditions are firmly entrenched, could put at risk any poor, black women who dared to march, as such acts could be seen as a direct challenge to patriarchal power. As a result, Stuart talked about the challenge of spreading SlutWalk's message to townships, who might interpret the march as some 'neo-colonial movement telling us what we should or should not do' (Macdonald, S. 2014).

While logistics and safety for participants were priorities for SlutWalk Cape Town, SlutWalk Singapore organizer Vanessa Ho had a very different experience. Operating in a nation in which the ruling People Action's Party (PAP) has shown 'little tolerance for free and open discourse', particularly on 'politically sensitive matters' (Lee 2010, cited in Gwynne 2013, p. 174), there is only one designated place for protests, called 'Speaker's Corner.' So, rather than having a 'march', which is not permitted, they held a 'gathering'. In fact, throughout the interview, Ho was careful not to use the word 'protest' which would draw unwanted attention from authorities, and make the approval of a police permit unlikely. While Ho and her co-organizers were freed from the burden of planning a march route, there was confusion in 2011 over whether they needed to apply for a police permit to gather. And although it looked like the event might not happen when the Singapore Police Force (SPF) decreed a permit was in fact necessary, just days before the gathering, it was approved (and then waived) in the end, and the event took place as scheduled ('Singapore Allows SlutWalk' 2011).

From my discussion with organizers who were new to activism, it became clear that many learnt the ropes along the way. In some cases, such as with SlutWalk Cape Town, they were criticized for their choices in terms of march logistics, while in other cases, organizers learnt not to stress the radical potential of their event. Overall however, none of my organizers felt that their lack of organizational or activist experience was a barrier to becoming involved in the movement, and they all developed strategies to cope with various challenges. For example, while some organizers turned to the internet to learn skills such as writing press releases, others turned to friends. And in fact, as we will see in the following section, while a number of organizers with media skills were involved in the movement, there was debate over how necessary these were for modern movements.

The media experts

Although several of my research participants had no prior activist organizational experience, many indicated that they or other members of the organizing team were media 'experts' and had used these skills to benefit the movement. Their areas of expertise were quite wide-ranging: journalists (mostly freelance), publicists, marketing agents, PR experts, web producers, TV presenters and graphic designers. For example, SlutWalk Bangalore 2011 organizer Dhillan Chandramowli worked in radio for seven or eight years and is now a freelance journalist (Chandramowli 2014). According to co-organizer Asqeer Sodhi (2014), Dhillan's experience and contacts were essential in securing a number of radio interviews in the run up to their march. Similarly, SlutWalk Winnipeg 2011 and 2012 organizer Deanna (2012) said she applied knowledge from her previous job in marketing and promotions to help publicize the march.

SlutWalk Melbourne also benefitted from its organizers' extensive media experience. For example, one of the key organizers from 2011 was well-known feminist and journalist Karen Pickering, who co-organizer Amy Gray argued came up with 'lots of interesting angles to generate mainstream media interest' (Gray 2014a). As a writer and web producer herself, with over 25 years of experience as an activist (Gray 2014a), Amy also drew upon her media skills to 'write documents and promotional material', particularly for the web and social media accounts. The amount of effort put into social media, rather than simply mainstream news, is due to recognition of the changing forms of modern feminist activism. As Amy stated: 'One of the things about SlutWalk, and the changing face of activism is that it is equally online as it is offline' (Gray 2014a). This supports scholars' assertions about the ways that modern social media protest involves the intersection of on and offline activities (Gerbaudo 2012; Postill & Pink 2012).

A number of SlutWalk satellite groups benefitted from having individuals with PR experience. For example, for the original march in 2011, SlutWalk co-founder and organizer Heather Jarvis noted that their organizing committee had at 'least one person who has strong experience in PR' (Jarvis 2012). Similarly, SlutWalk Chicago 2011 organizer Stephanie Sutton explained that their media outreach was handled by a volunteer who worked in the PR industry. Because he was good at writing press releases and attracting media attention, Stephanie gave details about how she could then direct her efforts to reaching out to the local arts community – which was where her interests lay. SlutWalk Johannesburg 2013 organizer Karmilla Pillay-Siokos stated that, while not on the organizing committee, a professional publicist was 'advising' the team (Pillay-Siokos 2013). In 2012, a freelance PR consultant joined the SlutWalk Newcastle organizing team, an addition that organizer Lizi Gray argued ensured the smooth sailing of several events (Gray, L. 2014). While having individuals with professional media skills was certainly highly valued by some satellite groups and individuals, what emerged from my research was also the importance of bloggers.

The bloggers

While most of my questioning towards SlutWalk organizers sought to find out if anyone on the organizing team had specific media skills such as journalism, PR or marketing, one organizer pointed out an area I had overlooked – the importance of blogging and being media savvy in general. Given the important role social media has played not only in SlutWalk, but in modern protest (see Castells 2012; Gerbaudo 2012), organizers such as Stephanie Sutton explained how having a background in blogging was an asset to the movement. Whereas SlutWalk Chicago had one PR expert in 2011, Stephanie explained that the other three organizers, herself included, 'came from blogging backgrounds.' As a result, they were able to draw upon their knowledge and skills to discuss issues such as race and the reclamation of the word slut, which were just emerging as serious issues in need of addressing. While there is no doubt that the mainstream media play an important role in alerting the public to the existence of various social causes, movements and activism, Stephanie's comments illustrate the growing importance of how new media technologies are used in some ways to bypass the mainstream media, and in other ways to advance the movement's aims and key theoretical debates.

For example, Stephanie argued that the movement's main means of reaching people was not through the mainstream media, as might have been the case for the First and Second Wave, but through *social media*. This strategy was confirmed by SlutWalk Melbourne 2012 and 2013 organizer Amy Gray, who talked about the importance of using blogging, social media and other female spaces to spark debates about rape and rape culture. Using the format of the personal opinion piece, or the 'feelpinion', Amy said a range of women were recruited to write about their own experiences with sexual violence, and then link these with the theory behind SlutWalk. As Amy noted, these pieces generated a lot of attention on social media (Gray 2014a). As a result, it is worth addressing the importance organizers placed on having professional media or PR experts, as my research indicates that those with more general social media, blogging or writing skills are becoming increasingly important in a potentially 'postmedia' age (Castells 2012).

The importance of media experts and outreach

As indicated in the sections above, SlutWalk involved a range of people with varying levels of media 'skills.' Some, such as SlutWalk Perth 2011 organizer Beth Castieau admitted that not having anyone on their team with media expertise was a real area of weakness: 'It is an area of weakness in Perth that we don't have an expert in journalism or PR, and we are cobbling along the best we can as a result' (Castieau 2012). For others however, it became clear that they put no or very little effort towards media outreach and thus were not overly concerned with having media experts on the organizing team. This attitude emerged right from the movement's foundation, when SlutWalk Toronto co-founder Heather Jarvis stated, 'We never intended to get media attention. That was not was it was about. Through my activism I had never done that' (Jarvis 2012). However, Heather revealed that media outreach was something her co-founder Sonya Barnett had thought about it in the first few weeks. As it turned out, the media got wind of their march and contacted them before they had a chance to send out press releases. However, when planning their second march in 2012, Jarvis acknowledged sending out press releases, but insisted that they put more effort on community outreach, which they felt was more important (Jarvis 2012).

In a similar vein, SlutWalk Vancouver 2013 and 2014 organizer Caitlin MacDonald stated that community outreach was more important than media outreach, noting that 'I don't think any of our attendees would have come because of what was published [in the media]. I didn't hear anybody say they came because they saw this in the newspaper' (MacDonald, C. 2014). Instead, Caitlin noted that everyone who attended seemed to have found out about the march from their own networks, and as a result, the organizers directed a lot of attention to community outreach, liaising with feminist and other anti-rape networks. SlutWalk Seattle 2013 and 2014 organizer Laura Delgado expressed similar views. She stated that their satellite group didn't 'particularly reach out to them [the media].' Instead, she argued:

> I think we are more interested in reaching out to people. We are more interested in pairing with feminist organisations on college campus, and there are some established feminist groups and anti-rape groups. (Delgado 2014a)

That feminists have different media strategies is nothing new. As far back as the 1960s, mainly liberal feminists made a concerted effort to reach out to mainstream publications, and viewed them as legitimate and effective outlets for disseminating information on feminist issues (Mendes 2011a). Conversely, it was routine for some, mostly radical feminists, to reject the mainstream media completely (se Bradley 2003). Instead, they often produced their own alternative publications, which gave them control over their representations and the message, which many felt was more important than mass reach (Barker-Plummer 2010; Hole & Levine 1971; Steiner 2005). While the SlutWalk movement has not led to the production of general feminist publications such as *Spare Rib, Off Our Backs* or *Ms. Magazine*,[2] it has used blogs, leaflets, posters, poetry and social media platforms to disseminate views, intervene and disrupt mainstream discourses, develop theory on rape and rape culture, and reach out to the public more generally – acts which several organizers valued more highly than mainstream media outreach.

Concluding thoughts

Like many other new social movements, which are based around cultural change, SlutWalk has attracted a diverse range of supporters, both as participants and as organizers. At the time of their involvement in the movement, the oldest organizer was in his early 40s, but the majority were in their 20s, and the youngest was 17. And while some came from activist backgrounds, for others, SlutWalk was their first foray into (feminist) activism. Although it is difficult to make generalizations about my 22 research participants' experiences, my research does indicate the ways social media is replacing the mainstream media as the means through which people find out about, and decide to become involved in social protests. As a result, one of the main things I hope to have demonstrated in this chapter is the vital role social media has played in the movement. Whether they were the spaces in which activists first heard about SlutWalk, or the avenues through which they first reached out to fellow organizers to become involved, social media platforms, Facebook in particular, were vital to the movement's success and growth. As SlutWalk Singapore organizer Vanessa Ho explained, operating in a controlled nation such as Singapore, where the state owns the mainstream news media, Facebook and Twitter were 'our only alternatives' to get their message out (Ho 2012).

Even in nations with where the media were seemingly free of government control, organizers turned to social media because they were free, cheap and easy to use (Castieau 2012; Gray, L. 2014; Jarvis 2012; Wraith 2013). As SlutWalk St. Louis 2012 and 2013 organizer David Wraith explained: 'I don't know how we would have done it without the internet' (Wraith 2013). Crucially, operating in an online environment also meant being able to cross geographical distances, which would have been impossible 20 years ago. As SlutWalk co-founder Heather Jarvis recounted: 'Within the first two weeks after putting up one simple Facebook community page, we had people from all over the world saying we have the same problem here' (Jarvis 2012). And as a movement with no source of income (aside from donations, or money raised in fundraising), they quickly learned that the 'best way to function is online' (Jarvis 2012). As SlutWalk Victoria 2013 organizer Diondra argued:

> Social media has absolutely been one of the most crucial parts of our movement, especially our Facebook page. We let people know about events and fundraisers through social media. We answer a number of messages from our followers via social media. We are also constantly sharing articles relevant to our movement. (Diondra 2013)

So, although all of the organizers I spoke with emphasized social media's important role in the movement, they disagreed on the need for or importance of pre-existing professional media skills. While some satellite groups felt this was extremely important (Castieau 2012), others prioritized having social media 'savviness', and knowing how to write effective blogs, or make better use of social media platforms (Gray 2014a; Sutton 2014). And similarly, while some satellite groups made a concerted effort to target national or local media, others were more interested in community outreach – and ensuring the movement's message would have the greatest impact. This often meant targeting marginalized communities who might not pay attention to the mainstream news in the first place. As a result, although I do not wish to argue that the mainstream news does not matter, it is clear that organizers are divided in their opinions, and that many would be happy to bypass the mainstream media completely. While this is clearly not a new strategy, as radical feminists have ignored the mainstream media for decades (Bryson 2003), online technologies meant that they were able to distribute their materials much more widely than before. This chapter also provides credence to Manuel Castell's (2012) theory of postmedia movements, which bypass traditional media in favour of social media. The implications of this are indeed worthy of further research.

7
SlutWalk, Community and Cyberactivism

As the second of two chapters exploring results from interviews with 22 SlutWalk organizers from around the world, who were involved in the movement between 2011 and 2014, this chapter analyzes ways that satellite groups connected with one another, formed feminist communities, and fostered a larger SlutWalk movement. And while there is no doubt that offline activism (e.g. SlutWalk marches) was crucial to the movement's success, this chapter highlights the ways social media fostered *networked counterpublics,* or online spaces for feminists to regroup, connect with one another, form opinions, express emotions and draw attention to certain issues which may require action. These networked counterpublics were fostered through speaking to one another directly (often via Twitter), identifying issues in need of addressing (often through mainstream or feminist media) and developing feminist discourses around these issues. And although there is evidence of many strong connections, my research also highlighted a range of other superficial or weak connections, in which satellite groups do not interact beyond 'liking' each others' Facebook pages, or 'following' one another via Twitter. Yet, despite this, these interlinkages at least provide a *sense* of a united SlutWalk movement, which gives it credibility and demonstrates the ways feminists around the world are working together to end rape culture.

The chapter concludes by addressing the ways that, although the internet undoubtedly makes it easier for feminists to connect with one another, it also makes them vulnerable to online harassment and trolling. Unfortunately, all of the organizers I spoke to about trolling had experienced it, in some cases in very personalized ways. What emerged from my interviews was not only various responses to trolling – sometimes laughing it off, while in other cases being disturbed by it – but various ways of managing trolls. For example, some organizers deleted (or censored) offensive messages, while others left them but included 'trigger warnings.' Others still left them up and either responded themselves, or had help from the online community, which responded for them. The results however indicate that although organizers recognize trolling as a problem, they differ in what they view to be the appropriate response – something feminists will increasingly have to consider as they take to the web in their fight for social justice.

The relationship between satellite groups

Unlike other contemporary social movements such as the Arab Spring, Spanish Indignados, and Occupy Movement, which are geographically contained within local, regional or national borders, SlutWalk is a movement with a truly global reach, with walks taking place in over 200 cities and 40 nations (Carr 2013). And although this book focuses on the eight English-speaking nations in which the movement emerged, its reach was much wider than what is presented here. As a result, a question worth asking is what makes SlutWalk a *global movement,* rather than just a series of individual marches? In what ways do the national movements within it connect with each other, and who, if anyone, do they turn to for leadership or support? What I argue in the section below is that, despite being locally organized without any overarching 'blueprints' or 'bylaws' (Carr 2013, p. 26), many of the SlutWalk organizers I interviewed did indeed feel part of, and foster, an *international* SlutWalk community, which was accomplished primarily via social media platforms such as Facebook and Twitter. And while many were intent on staying 'true' to the message put forth by SlutWalk Toronto, others took leadership roles and adapted the movement to suit local needs and pressures.

Guidance from SlutWalk Toronto

As a grassroots movement, scholars have noted the ways that SlutWalk has been 'locally organized with independent initiative and without any overarching organization, blueprint, bylaws, etc.' (Carr 2013, p. 26). As a result, it comes as no surprise that local organizers have tailored the movement to suit local needs and respond to local pressures. For example, as discussed in Chapter 3, several organizers in India, Central and South America used parallel or translated names. Other organizers, such as those in Singapore, were keen to stress the ways the movement discouraged participants from dressing provocatively, in order to avoid unwanted government and police attention (Ho 2012). While these satellite groups tailored the movement and made it culturally relevant, it is clear that several others took their lead from the movement founders – SlutWalk Toronto. In some cases this involved feelings of responsibility for ensuring SlutWalk was positively represented.

For example, when talking about how SlutWalk Vancouver saw itself, 2013 and 2014 organizer Caitlin MacDonald explained: 'We are a satellite of SlutWalk Toronto and we ... don't want to go off and make the movement look bad. That's really important to us' (MacDonald, C. 2014). Caitlin's comment reflects her belief that they were not just an individual satellite group fighting rape culture, but were part of a larger (transnational) community of feminist activists working towards the same cause. Yet while maintaining a good reputation was important to Caitlin, she also noted the challenge they faced in keeping 'true' to SlutWalk Toronto's message, but adapting the movement to local issues (MacDonald, C. 2014). This was also a challenge faced by SlutWalk Bangalore organizer Asqeer Sodhi (2014), who, when asked about why they used a parallel name, stated that while they recognized the ways that keeping 'SlutWalk' in their title could possibly alienate them from local communities, it was really important to indicate that they were not a stand-alone march, but were part of a broader movement.

Branding and promotion

One of the most visible ways many SlutWalk satellite groups followed Toronto's lead was in their branding. For example, although a number of groups created their own logos, many more, at least at some point, adapted the SlutWalk Toronto logo, by using the same font, style and colours, but inserting their own city's name in place of Toronto. Others, such as SlutWalk LA, inserted an 'X' over the word 'slut' in 'SlutWalk' (SlutWalk LA 2014b), while SlutWalk Vancouver added a drawing of a woman's clenched fist which represents solidarity over the words 'SlutWalk Vancouver' (SlutWalk Vancouver 2014). SlutWalk Perth added lipstick marks over their logo (SlutWalk Perth 2014). Others used SlutWalk Toronto's logo, but included their own taglines. For example, SlutWalk Melbourne (2014) added the phrase 'It's a controversial name, not a controversial message' to their logo, while SlutWalk London (2012) included the tagline: 'The radical notion that no one deserves to be raped.'

A number of other satellites have also used rhetoric, and background information taken off of SlutWalk Toronto's website including how the march came about, and why it was important. For example, although various satellite groups used various blurbs from the SlutWalk Toronto website, perhaps the most commonly cited part was this:

> We are tired of being oppressed by slut-shaming; of being judged by our sexuality and feeling unsafe as a result. Being in charge of our sexual lives should not mean we are opening ourselves to an expectation of violence, regardless if we participate in sex for pleasure or work. No one should equate enjoying sex with attracting sexual assault. (SlutWalk Toronto 2011)

This one blurb was used in various SlutWalk satellite groups' Facebook pages (Amsterdam, Cape Town, London, Ottawa, Portland, San Francisco, Vancouver, Winnipeg) as well as other promotional material encouraging citizens to join the march.

When speaking with organizers, the ways that many turned to SlutWalk Toronto for guidance on how to plan a march also became clear (see Brodie 2014; Castieau 2012). In addition to providing material such as poster templates, ideas for placards and fundraising events, they also provided practical information such as how to write a press release. And while SlutWalk Toronto might have been the original port of call for information, guidance and support, over time, organizers began turning to other satellite groups, and became sites of support themselves. As SlutWalk St. Louis 2012 organizer David Wraith explained, their satellite group had supported and advised newer Slutwalk groups on various aspects of organization. David gave one specific example of how SlutWalk Munich borrowed one of SlutWalk St. Louis' poster designs (Wraith 2013). A number of other organizers talked about the importance of secret international Facebook SlutWalk groups, which only invited members had access to, or could even see existed. Because these groups are truly invisible to anyone who has not been invited as a member, I was truly surprised by how many organizers I interviewed were either familiar with their existence, or had participated in them, suggesting the extent to which the movement truly fostered a global network of activists.

Interestingly, although it might be presumed that these secret Facebook planning groups originated with, and were administrated by, SlutWalk Toronto, Heather Jarvis (2012) admitted that although she participated in them, she had no control over them. And while some of these groups have shut down over the years, several organizers shared the ways they have been important places to share ideas, resources, discussions, and emotional support (see Castieau 2012; Delgado 2014a;

Jarvis 2012). As SlutWalk Perth 2011 organizer Beth Castieau said, these international groups are spaces where:

> We talk about lots of things – philosophical discussions, practical discussions, we provide emotional support. They are just a safe place to discuss things and share ideas, and to track where every single SlutWalk is taking place all over the world. (Castieau 2012)

According to Beth then, while these groups serve practical purposes such as the sharing of information, they are also used to track and monitor the movement's progress, watching it grow and spread. She also added that they are places where individuals could post specific questions such as 'What do I do when someone is staring at me?' or 'How do I do X, Y and Z?' As a result, these groups enabled the development of SlutWalk as both a global movement, and an international community of organizers: 'I might be in Perth, Western Australia, and we are so far away, but I am regularly chatting with people from all over the world, like in Canada, the US, France, and Korea. It's really cool' (Castieau 2012).

SlutWalk communities

This idea of 'community' is something that online scholars have spent a lot of time thinking about (see Keller 2013; Kozinets 2010). As people are increasingly turning to 'computer networks to partake in sources of culture' (Kozinets 2010, p. 7), it is clear there is debate about what constitutes a community, what is the minimum number of participants required, and what things they must do for it to be considered a community. According to Keller (2013), community-building is something many feminist activists do *unconsciously*, and is a natural part of engaging with web 2.0 platforms, which facilitates the sharing and circulation of content via community networks. And although community boundaries are 'indistinct', Kozinets (2010) argued that they 'must be understood in terms of self-identification as a member, repeat contact, reciprocal familiarity, shared knowledge of some rituals and customs, some sense of obligation and participation' (2010, p. 10). So, to what extent have communities formed between various SlutWalk satellite groups? How deep do these communities appear to be? And how are they maintained?

As indicated in the section above, many, although certainly not all organizers regularly communicate with organizers from other satellite groups. While these individual connections were frequently made via the international Facebook planning groups, broader satellite connections were made directly through interacting with each other's public Facebook pages and Twitter accounts. An examination of SlutWalk Facebook pages from all over the world provides evidence of the ways various satellite groups regularly comment or share items, posts or news stories from fellow satellite groups social media accounts. These may at times be announcements about the next march, fundraiser or other events. For example, in September 2014, SlutWalk Omaha (2014) retweeted a post from SlutWalk Melbourne: '@SlutWalkMelb because no one should be blamed for being assaulted.' Although the act of retweeting can simply be seen as 'the act of copying and rebroadcasting', scholars argue it is in fact part of a 'conversational ecology in which conversations are composed of a public interplay of voices that give rise to an emotional sense of shared conversational context' (boyd et al. 2010, p. 1). As a result, tweeting is not just about reaching new audiences, but validating and engaging with others (boyd et al. 2010).

At other times, satellite groups used Twitter to 'speak' to each other by using the '@' sign along with a satellite group's user name (also known as @replies). For example, in December 2011, SlutWalk NYC retweeted a post from SlutWalk DC which sought to draw the satellite group's attentions to a petition to get Facebook to remove pro-violence and pro-rape pages:

@SlutWalkTO @SlutWalkLA @SlutWalkNYC @Fem2pt0 PLEASE RT: #StillNotFunnyFacebook http://www.change.org/petitions/facebook-ceo-remove-pro-rape-pages-dont-just-label-them-as-humor-or-satire. (SlutWalk NYC 2011)

According to Honeycutt and Herring (2009) the use of @users is a form of 'addressivity' that is used to gain specific people's attention in order to facilitate conversation or activism (cited in boyd et al. 2010, p. 2). The result when examining SlutWalk Twitter accounts, however, is the particular visibility of connections between satellite groups.

These connections are also made visible by being able to see which groups are following, and being followed by whom. For example, SlutWalk DC is being followed by SlutWalk London, Delhi, France, Hamilton, Britain, Hamburg, Grahamstown, Hong Kong, Chile, Singapore, Winnipeg, NYC, Manchester, Houston, Philadelphia and more. Similarly, SlutWalk Toronto is not only followed by dozens of satellite groups, but follows dozens more in return. And while some of these connections are superficial, after all, not all SlutWalk Twitter accounts remain active, there is evidence that SlutWalk satellite groups are paying attention to each others' tweets, speaking with one another, and re-tweeting those they particularly like or find useful or important.

While at times re-tweeting is used to show solidarity or support, at other times it is used to share information, articles, or other feminist campaigns. For example, in March 2014, SlutWalk Singapore retweeted SlutWalk Toronto's post about the trending hashtag #rapecultureiswhen: 'The hashtag #rapecultureiswhen has been trending since last night. It brings forward more powerful comments from survivors & advocates' (SlutWalk Singapore 2014). This hashtag trended in response to a range of op-eds which insisted that rape culture did not exist (Kingkade 2014). In fact, unsurprisingly, rape culture in general was a frequent topic of articles shared amongst satellite groups. For example, even three years earlier, back in October 2011, SlutWalk Grahamstown (2011) retweeted a link to an article posted by SlutWalk San Antonio about rape culture. Other feminist scholars have also noted the ways that rape culture is a common discussion point amongst feminist communities (see Keller 2013; Rentschler 2014).

The community ties visible on Twitter are also found on Facebook, where it is possible to see which satellite groups 'like' their page. For example, at the time of this writing SlutWalk Seattle is 'liked' by at least 30 other satellite groups, each of whom Facebook gives the option of 'liking' in return. Scholars have of course raised questions about the 'depth' of such connections, noting that in many cases, groups follow one another out of a sense of obligation or being polite (Postill & Pink 2012). And there is no doubt that some of the connections between satellite groups on Facebook are indeed 'weak', in the sense that there is no other visible contact between these groups aside from seeing that they 'liked' each other. Yet despite this, the mere fact that these connections are, at least superficially visible, nonetheless contributes to the *sense* of global SlutWalk community.

While connections between satellite groups were at times weak or superficial, on the other hand, some satellite groups regularly shared and re-posted messages amongst each other. For example, on 2 September 2012, SlutWalk Seattle posted the following status update:

> Congratulations to SlutWalk SL,UT and SlutWalk Melbourne on their hugely successful demonstrations yesterday! Both events were VERY well attended which goes to show that the SlutWalk movement is going strong! (SlutWalk Seattle 2012, underlined to indicate hyperlinks in the original)

The status update contained hyperlinks so that readers could follow on and find out more about these other groups or the movement in general. As noted by Postill and Pink (2012), a common feature of taking part in online communities is the way it facilitates exploration – the following through to other links and then making one's way back 'home.'

Enhancing posts/tweets

According to Postill and Pink (2012), one common practice amongst those who participate in online communities is the 'enhancement' of posts or tweets by adding one's own comment to shared items. For example, in June 2014, SlutWalk Newcastle shared a link via SlutWalk Seattle titled 'After a School Slut-Shamed her Daughter, This Mom Provided an Incredible Response' (Ross 2014). In addition to sharing the link, SlutWalk Newcastle added their own comment on the article: 'Awesome read, after having gone to a school where we had to kneel on the floor to see if our skirt was a suitable length it's great to see young women fighting back against "being distracting to male pupils"' (SlutWalk Newcastle 2014). While not all groups contributed to this 'enhancement' of posts, it was a common practice found amongst some Facebook pages. For example, SlutWalk Toronto Facebook administrators regularly added their own comments to shared articles or links. In April 2014, they shared a link via SlutWalk Edmonton to an article titled 'The Dangers of the Monster Myth' (Meagher 2014). However, unlike SlutWalk Newcastle, whose administrators posted their own comments to the article, a more common practice within SlutWalk Toronto is to highlight a few relevant quotes from the article, presumably as a way of enticing the reader to click through and read the whole thing. In their re-post of 'The Dangers of the Monster Myth', written by the husband of Jill Meagher, an Irish woman living in Melbourne who was raped and murdered walking home at night, SlutWalk Toronto highlighted quotes about why it's problematic to view men who commit sex crimes as monsters, and explained how such myths prevent 'the self-examination required to end the cycle [of violence against women]' (SlutWalk Toronto 2014). Of course, as previously stated, not all satellite groups added their own 'value' to posts, and when they did, the tactics differed. Although I did not ask any of my organizers why they did (not) add their own comments, one possibility is that, particularly for groups which posted several articles/updates/links daily, adding their own comments to everything would have been too time consuming. However, further research could explore these social media practices in greater depth.

So, without claiming that all satellite groups engaged in community building activities, a careful reading through many SlutWalk Facebook pages and Twitter accounts demonstrates the ways that satellite groups did make use of tools of connectivity – such as liking, re-tweeting, speaking to one another, commenting or sharing posts or links. While satellite groups often connected with one another, most of the community-building I encountered was actually not amongst themselves, but with organizations and individuals interested in sexual assault prevention, support and awareness.

Connecting with feminist organizations and individuals

In April 2013, SlutWalk Victoria, BC shared a link via the Victoria Sexual Assault Centre titled 'What is Rape Culture?' (SlutWalk Victoria 2013). Similarly, in January 2014, SlutWalk Aotearoa shared a status update from the Wellington Women's Boarding House, which was seeking community volunteers. In August 2014, SlutWalk Johannesburg (2014b) shared the article 'An open letter to the man who raped me' via The Unspoken Spoken – Speaking Out Against Abuse. And in August 2014, SlutWalk Baltimore posted a photo of a 'monument quilt' that displayed thousands of stories from rape and abuse survivors (SlutWalk Baltimore 2014). In their caption, SlutWalk Baltimore stated that the image came from 'Our friends at FORCE' – a feminist group dedicated 'to upsetting rape culture' (FORCE 2014). Clearly then, SlutWalk satellite groups were not only forming communities amongst themselves, but with a range of other feminist organizations, individuals and communities who are committed to ending rape culture. As SlutWalk Newcastle 2011–2013 organizer Lizi Gray argued, one of the most important aspects of social media was the way it allowed them to 'get in touch with other existing feminist groups that we didn't know were out there' (Gray, L. 2014). Lizi added that not only was the use of social media a great way to get 'momentum going between marches' but, most importantly, it enabled groups 'to support each other' (Gray, L. 2014).

And support one another they do. It is rare to come across any SlutWalk Facebook pages which are not filled with 'likes', shared articles, posts or status updates from other feminist organizations or supportive individuals, many of whom contribute to these pages time and time again. Through engaging in these various practices, they fulfil Kozinet's definition of community, which requires 'identification as a member, repeat contact, reciprocal familiarity, shared knowledge of some rituals and customs, some sense of obligation and participation' (2010, p. 10). The sense of community that feminists generated was often visible. For example, on 1 September 2012, SlutWalk Melbourne retweeted Little Lion's update: 'Thanks to all at @SlutWalkMelb today. It was a revelation to be with supporters, fighters & survivors. 2day was a huge marker in my recovery' (SlutWalk Melbourne 2012). Little Lion's tweets show a clear sense of identity, as she marks herself as an insider – in this case a sexual assault survivor, by noting how it was a 'revelation' to be with *other* 'supporters, fighters & survivors.' The tweet also demonstrates evidence of shared knowledge (about rape culture and sexual assault) and rituals (fighting back through the SlutWalk).

As a result, these examples provide ample evidence of common practices amongst these online feminist communities, which, in drawing upon Keller's work, in fact constitute *networked counterpublics* (2013). Rather than being a homogenous group with an agreed upon set of aims and goals, these networked counterpublics are held together by 'particular, pertinent issues that are often responding to public conversations and debates' (2013, p. 179). In the case of SlutWalk, I would argue that their social media pages, although technically 'public', do in fact function as spaces for feminists to regroup, connect with one another, form opinions, express emotions and, crucially, draw attention to certain issues which may require action (see Shaw 2012b). Further evidence of this is provided below.

Signs of solidarity and calls to action

An examination of various SlutWalk Facebook and Twitter pages reveals the ways these networked counterpublics function as a means of providing support and solidarity with one another. In December 2012, in the wake of the gang rape and murder of an Indian woman on a moving bus, SlutWalk Perth updated its status to read:

> In Perth, Hong Kong and Singapore candle-light vigils are being held in honour of the death of India's victim of horrific gang-rape & torture; and this has shone light on the plight of Indian women who are at such great risk of violence and sexual violence.
> In solidarity. (SlutWalk Perth 2012)

As the gang rape and murder made international headlines, SlutWalk satellites across the world used this as an opportunity to demonstrate the ways sexual assault is a global issue, to highlight the 'solidarity' amongst women and victims, and using this incident as a catalyst to take to the streets in protest. So, while satellite groups undoubtedly wanted to attract the public to SlutWalk events, they also used social media posts to engage in other types of anti-rape activism. In June 2014, SlutWalk Vancouver posted:

> Been street harassed lately? Know someone who has?
>
> To demonstrate how pervasive this is (and to support those who've been targeted), some Vancouver people have opened a local chapter of Hollaback!
>
> Hollaback! Vancouver is a way to share harassment stories and locations online, including by mobile app. Local Hollaback! teams ... work with law enforcement and their communities with the goal of ending street harassment ... and the brand new Vancouver chapter could use your help. (SlutWalk Vancouver 2014, underlined text to indicate hyperlink in original)

Not merely empty gestures, these activities are important in making 'visible the connections that comprise feminist networked counterpublics' (Keller 2013, p. 162). In doing so, these posts challenge the postfeminist sensibility in which feminism is seen as irrelevant, redundant and passé, and where women are told they have more important things to think about than equality, bodily autonomy or oppression (Douglas 2010; Gill 2007; McRobbie 2009; Mendes 2012). Instead, these SlutWalk satellite groups are making sexism, oppression and other gender inequalities 'perceptible' (Frye 1983) to others, which in turns provides the impetus and emotion necessary for change.

One of the key spaces in which SlutWalk satellite groups sought to make sexism 'perceptible' was the mainstream media. Because the mainstream media is a key site of the (re)production of patriarchal discourse, it also provides fodder for *discursive politics* which intervenes in discourse to 'expose its dislocated nature' (Shaw, F. 2011).

Mainstream media critiques via social media

In her research on the Australian blogging community, Frances Shaw wrote about the ways bloggers *'feel it necessary* to show the absurdity of mainstream discourses' (Shaw, F. 2011, italics original). Confirming this, SlutWalk Victoria 2011 organizer Diondra (2013) acknowledged the ways that social media were particularly useful spaces for 'discussing problematic media coverage' of sexual assault and rape culture. While emotion is a natural part of all social movements, it is clear that many SlutWalk satellite groups used mainstream news articles as a way to construct 'an emotional space within which collective action can unfold' (Gerbaudo 2012, p. 5). Although mainstream news articles were re-posted on Facebook, my observations indicate that Twitter was a better platform for this (see also Penney & Dadas 2014), perhaps because the sharing of URL's appears to be a very common practice amongst Twitter users, particularly when retweeting (boyd et al. 2010). Mainstream news articles were regularly shared, sometimes with short comments directing followers to become outraged or angered by its contents, but often without. In September 2014, SlutWalk DC tweeted a link to a Huffington Post article titled '80% Of Central American Women, Girls Are Raped Crossing Into The US' (Goldenberg 2014). As the headline indicates, the article documents the staggeringly high incidences of rape for women making their journey to the US. Yet, despite these figures, the article notes how women are reluctant to come forward to authorities, in fear of being sent back home.

In August 2013, SlutWalk St. Louis shared a link to a story in *USA Today* via Twitter about how a judge who commented that a rape victim was 'older than her chronological age', and apologized for this remark, but not his sentence for the rapist (30 days), after the girl committed suicide (Bacon 2013). Tweeting 'Rapist, Judge, Girl – which one suffers the most in this case? Well the girl killed herself. The guys said they are sorry' (SlutWalk St. Louis 2013). Explaining how he regularly used Twitter and Facebook to post news articles he thought were relevant, organizer David Wraith also stated that this meant: 'For better or worse the SlutWalk page gives us an outlet for less cheery news' (Wraith 2013).

Yet this 'less cheery news' definitely serves a purpose. As Jasper (1997) noted, anger and outrage are useful emotions to foster when trying to instigate social change, as most people will only become 'open to the possibility of protest' in response to a 'moral shock' or something truly upsetting or disturbing. And Gerbaudo (2012) wrote about the importance of using social media to construct the 'emotional space within which collective action can unfold' for movements (p. 5). Therefore, while perhaps not 'cheery', these types of articles are likely to strike a nerve with (potential) participants, many of whom have experienced sexual assault, or live in fear or shame of it. Whether this involves cat calling, street harassment or eve teasing; stalking, battery or rape – sexual violence in its various forms is an almost universal experience for women (and many men). Perhaps unsurprisingly, while many SlutWalk satellite groups used their social media accounts to identify rape culture via the mainstream media, it was also extremely common to use these platforms to showcase feminist responses or perspectives on rape culture.

Promoting feminist mainstream coverage

Just as social media platforms such as Facebook and Twitter were often used to criticize the mainstream media, there are a number of examples where satellites promoted articles which were either written by known feminists (such as Jessica Valenti or Soraya Chemaly), or utilized feminist perspectives and discourses. In September 2014, SlutWalk Seattle shared a link from *New York Magazine* about the story of a college rape victim who vowed to carry a mattress with her everywhere until her rapist was expelled (Roy 2014). With 22 'shares' and 114 'likes', this was seen as a particularly creative way of a survivor taking action against rape culture. And this particular story, covered by a host of mainstream media outlets, also did the rounds on other satellite Facebook accounts.

In October 2013, SlutWalk Perth shared a link to a column in *The Guardian* titled 'How not to raise a rapist', in which parents are advised not to lock up their daughters as a means of preventing rape, but 'to proactively raise sons not to rape' (Badham 2013). This post had 11 'likes' and three 'shares.' Similarly, in August 2011 SlutWalk Aotearoa shared an article titled 'Myths about rape' (Townsend 2011) from *The Wellingtonian* about the misconceptions of rape and sexual assault, which garnered 12 'likes' and three 'shares.' Although not every post or link generated 'likes' or 'shares', some satellite groups such as SlutWalk Aotearoa did, typically, receive at least one comment, like or share per post, perhaps suggesting a dedicated group of followers, or community.

Although other scholars have talked about the ways that feminists turn to online spaces to critique the media (Keller 2013; Mowles 2008; Rentschler 2014), my research also found evidence of the ways that SlutWalk satellite groups regularly shared examples of 'good feminist practice.' So, although feminists operating online have been known to identify the 'dislocated nature' of mainstream discourse (see Shaw, F. 2011), they also use it as a means of supporting feminist views, as in: See? Even some people in the mainstream media 'get' rape culture or understand how to dismantle it. The result then is the sense that not only are other people also angry about rape culture, and interested in making it perceptible to others, but they are also willing to share ideas on how to challenge it. As a result of these various practices – from speaking with fellow satellite groups, to sharing articles, posts, comments or tweets from fellow feminist individuals' organizations – many SlutWalk social media sites provide evidence of the ways networked counterpublics are formed and sustained.

And while social media is a common method used to disseminate these examples of supportive mainstream articles, it is also unfortunately a space which enables abuse, misogyny and harassment, otherwise known as cybersexism or trolling.

Cybersexism and trolling

The internet, according to many techno-optimist feminists, offers a liberatory potential for women and other traditionally marginalized groups. Although the initial infrastructure is expensive, once purchased, it has enabled feminists to establish and participate in a range of discussion threads, chat rooms, blogs, social networking sites and explicitly feminist spaces. Because the internet offers users relative anonymity, it can make people feel safe talking about issues, such as feminism, that might be considered sensitive, inappropriate or dangerous if discussed face-to-face (Herring et al. 2002). Therefore, the internet is often not only presented as a 'safe' space, but as one inherently suitable for promoting women's activism. This is because it holds the promise of providing women-only platforms where counterhegemonic ideas can be discussed and fleshed out (Herring et al. 2002; Puente 2011).

While there is no doubt that many feminists are finding support structures in online spaces, and developing feminist communities (see Keller 2011, 2013; Mowles 2008; Rentschler 2014; Shaw, F. 2011, 2012b) there is growing evidence of the ways the virtual world has made 'misogyny routine and sexual bullying easy' (Penny 2013; see also Bamberg 2004; Gorton & Garde-Hansen 2013; Jane 2014; Piepmeier 2009). As Herring et al. (2002) write, 'When women gather online, and especially when they attempt to discuss feminism, they are not uncommonly the target of negative attention from individuals, mostly men, who feel threatened by or otherwise uncomfortable with feminism' (p. 373). This 'negative attention' has been referred to as flaming (Herring et al. 2002), cybersexism (Penny 2013), cyberstalking, online sexual harassment (Chawki & el Shazly 2013; Piepmeier 2009), e-bile (Jane 2014) and trolling.

According to scholars, a troll is an individual who baits, harasses and seeks to *disrupt* online communities (Herring et al. 2002). The name was derived from the practice used in fishing, where a baited line is dragged behind a boat (Herring et al. 2002). Flaming on the other hand is defined as actions used to victimize, control and exclude individuals or groups such as women (Chawki & el Shazly 2013), often through the use of profanity or explicit threats. In recent years however, the mainstream media have changed the meaning of the word 'trolling' to equate online harassment (see de Castella & Brown 2011; Schwartz 2014), and it has become a more widely used term than 'flaming.' And although scholars have promoted their own definitions, such as e-bile (Jane 2014) I will refer to any hostile text or speech act as trolling.

I became interested in finding out organizers' experiences with trolling as the issue began attracting media attention from 2012. As one of the most high profile victims, blogger Anita Sarkeesian became the subject of a torrent of online trolls after she launched a crowdfunding project to create a short film series, 'Tropes vs. Women.' She used these films to explain 'the basic, lazy, sexist plotlines of many videogames' (Penny 2013). One troll even designed a game called 'Beat Up Anita Sarkeesian', where users could click on Sarkeesian's face and make blood, cuts and bruises appear (Penny 2013). Others e-mailed drawings of her being raped by video game characters (Lewis 2012). Feminist writer Laurie Penny also detailed her experiences with online trolls in her book *Cybersexism* (2013), sharing typical examples of online threats: 'There's nothing wrong with [her] a couple of hours of cunt-kicking, garrotting and burying in a shallow grave wouldn't sort out.' Penny even confessed to writing *Cybersexism* in a safe-house, 'after being one of several female journalists in the UK to receive a bomb threat. I could go on' (Penny 2013). Consequently, Penny argued that: 'Any woman active online runs the risk of attracting these kinds of frantic hate-jerkers, or worse.' And while merely being a woman with a public profile is seemingly enough to make oneself a target of abuse, the scenario appears to be more precarious for those fighting for gender justice, including those such as SlutWalk organizers who are involved in anti-rape activism.

Organizers' experiences with online trolling

In several of my early interviews, before trolling became a widely discussed issue, some organizers talked about the 'negative' responses they received on their social media accounts, namely their Facebook page. For example, SlutWalk St. Louis 2012 organizer David Wraith talked about qualitative differences in the 'negative' comments their Facebook page received. While he stated that he engaged with 'legitimate criticisms' such as how the movement excluded women of colour, and those from poorer socio-economic backgrounds, he admitted that it was hard to know how to respond to those claims meant only to insult or wound SlutWalk supporters (Wraith 2013). However, David explained that they eventually developed a policy of deleted things they found 'hurtful and insulting', but responding to those which he felt were 'ignorant and worth keeping on the [Facebook] page so people could have a public debate about them' (Wraith 2013). Therefore, although we did not have this conversation using the language of 'trolling', this was really the first interview in which I realized online harassment was an issue worth exploring with other organizers.

When I asked about her experiences with online trolling, SlutWalk Newcastle 2011–2013 organizer Lizi Gray stated that trolls usually only emerged in the run up to the marches or other big events. For example, just before their women-only comedy night fundraiser, Lizi explained how they received a number of abusive messages (Gray, L. 2014). She also recounted how she was trolled by boys she went to secondary school with, who insisted that men who are falsely accused of rape have it much worse than actual victims. This type of trolling in which men accused the movement of ignoring their needs, or claims that they are the 'real' victims, was also documented by other organizers. For example, SlutWalk Bangalore 2011 organizer Asqeer Sodhi explained that their Facebook page was targeted by a bunch of men who called themselves 'masculinists, who were posting all over our walls' (Sodhi 2014). These sorts of discourses are typical of the general backlash that accompanies women's activism, and I documented similar discourses on the ways women's activism was constructed as being harmful for men during the Second Wave (Mendes 2011b). And while SlutWalk Facebook pages were often targeted, organizers explained the ways that they were at times individually trolled.

Personal attacks

Several of the organizers I interviewed shared the ways they were individually, and personally, harassed as a result of their involvement with the movement. For example, Australian writer Amy Gray told me about the backlash she received after writing an article about why she took her young daughter to SlutWalk. As she recounted, the 'reaction to the article was really vehement' and she even received a message from a child protection worker who threatened to take her daughter into social care (Gray 2014a). When I asked Amy how she felt about this abuse, and if she responded to this incident, she exclaimed: 'Hell no! An empty threat is an empty threat.' Perhaps Amy's relaxed reaction to trolling can be credited to her 25 years of experience as an activist, as she was the only organizer I spoke with who was able to really 'laugh off' such abuse. As Jane (2014) noted, common reactions to trolling include: distress, fear, irritation, anxiety and feelings of violation and vulnerability (p. 536). And although

Amy was seemingly not bothered by trolling, she admitted that some of her co-organizers were indeed affected. For example, Amy explained how SlutWalk Melbourne leader Karen Pickering felt emotionally exhausted from her experiences of trolling: 'I think for Karen it can actually be a draining thing, to constantly deal with rape threats, death threats, or just, "you're just all fucking whores," and general sexist things' (Gray 2014a). This was particularly true in the run up to the march when:

> You deal with a lot of people who suddenly realize a bunch of women are getting together to ask for equality – fuck them! I'm going to tell them that they're all fat [she laughs]. Personally, it was never an issue for me. (Gray 2014a)

That Amy was seemingly not affected by online trolls does not, however, mean that the organization did not take them seriously. Instead, she noted how SlutWalk Melbourne liaised closely with the police, and made a policy of registering all actual threats. However, according to police advice, it was not the explicit bomb or rape threats that organizers were told to worry about. Instead, they were advised that it was 'the ones who wanted to almost spook you or make you uncomfortable if that makes sense, that you had to worry about' such as the ones would try to friend you and offer themselves as 'a kind of white knight' (Gray 2014a).

One organizer who experienced this sort of 'spooky' trolling was SlutWalk Chicago 2011 organizer Stephanie Sutton. Stephanie explained how after posting her personal email address on the Facebook page so volunteers could contact her, she received a long email, meant to look like it was coming from her mother, 'Ms. Sutton.' The email began with: 'Dear Stephanie I am so proud of you, I can say with absolute pride that my daughter is a slut' (Sutton 2014). As Stephanie explained, although the email didn't bother her at first, 'it was kind of triggering to get an email like that, and kind of upsetting' (Sutton 2014). Although this experience was the one that stood out, when asked about trolling in general, she said:

> It's just kind of upsetting to know that there are people out there that really believe that women deserve to be raped, and that it's the victim's fault for rape happening, and that woman can and should be raped as much as possible. That's kind of crazy. (Sutton 2014)

Although it does not make this abuse any easier to digest, Stephanie recalled her co-organizers arguing that the trolling they experienced was a sign they were doing something right, because challenging rape culture was inevitably 'going to make people upset' (Sutton 2014).

SlutWalk Chicago 2013 and 2014 organizer Ashley Broher also had disturbing experiences with online trollers. When attending the 2012 protest, she 'got a little brazen' and removed her top (Broher 2014). Wearing nipple-patches over her breasts, she wrote the words 'Still Not Asking for It' across her chest. Although many people took photos of her that day (mostly with her consent), one of those photos vent viral several months after the march. Standing with her eyes closed, arm in the air holding a cigarette, the photo was re-blogged and shared over two million times, at which point Ashley became the target for vitriolic online abuse. The type of abuse was wide ranging. While most included body-shaming comments, such as how she must have had plastic surgery, was too fat or thin, others claimed she was just an attention-seeking 'whore' and 'slut' (Broher 2014). Others rejected the message written on her chest, and countered that by exposing her body, she was indeed 'asking for it' (Broher 2014). Ashley also experienced direct threats, such as men stating that if they saw her dressed like that, 'I would hold you down and rape you' (Broher 2014). From Ashley's perspective, one of the worst experiences was when 'some misogynist' photoshopped the image so that only the words 'Asking for It' were left (Broher 2014).

When asked how she responded to such online abuse, she stated that she 'stopped reading the comments after a while', and admitted that seeing the photoshopped image made her feel violated. However, as a seasoned activist (she had attended around 14 protests or demonstrations in the *two weeks* before our interview alone), Ashley explained that she was prepared for this reaction: 'It wouldn't have made a statement if I didn't expect the backlash' (Broher 2014). And although this experience showed her that 'the horrible, dark, scary corners of the internet were there', she claimed that 'by far' most messages were supportive. For this, she credited the online feminist community and talked about the ways that hundreds of people reached out to her to say what a great photo it was. In fact, Ashley noted that after exchanging online correspondence, several of these people have become 'good friends over the years' (Broher 2014).

What is clear from speaking to my organizers is that trolling is both routine, and potentially triggering, something of great concern given that many organizers are survivors of sexual abuse themselves. Where trolling was once seen by academics and commentators as a string of isolated incidents, it is now widely recognized as 'the status quo in the online world' (Lanier 2010, p. 60, cited in Jane 2014, p. 540), particularly for feminist activists (Piepmeier 2009; Penny 2013). So, given the depressing 'reality' that SlutWalk organizers will inevitably encounter, or have encountered, trolling, I asked how they responded. In the next section I will outline not just their varying approaches to this phenomenon, but their strategies for managing this online abuse.

Strategies to manage trolls

Research into the online trolling of feminist groups has found that it is common for group members to debate 'When – and where – is it legitimate to draw the line?' (Herring et al. 2002, p. 372). Within various SlutWalk satellite groups, it became clear that there were very real differences and perspectives, strategies and policies when it came to trolls. For example, SlutWalk Aotearoa 2011 and 2012 organizer MJ Brodie noted their group's distinction between people who posted comments, often naïvely, perpetuating rape myths (e.g. provocative clothes *do* causes rape), and those who proclaimed 'let's rape some bitches!' (Brodie 2014). As MJ revealed, these different types of posts resulted in different strategies. For example, the group learnt quickly to delete the latter comments, which scholars have noted are simply there to silence, threaten or 'out-shout' everyone else (Jane 2014, p. 534). However, MJ insisted that they did not go as far as to simply 'censor' all negative comments from the Facebook page: 'We weren't just deleting every comment that didn't like SlutWalk, because it's really important to have those conversations' (Brodie 2014). As MJ explained, the group kept comments that started off asking things such as, 'well what about a man's urges?' because 'we've all been through that stage of "look what she's wearing"' (Brodie 2014). I think MJ's comment here is extremely important. After all, for most feminists reading this book, the idea that clothing does not cause rape is just 'common sense.' So much so, that it is hard to imagine a time when we thought differently. However, these concepts are still new to the majority of society, and it is therefore necessary to take a step back and assume that the public are not familiar with these feminist concepts. Therefore, rather than simply being dismissive of comments stating that clothes cause rape, in some cases it might be better to engage with such discourses and reveal their dislocations (see Shaw, F. 2011).

MJ was not the only organizer to emphasize that the purpose of the Facebook page was not to merely to show how great the movement was, but to act as an important space for learning about rape culture, and fostering discussions about how to smash it. As SlutWalk Seattle 2013 and 2014 organizer Laura Delgado stated, as a rule, 'I don't think comments should be hidden, I try to perpetuate the conversation because I think it's more helpful to everyone's learning experience' (Delgado 2014a). Similarly, SlutWalk Victoria 2013 organizer Diondra noted that their Facebook page was often a space for 'heated debate', which she found valuable (Diondra 2013).

Community policing

Although most SlutWalk organizers discussed *their* role in monitoring their social media accounts, deleting comments or blocking people when necessary, a few indicated the ways that the *online community* also helped out. For example, when it came to comments perpetuating rape culture, SlutWalk Chicago's Ashley Broher stated that many online community members were often the first to respond. As a result, she stated that deciding on whether or not to delete the post would depend on 'Whether or not the community responded or took care of it already.' As she explained, 'Other people on our page take care of things so we don't always have to' (Broher 2014). SlutWalk Cape Town's Umeshree Govender also shared her experience of community support and intervention. While explaining that responding to trolls did 'get tiring', she added: 'What was beautiful though was how many people took over the debate for us. We never censored any of the comments' (Govender 2014). The community 'policing' described by both SlutWalk Cape Town and Chicago is only really possible because of both groups' vibrant Facebook communities, and the dedication their supporters have to the cause (see also Govender 2014). Although the SlutWalk Cape Town Facebook site is now defunct, SlutWalk Chicago's page is still extremely active. With over 8,500 'likes', and five organizers managing it, it is normal for the site to publish multiple posts on a daily basis (Broher 2014).

Censorship vs. Free speech

As scholars have noted (Jane 2014; Penny 2013), knowing where to draw the line at hostile or threatening comments was easy for some, while for others, these decisions were complex, as the issue evolved into one around censorship vs. free speech. Yet, a common accusation towards those who have censored, blocked or un-friended trollers is that they are opposed to the principles of free speech (Jane 2014). And while one might assume this principle was particularly important to Americans, since free speech is protected by their constitution, it was also seen as important for organizers in other parts of the world. For example, SlutWalk Bangalore 2011 organizer Asqeer Sodhi explained how, alongside co-organizer Dhillan Chandramowli, they 'would go back and forth about how much free speech and how much allowance to give them [trollers]' (Sodhi 2014). As the subject of regular trolling, and a supporter of censoring abusive comments, Laurie Penny (2013) opined about the problematic way debates around trolling have centred on the issue of freedom of speech. In defending her point of view, she stated:

> [P]eople talk unironically of their right to free expression whilst doing everything in their power to hurt, humiliate and silence any woman with a voice or a platform, screeching abuse at us until we back down or shut up. They speak of censorship but say nothing of the silencing in which they are engaged. (Penny 2013)

And while I agree with Penny, it is clear from my interviews that organizers found it difficult to decide where to draw that line. In the end, Asqeer and Dhillan decided not to censor comments, but instead put 'trigger warnings' to alert readers about the presence of sensitive or disturbing issues. Trigger warnings are a common feature in feminist blogs, and it is seen as a sign of consideration so readers can choose whether or not to proceed in reading the article or post.

Ironically for Asqeer and Dhillan, despite giving trollers 'free speech' regarding the movement, SlutWalk Bangalore was itself 'censored', in a way. The night before the march, Dhillan received a phone call from a major political party, which threatened to 'thrash' anyone who turned up in skirts or other 'revealing' clothing (Chandramowli 2014). On the morning of the march, Dhillan and Asqeer were arrested when they turned up to let people know the march had been cancelled. And although it might be easy to conclude that the trollers won, Dhillan in fact insisted that these attempts to silence the movement instead raised its profile and generated much media attention. And instead of focusing on how many people turned up and how they were dressed, they were able to talk about how they were bullied and have deeper conversations about what fuelled the movement (Chandramowli 2014).

When thinking about censorship vs. free speech, SlutWalk Cape Town also decided not to remove any offensive posts. As 2011 organizer Umeshree Govender said: '[We] always left the posts up. Initially we would engage in debate but it did get tiring' (Govender 2014). SlutWalk Cape Town's decision not to censor comments was also likely informed by the libertarian political beliefs of co-organizer Stuart MacDonald who, when I asked why he was interested in the movement, told me: 'I want people to have as much freedom and autonomy as possible' (MacDonald, S. 2014). And, as indicated in Umeshree's quote above, instead of having to remove, hide or 'censor' comments, they found that, similarly to the case of SlutWalk Chicago, other members of the community were quick to deal with the trollers themselves. As Collins-Jarvis (1997) noted, some participants find that 'challenging prejudice online can be an empowering act of resistance' (cited in Herring et al. 2002, p. 372). Empowering or not, trolling is simply a fact of life for many women who wish to participate in the digital world. As Laurie Penny wrote, 'It's not every woman who writes online or runs a blog or plays videogames [who gets trolled], but it's many of us, and it could be any of us' (Penny 2013).

Cleary then, my discussion with organizers indicated the ways that SlutWalk organizers all around the world *are* subject to online trolling, and in some cases, verbal threats of abuse. While some trolls targeted specific individuals, sending them private emails or messages, the majority were directed towards the satellite group and posted on public social media platforms such as Facebook. In fact interestingly, although there have been high-profile examples of the way trolling has occurred on Twitter, all of my organizers' examples were in relation to Facebook, indicating once again the importance of this particular platform for the movement. And while trolling seemed to bother some organizers, others were able to laugh off what they saw as 'empty threats' (Gray 2014a). Yet, as Laurie Penny wrote, 'threats to hurt and rape and kill are not always less distressing when they don't come with an explicit expectation of follow-through in physical reality' (Penny 2013). In this way, what Penny argued is that we need to stop seeing the internet as an *imaginary* space, and recognize that what goes on online has material consequences and meaning:

> The Internet is public space, real space; it's increasingly where we interact socially, do our work, organize our lives and engage with politics, and violence online is real violence. The hatred of women in public spaces online is reaching epidemic levels and it's time to end the pretence that it's either acceptable or inevitable. (Penny 2013)

In thinking about the ways that feminist activism has historically been met with backlash and resistance to this activism (Faludi 1992; Mendes 2011b), it is therefore unsurprising that SlutWalk organizers are subject to trolling. However, just as Laurie Penny argued, it is an issue that must be taken seriously – by feminists, academics, social media platforms, online communities, policy makers and the general public. After all, just as feminism is experiencing a resurgence, we must do all that we can to prevent these voices from being threatened, humiliated, punished and, ultimately, silenced. And while my interviews with SlutWalk organizers demonstrate that feminists are not simply standing by and allowing trolling to happen, we need to learn more about the ways women are trolled, as well as their various responses. We need social media platforms to become more accountable for trollers and to provide more targeted strategies to prevent online abuse. While certain victories have been won, such as the #FBrape campaign, which forced Facebook to change its policy on removing content promoting gender-based violence (see Little 2013), we don't have time to let this issue become an even bigger problem. It cannot wait. Instead, the issue of trolling, and feminist responses to it needs addressing *now* (see Mendes et al., 2014).

Overall experiences with the movement

In the majority of cases, I concluded my interviews by asking organizers to reflect about their experiences with the movement. Some organizers, such as SlutWalk Toronto's Heather Jarvis, SlutWalk Seattle's Laura Delgado, SlutWalk Chicago's Ashley Broher, SlutWalk St. Louis' David Wraith, SlutWalk Victoria's Diondra, and SlutWalk Vancouver's Caitlin MacDonald and Margaret Haugen, were still involved in the movement and were gearing up for that year's march at the time of our interview. In other cases, such as with SlutWalk Cape Town's Umeshree Govender and Stuart MacDonald, SlutWalk Chicago's Stephanie Sutton, and SlutWalk Bangalore's Asqeer Sodhi and Dhillan Chandramowli, they hadn't been involved in the movement for several years, and their perspectives were shaped by hindsight and distance from the movement.

In speaking with these organizers, many expressed a range of emotions. For example, SlutWalk Chicago 2013 and 2014 organizer Ashley Broher described her experience as 'wonderful and transformative, and exciting' (Broher 2014). SlutWalk Bangalore 2011 organizer Dhillan Chadramowli said it was 'Enlightening, disillusioning, a re-birth, and an interesting journey' (Chandramowli 2014). His co-organizer Asqeer Sodhi noted that despite being 'consumed by it for three months' she 'loved every minute of it.' As she went on to explain:

> For me personally, it told me a lot about the kind of work that I would enjoy doing later on. It was like watershed for me personally.

I had never felt that energized you know? It was a whole other high. (Sodhi 2014)

That the movement meant something to these organizers was very clear. For example, SlutWalk St. Louis 2012 organizer David Wraith talked about how he was 'profoundly affected' by the movement, and imagined that 'others were affected the same way' (Wraith 2013).

And while most organizers talked positively about their experiences, this was certainly not the universal experience. Many, although not all organizers confided that they were sexual assault survivors, and as a result, there was the recognition that there is a 'lot of pain and healing' in the movement (Jarvis 2012). In several cases, organizers addressed how draining the movement could be, not only in confronting their own experiences, but in hearing story after story not just about sexual violence, but the 'second assault' – or their experiences of being shamed and judged afterwards (Wolburt Burgess et al. 2009). In fact, several organizers confided how their involvement in the movement was the first time they had been able to talk about their assault. Confronting their experiences was therefore very emotional. As one organizer explained:

It was really hard. My first SlutWalk I talked for the very, very first time about my sexual assault ... I had a lot of conversations with people, people I knew and people I was close to, who shared their experiences [of assault]. It was amazing and it's really, really important because it's one of those things everybody feels they can't talk about, but want to. Because no one believes that one in four or one in five will be assaulted. But from my experiences, these figures are absolutely true. (Brodie 2014)

When looking back on her experience with SlutWalk Chicago in 2011, organizer Stephanie Sutton described her relationship with the movement as 'complicated.' While on one hand she stated she was really happy to have participated in the movement, and as a survivor, she felt 'it was the only way I could take power over that situation and seek any form of justice', she also became exposed to critiques, particularly by women of colour about the ways the movement excluded them. It was these critiques that led to her, and her co-organizers stepping down after the first year. Movement co-founder Heather Jarvis (2012) also talked about how hard it had been, particularly in the first year, to receive so many criticisms from women of colour and fellow feminists they wanted to stand with in solidarity and support.

The movement's impact

SlutWalk Cape Town 2011 organizer Umeshree Govender described her involvement as a mixture of 'accomplishment', 'euphoria' and 'despondency' (Govender 2014). She felt a sense of accomplishment for realizing that 'ordinary people can make a difference and can make 2,000 people show up in solidarity and come together and march for a cause, I thought that was quite beautiful.' However, she also described her experience as 'heartbreaking':

> We had so many rape survivors, and so many of them thanked us for giving us a voice. And women were wearing what they wore on the day they were raped, and said thank you for making us see, and trying to convince others that it wasn't our fault. And if we did that for one person, that was enough. It was a beautiful experience but it was also heartbreaking, because through the movement we got involved with a lot of anti-rape organisations. You realize it's not just a statistic because you meet people affected. (Govender 2014)

In fact, several organizers spoke about the impact they felt the movement had. Many were proud of the ways it helped fuel discussions about rape culture, sexual assault and consent (Broher 2014; Diondra 2013; Gray 2014a; Ho 2012), while recognizing that the movement alone was not enough to shatter rape culture. However, as SlutWalk Melbourne's Amy Gray sated, it's easy to think 'oh, what am I doing? Am I actually contributing? Is this day actually going to mean anything? Is this going to help shatter one thing, or is it going to put pressure on another thing? Are we doing enough?' (Gray 2014a). While she argued that on its own, the movement isn't doing enough, 'If you see it in conjunction with other forms of activism and other forms of conversation, yeah, it's quite good' (Gray 2014a).

Several organizers also talked about how change need not be large-scale to be meaningful. For example, SlutWalk Winnipeg 2011 and 2012 organizer Deanna admitted how she had engaged in victim-blaming before learning about the movement. As a result, she noted that, 'If I've been educated because of the movement, then of course many others must have also grown in their understanding of this issue' (Deanna 2012). SlutWalk Vancouver 2013 and 2014 organizers Caitlin MacDonald and Margaret Haugen also recounted the ways they were 'visibly seeing the impact it's having, beyond the rally' (MacDonald, C. 2014). Margaret shared a turning point she had with one survivor who, until that conversation, had always blamed himself for the childhood abuse he suffered (Haugen 2014), while Caitlin talked about the change she has seen in several of her male friends who had previously promoted rape culture. However, after learning more about the movement, they admitted:

> 'I didn't see what I was doing before but now I get it.' And they are now totally supportive. To the point where, they say, I want to host a workshop where I can tell men how they can end rape culture. So, yeah, that's been amazing, and people want to help. (MacDonald, C. 2014)

While the organizers I spoke with all clearly had different experiences with the movement, perhaps the most common sentiment they all shared was the continued need for more to be done. As SlutWalk Melbourne 2012 and 2013 organizer Amy Gray explained, she took her daughter to SlutWalk because she needs to know that it's important to 'make a stand together with other people for things that matter for them. And I want her to know that democracy requires her action, not every four years when it's an election, but every day' (Gray 2014a).

Concluding thoughts

This chapter explored the various connections, communities and activism SlutWalk organizers engaged in via social media platforms. What emerged from interviews with 22 organizers from around the world was that, in addition to connecting the movement with supporters, Facebook has played a special role in connecting organizers with one another. The various secret Facebook planning groups that emerged were used by many of the organizers I interviewed and, I am told, by hundreds of other organizers from all across the world (Castieau 2012; Delgado 2014a; Jarvis 2012). In addition to being spaces where organizers shared resources, helpful tips and philosophical questions, and provided emotional support, they were essential in forging the connections that transformed SlutWalk from a host of individual marches, to a transnational feminist movement (see also Carr 2013). These connections were displayed in different ways. For example, they were made visible by the ways satellite groups followed one another on Twitter, 'liked' one another on Facebook, and regularly re-posted or re-tweeted each others' posts, status updates, or articles of interest. At other times, the solidarity was evident in the ways that marches were organized to take place on the same day. For example, on 20 May 2012,

SlutWalks were held in Wellington and Christchurch, New Zealand. And on 4 December 2011, SlutWalks were organized in Singapore, Mumbai, Hong Kong and Bangalore.[1] In the run up to these marches, SlutWalk Singapore interviewed organizers from Mumbai, Hong Kong and Bangalore and posted these interviews on their blog (see SlutWalk Singapore 2011a, 2011b).

And while SlutWalk satellite groups inevitably promoted their own events or marches, they also regularly posted events, issues or activism highlighted by other (feminist) individuals or organizations. Many also used their social media accounts to share mainstream news articles – either examples of rape culture in action, or evidence of ways that citizens were challenging it. As a result of these connections and practices, I argue that these social media platforms contributed to the creation of *networked counterpublics* (Keller 2013), which formed around sexual assault and rape culture, and provided space for the creation of feminist discourses and identities to take place (see Shaw, F. 2011).

Yet, as this chapter has demonstrated, although social media platforms have provided spaces in which feminist articulations occur, and feminist communities are formed, it is wrong to assume they are inherently 'safe.' In fact, all of the organizers I asked were victims of trolling – or online harassment – which included offensive sexual messages, gender-humiliating comments, threats of violence, sexual remarks or dirty jokes (see Chawky & el Shazly 2013; Jane 2014; Penny 2013). Caught between debates around freedom of speech and personal safety (including mental health), organizers took vastly different approaches to their responses to trolling, with some deleting (or censoring) comments which were simply meant to offend or intimidate online users, and others keeping them, but including 'trigger warnings' to indicate they contained sensitive or offensive information. Some simply left these posts as they were, and either responded themselves, or allowed the community of online users to intervene. My interviews therefore confirm that that when it comes to trolling, feminists don't always agree on where, how and when to draw the line (see also Herring et al. 2002). Despite this, it is clear that trolling is an expected part of the backlash that historically takes place when women fight for greater rights (see Faludi 1992; Mendes 2011a).

This chapter concluded with an overview of organizers' experiences, which are once again varied. While a few left the movement feeling despondent, and even critical, the majority of organizers felt energized, proud and amazed by what they had helped accomplish. Recognizing that there was still a long way to go in ending rape culture, many insisted that the movement was making a difference, even if it was just one individual at a time. And while organizers disagreed on whether there could ever be an end to sexual violence, many felt that the movement helped those who had experienced it, allowing them to recover and heal with dignity and the knowledge that they were not to blame.

8
Conclusion

Representing SlutWalk

There is no doubt that the past several years have witnessed the beginnings of cultural change. For the first time, perhaps ever, feminism is enjoying not only a resurgence, but mass popular approval (Valenti 2014c). Celebrities such as Beyoncé, Taylor Swift, Emma Watson, Lena Dunham and Joseph Gordon-Levitt have all recently announced to the world that they are feminists (Vagianos 2014; Valenti 2014c). Women's issues, particularly domestic and sexual violence, are at the forefront of public and policy agendas, and not just in Western nations such as the US, Canada and the UK, but in other parts of the world such as India, South Africa, Australia and New Zealand. Given the cultural shift in global efforts towards gender equality, what does my research into representations of SlutWalk in mainstream news and feminist media tell us about women's position in society?

Firstly, I argue that, given the seemingly unprecedented amount of media attention the movement received, there was indeed a hunger for a grassroots response to rape culture. This was particularly true within the feminist blogosphere – a space in which rape culture is a commonly discussed issue (see Keller 2013; Mowles 2008; Rentschler 2014). And while it would be nice to think that the mainstream media covered SlutWalk because they were pleased to see a challenge to rape culture, it is more likely that, given their inherently capitalist and patriarchal nature (see Byerly 2013; Freeman 2001; Global Media Monitoring Project 2010), they were drawn to the movement because of its potential for sexy photo opportunities, used to generate revenue. Given that the news media is increasingly responsive to social media trends

(Drezner & Farrell 2008; Mowles 2008), the fact that SlutWalk had gone 'viral' certainly also made it more newsworthy and appealing.

Yet, at the same time, over a third of coverage in both the mainstream news and feminist media discussed specific marches *before* they took place. As I previously argued, this is significant because such posts/texts were not merely focused on what participants would or would not wear, or how many would turn up. Instead, these texts often allowed the authors to interrogate the march's aims, purposes and message, and provided potential participants with information about its start time, location and route, information which enabled them to take part if they so desired. The majority of texts, however, were *reactive* towards the movement, reporting on events after they had happened. These texts focused on aspects such as how many and who attended, and what protestors wore, interspersed with interviews with participants and organizers. And although my feminist media sample were more likely to report on local marches, demonstrating the highly personalized and localized nature of blogging (Simmons 2008), the mainstream news often reported on the global nature of the march, paying particular attention to its movement to places such as India, Australia and New Zealand. Such coverage not only created a sense of collective activism, and represented a shift away from the neoliberal focus on the individual, but also provided it with credibility. In fact, SlutWalk Cape Town 2011 organizer Stuart MacDonald (2014) argued that it was mainstream news coverage of the march's international growth to the UK that had convinced him it was worth doing in South Africa (2014b).

At the same time, it was precisely the movement's international nature that led to a variety of criticisms, particularly in nations such as India, South Africa and Australia. These included statements that the movement was 'irrelevant', 'dangerous' and 'Western.' And although I would argue that rape culture is not limited to the Western world, such criticisms do highlight the ways social movements must 'Think Global, Act Local' in order to be successful. Rather than simply trying to 'ape' Western SlutWalks, organizers in other parts of the world adapted its aims and names as a result (see also Carr 2013; Gwynne 2013). For example, SlutWalk Singapore de-emphasized aims to reclaim the word 'slut' – a goal they knew would not be widely supported in such a conservative and highly policed state. Similarly, organizers in India used parallel names in local languages, which they knew gave it a higher chance of attracting supporters (Chandramowli 2014; Sodhi 2014), while also adapting its goals to focus on widespread issues such as street harassment.

Supporting feminism

Because feminist activism has not historically been given much mainstream media support (see Bradley 2003; Douglas 1994; Hinds & Stacey 2001; Mendes 2011a; Morris 1973a, 1973b; van Zoonen 1992), I was surprised to discover that the vast majority of my mainstream news sample, taken from eight nations which hosted SlutWalks between 2011 and 2013, was in fact supportive of the movement. This was not only evident in headlines that legitimized the need for the movement, but in the ways the mainstream media constructed it as part of a global stand against sexual violence, victim-blaming and slut-shaming. And even though the movement has no doubt sparked sharp disagreements, particularly amongst feminists (Carr 2013; Dow & Wood 2014), it was overwhelmingly supported by the feminist media. In fact, I argue that the feminist media served as a particularly important space for the development of online feminist communities, or *networked counterpublics* (see Keller 2013), which debated, discussed and analyzed rape culture. Unlike the mainstream news, which often presented superficial accounts of the movement, feminist media posts, which are for the most part unrestricted by traditional journalistic conventions such as objectivity, narrative style or organizational, political or economic constraints, connected with one another via hyperlinks and blogrolls, in order to share information and feminist discourses on the nature of rape and strategies to end rape culture. As a result, their posts not only contained much more nuanced analyses of rape culture, but often provided readers with directions for where to turn for more information on particular topics.

While I do not want to go as far as to say that feminists should ignore the mainstream news media, as it certainly alerted many members of the public to the movement's existence who would not have known about it otherwise (namely those not connected to the feminist blogosphere), I do maintain that traditional 'hard' news articles are simply incapable of challenging patriarchal discourses because they lack the space and narrative freedom to interrogate these ideologies fully. That said, columns and features are much more amenable to this type of work, and many mainstream news publications included detailed explanations of rape culture via these genres. As I have previously argued, although not traditionally seen as as important as 'hard' news, these 'soft' genres play an important role in making visible feminist ideologies and values (see Mendes 2012), and should be the continued focus for feminist media scholarly inquiry.

Opposing SlutWalk

Although the movement was overwhelmingly supported in my two samples, there is no doubt that it came under much criticism, particularly

from feminists. Women of colour in the US and Canada early on identified the ways that they felt excluded from the movement because of
its focus on the word 'slut', a pejorative term rarely used against them.
As women who had historically been sexualized and seen as legitimate
targets of assault, they pointed out the ways the movement needed a
more intersectional approach to the problem of sexual violence. Many
feminists were also wary of the ways the movement played to the male
gaze, prompting fears that rather than challenging patriarchy, it was
instead making it 'pleasurable for women' (Douglas 2010; see also Dow
1999; Dow & Wood 2014).

It is also worth pointing out how these critical arguments differ
qualitatively from those that opposed Second Wave activism. Where
these traditional 'backlash' discourses rejected feminism or feminist
activism, the vast majority of articles opposing SlutWalk approved of
its goals (smashing rape culture), but disagreed with its tactics. As a
result, I argue that SlutWalk presents evidence of a shift away from our
current postfeminist sensibility (Gill 2007), in which feminism is seen
as dead, redundant, harmful or passé (McRobbie 2007, 2009; Mendes
2011a, 2011b).

And while, as an advocate of feminist activism, it is tempting to label
such critiques 'bad' as they might deflect support away from the movement, I argue instead that these dialogues are necessary in thinking
through what we think feminism is and should be about. And as other
scholars have reminded us, there have been 'clashing political invest-
ments in feminism, disagreements over strategies, tactics, and priorities,
and related conflicts over theories of social change' amongst feminists
for centuries (Dow & Wood 2014, p. 23). And like Dow and Wood,
rather than viewing these disagreements over tactics, visual politics,
and messages as an area of weakness, I too believe they are a sign of
feminism's 'vitality' (2014, p. 23).

In fact, some of the critiques raised by feminists did lead to change,
with many satellite groups dropping their aim of reclaiming the word
'slut', discouraging provocative attire at marches, or changing the
movement's name to make it more inclusive. In some cases however,
organizers simply felt that they had to step away from the movement
or disband when they were unsure of how to resolve these issues
(Marturano 2013; Sutton 2014). And while their retreat from SlutWalk
could be interpreted as a loss for feminism, some, such as SlutWalk
Chicago 2011 organizer Stephanie Sutton, instead argued that such
critiques made her a 'better feminist and a better person down the line'
(Sutton 2014). Similarly, those involved in the disbanded SlutWalk NYC

didn't leave anti-rape activism completely, but instead became involved in other organizations which combatted rape culture, 'taking the mistakes we made during SlutWalk NYC very seriously in order to ensure that our activism is doing whatever it can to fight for a world without rape culture for all people and not just the privileged' (Marturano 2013).

When thinking about how the movement was represented, it appeared as though many feminists were particularly concerned about its visual representations, which unlike the text itself, tended to prioritize neoliberal constructions of a movement for, and about young, attractive, white women, who were intent on securing their personal rights and freedom to dress like a 'slut.' In this sense then, the feminist message that women have a right to dress how they want *without it being interpreted as a sign of inviting abuse* was often erased. As a result, I argue that it was the visual representations of the movement which led to many feminist critiques about the movement conforming to patriarchy. What my study revealed, however, was that far from accepting this 'storying' of SlutWalk, those active in feminist blogging communities often took it upon themselves to challenge mainstream accounts of the movement. They did this both through *discursive* interventions, in which they critiqued and called out the media for its superficial and raunchy coverage, and through the archiving of visual material such as photos and videos, which showed the diversity of protestors. As a result, I argue that these feminist bloggers came together as networked counterpublics to create their own 'counter-memories', and meanings of the movement.

Organizers' experiences with the movement

Although I didn't begin this research with the intention of interviewing so many organizers, the more I spoke with them, the more I became interested in their roles, routines and practices. This ranged from how they first heard of SlutWalk, to how they actually became involved as an organizer, and why they left. I was also interested in identifying their media strategies, priorities, and organizational tactics, as well seeking to understand their overall experiences of grassroots activism. What became clear throughout my 22 interviews was the vital importance of social media. Without it, they were all certain that the movement would not have happened. Although Twitter was cited as being an important tool, by far, most users identified their Facebook pages as the most important platforms. Acting as a homepage, organizers could use its functions to share information about the movement, create events, post relevant articles about rape culture/slut-shaming, and attempt to open up dialogue about the march's aims and purpose. Like Gerbaudo (2012), I also found that social media were instrumental in setting the emotional scene of activism, and were valued for the ways they opened up the possibility of dialogue *and* mobilization.

As a result, while traditional professional media skills such as journalism, PR, marketing, advertising and so forth were still considered valuable by some (Castieau 2012; Gray, L. 2014; Jarvis 2012), others identified the ways in which general media savviness, blogging and writing skills were becoming increasingly important (Gray 2014a; Sutton 2014). Furthermore, that several satellite groups simply did not pay much attention to mainstream media outreach indicates the extent to which they believe social media and other forms of communication are the way forward in movement organization (see Delgado 2014a; Gray 2014a; Haugen 2014; MacDonald, C. 2014), confirming Castell's (2012) view of a move towards 'postmedia' movements.

And while there is no doubt that connectivity afforded by social media has its advantages, the absolute ubiquity of trolling and online harassment indicates the ways in which those fighting for gender justice are also exposed to insults and threats meant to scare, humiliate, punish and silence them. And while trolling has certainly gained widespread media attention since 2012, I argue that more scholarly work is needed to examine the different forms it takes, as well as personal and collective responses to it. As an act which is used to silence others, trolling will only become an increasing concern as feminist media (and activism) becomes more prominent and visible.

So, what lessons have we learnt from SlutWalk and what can be said about its legacy?

SlutWalk's legacy

Contrary to popular belief, sexual assault is not a random or isolated event that a few unfortunate people will experience in their lives. Instead, sexual assault is a systematic tool that has been used for thousands of years to enforce various systems of oppression such as racism, sexism, classicism, colonialism, imperialism and heterosexism (Bevacqua 2001; McNicol 2012). However, it wasn't until the 1960s and 70s that feminists began to really theorize sexual assault and recognize the ways in which it was not an *individual* problem for which the individual was to blame, but a political problem which needed addressing (Bevacqua 2008; McNicol 2012). Since then, anti-rape activism has emerged around the world, scoring some major successes along the way, such as the formation of rape crisis centres and hotlines, the introduction of rape testing kits, specialized sexual violence assault police units, public awareness campaigns, self-defence classes, and public protests and marches such as Reclaim the Night.

It is in the context of over 50 years of anti-rape activism that SlutWalk emerged and helped bring sexual violence back onto the public agenda. Although SlutWalk marches did not attract even a fraction of the mainstream news or feminist media attention in 2013 that they did in 2011, they are regularly used as a reference point to signal the (re)emergence of anti-rape activism around the globe. For example, amongst my feminist media sample, SlutWalk was praised for allowing 'women who didn't feel comfortable discussing feminism in more "intellectual" terms to identify with the movement nonetheless' (Baker 2013a). It was also credited as helping bring street harassment to the public's attention (Baker 2013b). In the mainstream news, one *Canberra Times* article praised SlutWalk for 'dragging' the term rape culture 'out of academe and into popular culture', thus providing the public with language with which to understand the ways in which 'sexual violence is both made to be invisible and inevitable' (Brooks 2013; see also Fondas 2013). When British celebrity Joanna Lumley was quoted advising women to dress 'demurely' at night to avoid being raped or robbed, a Twitter storm erupted and noted that such 'depressing ignorance' persisted despite efforts such as SlutWalk to challenge the view that 'women are ever to blame for the sexual violence of men' (Cox 2013). That this vehement critique of Lumley was published in Britain's conservative *Daily Mail* – a newspaper that is known for its anti-feminist views (see Mendes 2012) – is particularly surprising, and suggests the movement has introduced feminist consciousness even into society's most conservative spaces. As British feminist Finn Mackay (2012) argued, there is growing evidence that feminism has 'seeped into people's consciousness.'

Putting feminism (back) on the agenda

Although it would certainly be an overstatement to claim that SlutWalk alone brought sexual violence and rape culture onto the public agenda, at the time of this writing, there is no doubt that it played an important role in making this topic visible. In fact, in 2014, rape culture and feminism are 'hot' topics amongst both the mainstream news and feminist media. Speaking about the Australian context, SlutWalk Melbourne 2012 and 2013 organizer Amy Gray stated that it was 'undeniable' that SlutWalk 'put feminism back in modern media discussion'

(Gray 2014a). She also argued that the movement 'brought back wide-scale feminist activism' to Australia (Gray 2014a). Acknowledging that 'deeply ingrained attitudes aren't going to change overnight', SlutWalk Newcastle 2011–2013 organizer Lizi Gray stated, 'if we can just make one victim/survivor see that they were not to blame then I really think we've done our job right' (Gray, L. 2014). There was also consensus about the movement's ability to raise awareness and change people's minds about sexual assault and victim-blaming. As SlutWalk Johannesburg 2013 organizer Karmilla Pillay-Siokos and SlutWalk Victoria 2013 organizer Diondra declared, while acknowledging that 'there is lot of work to be done in translating that into a real change in the attitudes of the major-ity of people at grass roots level' (Pillay-Siokos 2013), the movement definitely created much more awareness of the issue of victim-blaming and consent (Diondra 2013).

A more pessimistic view

Yet despite these optimistic claims, other organizers were more reserved in their judgements. For example, SlutWalk Singapore 2011 and 2012 organizer Vanessa Ho stated, 'I personally don't think we've gone far in challenging the victim blaming attitude. Rather, I think what we have done is to equip people with the tools [mostly language] to start doing that' (Ho 2012). Acknowledging that the movement faced 'an uphill battle', SlutWalk Winnipeg 2011 and 2012 organizer Deanna (2012) insisted that 'it is impossible for the movement to not have educated many people on the issue.' In a similar vein, while SlutWalk Aotearoa 2012 and 2013 organizer MJ Brodie felt that the movement had achieved success on an 'individual level', by getting people talking about 'issues that we have been quiet about for a really long time', she stated that on a wider scale, its success rate was 'maybe not so much' (Brodie 2014). She came to this conclusion after noting how she had to have the same conversations about rape culture year after year after year. SlutWalk Cape Town 2011 organizer Umeshree Govender was also disheartened by the movement's impact. As she stated:

> I don't want to sound pessimistic, but once we started the event Facebook page, we constantly had guys saying this was the dumbest thing, guys saying if you are going to walk down the street at night in a Rolex and you know you are likely to get robbed, would you wear a Rolex? I mean using a Rolex for a metaphor for a woman is insult-ing. It didn't matter how much we engaged with these individuals or how much we tried to debate it, I don't think we changed minds. (Govender 2014)

On the other hand, Umeshree argued that the movement was useful for exposing the prevalence of victim-blaming attitudes in seemingly 'normal' people, both men and women of all races, classes and ages (Govender 2014).

When thinking about the movement's overall impact, SlutWalk St. Louis 2012 organizer David Wraith agreed that marching down the street once a year was not going to stop rape. However, he stated that, 'I firmly believe that doing something is better than doing nothing. I don't know what kind of impact it will have on our community, but I do know what kind of impact staying home and doing nothing is having' (Wraith 2013). And I think David is right here. While sexual assault certainly has not stopped since SlutWalks began, and while victims continue to be blamed for their assault, and while assailants continue to go unpunished for their crimes, these things are not happening unchallenged. Judges are routinely criticized for giving light sentences to convicted rapists, or for making comments in their rulings that perpetrators should 'forgive' their attackers (Pearce 2014), that they were not the victim they claimed to be (Belle 2014), or that they 'dressed older' than their chronological age (Brown 2013). The news media comes under attack when writing accounts sympathizing with the attackers, rather than the accusers, even when such acts are caught on film (McKinley 2011). And anti-rape activism is springing up everywhere. So, what hope for change is there out there?

Hope for change

While it is clear that rape is still an issue, at least there are signs that rape culture is being addressed. For example, in 2014 the Egyptian government criminalized sexual harassment for the first time. Offenders face a minimum of six months in jail and a monetary fine, both of which can increase for repeat offenders (Kingsley 2014). In a nation in which sexual assault has been used as a weapon to keep women from participating in public protest, and ostensibly public life ('Egypt Keeping Women Out: Sexual Violence Against Women in the Public Sphere' 2014), this is a bold first step. In light of their failure to bring sexual violence offenders to justice, Britain's Metropolitan Police announced it was going overhaul and review its policies and practices, admitting that 'unconscious bias' was preventing officers from taking many rape allegations seriously (Dodd 2014). The review is not only meant to improve how allegations are investigated, but also comment on how they are prosecuted. In June 2014, the UK hosted the Global Summit to End Sexual Violence in Conflict – the largest gathering to date on this topic (UK Government 2014). And although it certainly did not end sexual violence, it has brought this important and often neglected issue to the forefront.

In fact, scarcely a day that goes by without at least one mainstream news story related to sexual violence prevention/management. Whether it's India's newly elected government pledging a zero tolerance policy on sexual violence (Burke 2014), or even professional sports associations such as the National Football League (NFL), National Basketball Association (NBA), Major League Baseball (MLB) and Ultimate Fighting Championship (UFC) revising their policies on domestic violence (Armstrong 2014; Conway 2014; Gambino 2014; 'MLB Meets with Groups on Domestic Violence Policy' 2014). As institutions that cultivate and glorify aggressive masculinity, their intolerance towards abuse and seeming recognition that it is a serious problem, is at least an important gesture, which I hope translates into education and prevention programmes.

In some cases, we are in fact seeing initiatives that aim to tackle sexual violence before it happens. In the Balkan region, the NGO CARE is entering the third phrase of its 'Young Men Initiative' which aims to promote 'gender equitable social norms, healthy lifestyles and discourage violent behavior against community, women and peers' (CARE 2014). This programme is especially important because it focuses on challenging aggressive masculinity and preventing the problem before it begins. Similarly, in 2011, the US government launched its '1 is 2 Many' initiative, which aims to use technology, such as apps, and outreach to reduce violence and sexual assault on teens, students and young adults (The White House 2014). In 2014, it followed this up with an 'It's On Us' campaign which encourages the public to both 'Intervene in situations where consent has not or cannot be given' and 'To create an environment in which sexual assault is unacceptable and survivors are supported' (It's On Us 2014). That governments and policy-makers are finally recognizing the ways that rape prevention requires *collective,* rather than *individual* solutions is a major development worth celebrating. Furthermore, it acknowledges a feminist conceptual shift of sexual violence, from being a personal issue to a truly political one.

What next?

While the developments discussed above are all positive steps in the right direction, they are no guarantee that anything will change. After all, sexual assault is the result of various systems of oppression (capitalism, colonialism, racism, patriarchy, heterosexism, etc.), which, despite global efforts, are still deeply entrenched. All that we can really do is make the most of the current feminist 'zeitgeist' (Valenti 2014c) to talk about these issues, call out people or the media who promote rape culture, engage in discursive activism, and occupy public spaces where necessary. And why must we do this? Well, as the slogan for SlutWalk states: 'Because We've Had Enough.'

Notes

1 Introduction

1. In 2013, the group changed the name of the event to 'The March to End Rape Culture' (SlutWalk Philadelphia 2013). However, the SlutWalk Philadelphia Facebook page is still extremely active and is used to promote this march.
2. Unfortunately, just days before the walk was scheduled to take place, SlutWalk Seattle had to cancel their event after their sound specialist volunteer pulled out at the last minute and they could not find someone to replace them. As organiser Laura Delgado explained, 'it seemed impractical to keep trotting on right up to the deadline without that element planned out' (Delgado 2014b).
3. Websites and Facebook groups consulted include: SlutWalk Aotearoa, SlutWalk Bangalore, SlutWalk Chicago, SlutWalk India, SlutWalk Johannesburg, SlutWalk London, SlutWalk Perth, SlutWalk Seattle, SlutWalk Singapore, SlutWalk Toronto, SlutWalk Winnipeg.

2 Contextualizing the Issues

1. In fact, there is even talk about a Fourth Wave of activists, who are defined by their use of new media technologies to create a new feminist movement online (see Cochrane 2013). However, although the term Fourth Wave has been coined, it has yet to be a label embraced by feminist scholars or feminists themselves (Keller 2013).
2. Surprisingly, although Reclaim the Night marches have been staged since the late 1970s, I found no academic research exploring its representations in the news media.
3. Heather Jarvis (2012) told me that the first secret organising group she heard of started out of Atlanta, but that there are several in operation, many of which are in languages other than English. She also added that certain groups have closed down over the years due to disagreements which she sees as 'natural', given most organisers are survivors of sexual assault and are dealing with a lot of pain and healing.
4. Others, such as Gerbaudo (2012) questioned the extent to which any social movement can truly be leaderless, and instead argued that although many new social movements refuse to have identifiable leaders, they do develop their own kinds of hierarchies (see also Freeman 1972).
5. In fact, the sexual assault of female protesters has become such an issue that several groups have formed which aim to 'rescue' women who are attacked. These include Operation Anti-Sexual Harassment (OpAntiSH) and Tahrir Bodyguard.
6. Keller (2013) initially limited her study to girls aged between 15 and 21, although she recognises that the term 'girl' is not necessarily age-related and that older women can also identify as 'girls'.

7. These included organisers for SlutWalk LA, Victoria (Canada), Newcastle, New York City, Johannesburg, Singapore, and Winnipeg.

8. This is despite the fact that some marches were cancelled at the last minute. For example, the SlutWalk Bangalore 2011 march was cancelled the night before when police revoked the march permit. Similarly, SlutWalk Seattle 2014 was cancelled around a week before its scheduled date. In both cases, however, I included my interviews with those who had organised these marches as both were cancelled due to unforeseen circumstances.

9. My mainstream news sample consisted of the following: *Australian Broadcasting Company* (Australia); *The Australian/Weekend Australian* (Australia); *Canberra Times* (Australia); *Herald Sun* and *Sunday Herald Sun* (Australia); *Hobart Mercury* and *Sunday Tasmanian* (Australia); *Sydney Morning Herald* (Australia); *Calgary Herald* (Canada); *CBC* (Canada); *Globe and Mail* (Canada); *Ottawa Citizen* (Canada); *Huffington Post* (Canada, UK and US); *Toronto Star* (Canada); *Indian Express* (India); *New Indian Express* (India); *The Telegraph* (India); *Times of India* (India); *New Zealand Herald* (New Zealand); *Sunday Star-Times* (New Zealand); *TV New Zealand* (New Zealand); *The New Paper* (Singapore); *The Straits Times* (Singapore); *Cape Times* (South Africa); *Daily Dispatch* (South Africa); *South African Broadcasting Company* (South Africa); *Sowetan* (South Africa); *BBC* (UK); *Daily Mail, Mail on Sunday* and *Mail Online* (UK); *The Guardian* (UK); *The Observer* (UK); *The Sun* (UK); *The Times* (UK); *Daily News* (US); *New York Times* (US); *Washington Post* (US); *Washington Times* (US).

10. My feminist media sample consisted of the following sites: *The Conversation* (Australia); *DragOnista* (Australia); *Dangers Untold and Hardships Unnumbered* (Australia); *Definatalie.com* (Australia); *Feminaust* (Australia); *Godard's Letterbox* (Australia); *Green Left Weekly* (Australia); *Hoyden About Town* (Australia); *Insanity Works* (Australia); *Two Feminists* (Australia); *Zero at the Bone* (Australia); *Emma W. Wooley* (Canada); *Feminist Catalyst* (Canada); *Feminist Current* (Canada); *Rabble.ca* (Canada); *Rmott62* (Canada); *SlutWalk Toronto* (Canada); *Asian Window* (India); *Crazy Dumbsaint of the Mind* (India); *The Dancing Sufi* (India); *From A SlutWalker, With Love* (India); *Just Femme* (India); *Pratiksha Baxi* (India); *Ramblings of a Feminist Abroad* (India); *Rendezvous* (India); *Textual Orientation* (India); *This Is My Truth* (India); *Women's Web* (India); *Open Democracy* (International); *Brooklynne Michelle* (New Zealand); *come again?* (New Zealand); *Craft is the new black* (New Zealand); *The Hand Mirror* (New Zealand); *Iced Chai* (New Zealand); *Ideologically Impure* (New Zealand); *Kiwiana* (New Zealand); *The Lady Garden* (New Zealand); *Lady News* (New Zealand); *Luddite Journo* (New Zealand); *News With Nipples* (New Zealand); *Pickled Think* (New Zealand); *Scuba Nurse* (New Zealand); *Too Fat for our Pants* (New Zealand); *Aware* (Singapore); *Diva* (Singapore); *Juice* (Singapore); *Rachel Zeng* (Singapore); *SlutWalk Singapore* (Singapore); *Feminists SA* (South Africa); *Just a South African Woman* (South Africa); *SlutWalk Johannesburg* (South Africa); *Thought Leader* (South Africa); *Bad Reputation* (UK); *The F-Word* (UK); *Here. In My Head* (UK); *Lesbilicious* (UK); *Rarely Wears Lipstick* (UK); *Red Pepper* (UK); *Slutwalk London* (UK); *Versatile Identities* (UK); *AfroLez femcentric perspective* (US); *AlterNet* (US); *Big Think* (US); *Bitch Media* (US); *Black Women's Blueprint* (US); *Bust Magazine* (US); *Crunk Feminist Collective* (US); *David Wraith* (US); *Dissent* (US); *The F*

Bomb (US); *Feminist Frequency* (US); *Feministe* (US); *Feministing* (US); *Feminists for Choice* (US); *Gender Focus* (Canada); *The Good Men Project* (US); *Hugo Schwyzer* (US); *I Blame the Patriarchy* (US); *Intersectional Activism* (US); *Jezebel* (US); *Life in a Pickle* (US); *Ms Magazine* (US); *People of Color Organize* (US); *The Pursuit of Harpyness* (US); *Queer Black Feminist* (US); *Racialicious* (US); *Rookie* (US); *Scarleteen* (US); *Stop Street Harassment* (US); *Thought Catalogue* (US); *To the Curb* (US); *Women's Views on News* (US); *Where is Your Line?* (US); *Yasmin Nair Blog* (US); *Clarisse Thorn* (US); *The Feminist Wire* (US).

3   Situating SlutWalk

1. Where only five news articles were 500 words or more, 28 columns and 14 features were this length. Although no news articles were 1,000 words or more, eight columns and five features were this length. Alternatively, where 87 news articles were 250 words or less, only 12 columns and 19 features were this length.
2. Gejje Hejje translates to 'anklet footsteps', and was used because anklets were worn by concubines, courtesans and sex slaves when performing dances used to entertain upper-class men.

4   Representing the Movement: SlutWalk Challenges Rape Culture

1. In both mainstream news and feminist media, I counted up to three feminist discourses per article/post.
2. However, Scully & Marolla (1985) found that some rapists admitted they did not orgasm and indicate rape was not done for sexual fulfilment.
3. Yet, in 2014 another instance of biological determinism emerged as a judge in Hull, UK, told a man accused of rape that: 'It's sad to see a man of generally good character in the dock for such a serious offence ... This was a case where you just lost control of normal restraint' (Shoesmith 2014).
4. For an interesting critique of neoliberal tropes inherent in current anti-victimization discourses, see Rebecca Stringer (2014).

5   Representing the Movement: SlutWalk is Misguided or Opposed

1. For example, SlutWalk DC was heavily criticised after it held a fundraiser at a 'gentleman's club'.
2. While my coding scheme allowed me to count the number of photos in each post, I only coded the content for the first image presented.
3. Interestingly, to my knowledge, this discourse has never been used as a justification for why men are raped.

6   SlutWalk Hierarchies and Organizers' Roles

1. I should point out that after their September 2014 march, Karen Pickering decided to step down from her role as organiser (Gray 2014b).

2. I have come across at least one example, from SlutWalk Winnipeg, of a home-made zine that the organisers photographed and uploaded as a PDF. The zine can be accessed from the SlutWalk Winnipeg website (2014). I have, however, come across calls for material to be published in a zine on the 2014 SlutWalk Chicago Facebook page, and SlutWalk Singapore 2011 and 2012 organiser Vanessa Ho told me they had sold zines as a means of fundraising (2012).

7   SlutWalk, Community and Cyberactivism

1. The Bangalore march was unfortunately cancelled the day before when opponents threatened to attack protesters and police revoked their permit amidst safety concerns (Chandramowli 2014).

References

Adams, K. (2011) 'SlutWalkers are Missing the Point', *The Sun*, 6 June, 11, online.

Adelman, L. (2011) 'The Feministing Five: Sonya Barnett and Heather Jarvis', *Feministing*, 16 April, online.

AF3IRM (2011) 'Women of Color Respond to SlutWalk: "The Women's Movement is Not Monochromatic"', *People of Color Organize*, 29 September, online.

Aguilar, E. (2011) 'Four Brief Critiques of SlutWalk's Whiteness, Privilege and Unexamined Power Dynamics', *People of Color Organize*, 16 May, online.

Alat, Z. (2006) 'News Coverage of Violence Against Women: The Turkish Case', *Feminist Media Studies*, 6(3), 295–314.

All Students for Consent (n.d.) 'Ask for It', *Facebook*, https://www.facebook.com/WhitmanASC?directed_target_id=0, date accessed 6 June 2014.

Amnesty International (2007) 'Maze of Injustice: The failure to protect Indigenous Women from Sexual Violence', *Amnesty International*, online.

Ana (2011) 'SlutWalk, Porn and the Future of Feminism', *Too Fat for our Pants*, 19 June, online.

Andersen, M.L. and Taylor, H.F. (2008) *Sociology: Understanding a Diverse Society: Fourth Edition* (Belmont, CA: Thomson Higher Education).

Anderson, D. (1991) *The Unfinished Revolution: Status of Women in Twelve Countries* (Toronto: Doubleday Canada Ltd).

Andrea (2011) 'Am I Troy Davis? A Slut?; or, What's Troubling Me about the Absences of Reflexivity in Movements that Proclaim Solidarity', *Racialicious*, 11 October, online.

'Are "slutwalk" protests the future of feminism?' (2011) *The Washington Post*, 6 June, online.

Armstrong, D. (2014) 'UFC Cuts Ties With Fighters Accused of Domestic Violence', *Bloomberg Business Week*, 22 September, online.

Arthurs, D. (2011) 'Scantily-clad "SlutWalk" Women March on New York after Police Tell them to "Cover Up" to Avoid Rape', *Daily Mail*, 10 May, online.

'Arrest over "revenge" rape in Jharkhand' (2014) *BBC*, 11 July, online.

Ashley, L. and Olson, B. (1998) 'Constructing Reality: Print Media's Framing of the Women's Movement, 1966–1986', *Journal of Mass Communication Quarterly*, 75(2), 263–77.

Asian Window (2011) 'New Delhi "SlutWalk" on June 25', *Asian Window*, 12 June, online.

Atkinson, J. (2009) 'Networked Activists in Search of Resistance: Exploring an Alternative Media Pilgrimage Across the Boundaries and Borderlands of Globalization', *Communication, Culture & Critique*, 2, 137–59.

AWARE (2011) 'SlutWalk Singapore: Happening this December', *AWARE*, 24 August, online.

Bacon, J. (2013) 'Judge Apologizes for Teen Rape Remark, Not Sentence', *USA Today*, 6 September, online.

Badham, V. (2013) 'Hot Not to Raise a Rapist', *The Guardian*, 29 October, online.

Baker, K.J.M. (2013a) 'Steubenville's Legacy: How a Rape Case in Ohio could Change History', *Jezebel*, 8 January, online.

Baker, K.J.M. (2013b) 'SF Street Harassment Stabbing is a Great Reminder that Cat Calling Isn't a Joke', *Jezebel*, 8 January, online.

Bamberg, M. (2004) 'Form and Functions of "Slut-Bashing" in Male Identity Constructions in 15-Year-Olds', *Human Development*, 249, 1–23.

Barbato, L. (2012) 'Scenes from SlutWalk LA 2012', *Ms. Magazine*, 8 August, online.

Barker-Plummer, B. (2000) 'News as a Feminist Resource? A Case Study of the Media Strategies and Media Representation of the National Organization for Women, 1966–1980', in A. Sreberny and L. van Zoonen (eds.) *Gender, Politics and Communication* (New Jersey: Hampton Press Inc), 121–59.

Barker-Plummer, B. (2010) 'News and Feminism: A Historic Dialogue', *Journalism & Communication Monographs*, 12(3), 144–203.

Barnett, B. (2005) 'Feminists Shaping News: A Framing Analysis of News Releases From the National Organization for Women', *Journal of Public Relations Research*, 17(4), 341–62.

Bates, L. (2014) 'Project', *The Everyday Sexism Project*, http://everydaysexism. com/, date accessed 6 June 2014.

Baumgardner, J. and Richards, A. (2000) *Manifesta: Young Women, Feminism and the Future* (New York: Farrar, Straus and Giroux).

Baxter, H. and Cosslett, R.L. (2014) *The Vagenda: A Zero Tolerance Guide to the Media* (London: Square Peg).

Baylor, T. (1996) 'Media Framing of Movement Protest: The Case of American Indian Protest', *The Social Science Journal*, 33(3), 241–55.

Beigh, N. (2012) 'Comment', *Facebook*, 2 June, https://www.facebook.com/notes/384408591596053/, date accessed 10 November 2014.

Belle, W. (2014) 'Legal SlutShaming', *Oye! Times*, 10 May, online.

Benedict, H. (1992) *The Virgin and the Vamp: How the Press Covers Sex Crimes* (New York: Oxford University Press).

Benford, R.D. and Snow, D.A. (2000) 'Framing Processes and Social Movements: An Overview and Assessment', *Annual Review of Sociology*, 26, 611–39.

Berridge, S. (2015) 'Empowered vulnerability?: A Feminist Response to the Ubiquity of Sexual Violence in the Pilots of Female-Fronted Teen Drama Series', in K. Silva and K. Mendes (eds.) *Feminist Erasures: Challenging Backlash Culture* (Basingstoke: Palgrave), 91–105.

Berrington, E. and Jones, H. (2002) 'Reality vs. Myth: Constructions of Women's Insecurity' *Feminist Media Studies*, 2(3), 307–23.

Bevacqua, M. (2001) 'Anti-rape Coalititions: Radical, Liberal, Black, and White Feminists Challenging Boundaries', in J.M. Bystydzienski and S.P. Schacht (eds.) *Forging Radical Alliances Across Difference: Coalition Politics for the New Millenium* (New York & London: Rowman & Littlefield), 163–76.

Bevacqua, M. (2008) 'Reconsidering Violence Against Women: Coalition politics in the antirape movement', in S. Gilmore (ed.) *Feminist Coalitions: Historical Perspectives on Second-wave Feminism in the United States* (USA: University of Illinois), 163–77.

Bhardwaj, A. (2011) 'It's a Walk Against the Besharam Men', *Indian Express*, 1 August, n.p.

Bhattacherjee, A. (2012) *Social Science Research: Principles, Methods, and Practices* (Tampa: University of South Florida).

Black, D. (1983) 'Crime as Social Control', *American Sociological Review*, 48, 34–45.

Black Women's Blueprint (2011) 'An Open Letter from Black Women to the SlutWalk', *Black Women's Blueprint*, 23 September, http://www.blackwomens-blueprint.org/2011/09/23/an-open-letter-from-black-women-to-the-slutwalk/, date accessed 30 December 2011.

Blackman, I. and Perry, K. (2000) 'Skirting the Issue: Lesbian Fashion for the 1990s', *Feminist Review*, 34(Spring), 67–78.

Blake, M. (2014) 'Father of One of Indian Girls Gang-Raped and Hanged from a Tree was Ignored and Ridiculed by Police When He Reported her Missing Because of his Caste', *Daily Mail*, 30 May, online.

blatantblithe (2011) 'SlutWalk London 2011: Full photo report!', *Catherine Elms*, 13 June, online.

Blogando, A. (2011) 'SlutWalk: A Stroll Through White Supremacy', *To The Curb*, 13 May, online.

Blumer, H. (1969) 'Social Movements', *Studies in Social Movements: A Social Psychological Perspective*, 8–29.

Bonnar, J. (2011) 'Protesters Unite Against Damaging Stereotypes of Sexual Assault Survivors', *Rabble.ca*, 5 April, online.

Bonnes, S. (2013) 'Gender and Racial Stereotyping in Rape Coverage', *Feminist Media Studies*, 13(2), 208–27.

Borah, R. and Nandi, S. (2012) 'Reclaiming the Feminist Politics of SlutWalk' *International Feminist Journal of Politics*, 14(3), 415–21.

Bouchier, D. (1983) *The Feminist Challenge: The Movement for Women's Liberation in Britain and the United States* (London: Macmillan Press).

boyd, d.m. (2008) 'Why Youth [Heart] Social Network Sites: The Role of Networked Publics in Teenage Social Life', in D. Buckingham (ed.), *Youth, Identity, and Digital Media* (Cambridge, MA: The MIT Press), 119–42.

boyd, d.m. (2010) 'Social Network Sites as Networked Publics: Affordances, Dynamics, and Implication', in Z. Papacharissi (ed.) *Networked Self: Identity, Community, and Culture on Social Network Sites* (New York and London: Routledge), 39–58.

boyd, d.m. (forthcoming) 'Making Sense of Teen Life: Strategies for Capturing Ethnographic Data in a Networked Era', in E. Hargittai and C. Sandvig (eds.) *Digital Research Confidential: The Secrets of Studying Behavior Online* (Cambridge, MA: The MIT Press).

boyd, d.m. and Ellison, N. (2007) 'Social Network Sites: Definition, History, and Scholarship', *Journal of Computer-Mediated Communication*, 13(1), 210–30.

boyd, d.m., Golder, S. and Lotan, G. (2010) '*Tweet, Tweet, Retweet: Conversational Aspects of Retweeting on Twitter*', *Proceedings of HICSS-42*, Persistent Conversation Track. Kauai, HI: IEEE Computer Society, 5–8 January.

Bradley, P. (2003) *Mass Media and the Shaping of American Feminism, 1963–1975* (USA: University Press of Mississippi).

Brodie, MJ (2011) 'MJ's SlutWalk Aotearoa Speech', *Kiwiana*, 15 August, online.

Brodie, MJ (2014) *SlutWalk Aotearoa 2011 & 2012 Organiser*, Personal Interview, 25 May.

Broher, A. (2014) *SlutWalk Chicago 2013 & 2014 Organiser*, Personal Interview, 27 July.

Brooks, L. (2013) 'We Must All Counter the Mood Music of Rape Culture', *Canberra Times*, 8 January, online.

Brown, L.M. (2013) 'In Montana, A Case Study in Rape Culture', *CNN*, 26 September, online.

Browne, R. (2011) 'Dressed Up for a Dressing Down', *Canberra Times Online*, 8 May, online.

Brownmiller, S. (1975) *Against Our Will: Men, Women and Rape* (Harmondsworth, New York, Victoria, Markham, and Oakham: Penguin Books).

Bryson, V. (1999) *Feminist Debates: Issues of Theory and Political Practice* (Basingstoke: Palgrave).

Bryson, V. (2003) *Feminist Political Theory: An Introduction, 2nd ed.* (New York: Palgrave Macmillan).

Buchwald, E., Fletcher, P.R., and Roth, M. (2005) *Transforming a Rape Culture, 2nd ed.* (Minneapolis, MN: Milkweed Editions).

Budgeon, S. and Currie, D.H. (1995) 'From Feminism to Postfeminism: Women's Liberation in Fashion Magazines', *Women's Studies International Forum*, 18(2), 173–86.

Burke, J. (2014) 'Indian Government Vows Zero Tolerance Over Violence Against Women', *The Guardian*, 10 June, online.

Buss, D.E. (2009) 'Rethinking "Rape As A Weapon of War"', *Feminist Legal Studies*, 17(2), 145–62.

Butler, J. (1990) *Gender Trouble: Feminism and the Subversion of Identity* (London and New York: Routledge).

Byerly, C.M. (1994) 'An Agenda for Teaching News Coverage of Rape', *Journalism Educator*, 49(1), 59–69.

Byerly, C.M. (2013) *The Palgrave International Handbook of Women and Journalism* (Basingstoke and New York: Palgrave MacMillan).

Campbell, B. (2013) *End of Equality: The Only Way is Women's Liberation* (London, New York and Calcutta: Seagull Books).

CARE (2014) 'Young Men Initiative' *CARE*, http://www.youngmeninitiative.net/en/?page=2, date accessed 10 June 2014.

Carmon, I. (2011) 'How a Victim Blaming Cop Inspired SlutWalk', *Jezebel*, 31 March, online.

Carr, J.L. (2013) 'The SlutWalk Movement: A Study in Transnational Feminist Activism', *Journal of Feminist Scholarship*, 4(Spring), 24–38.

Carter, C. (1998) 'When the "Extraordinary" Becomes "Ordinary": Everyday News of Sexual Violence', in C. Carter, G. Branston, and S. Allan (eds.) *News, Gender and Power* (London and New York: Routledge), 219–32.

Carter, C.J. and Harlow, P. (2013) 'Alleged Victim in Steubenville Rape Case Says She Woke Up Naked', *CNN*, 18 March, online.

Castells, M. (2000) 'Materials for an Exploratory Theory of the Network Society', *British Journal of Sociology*, 51(1), 5–24.

Castells, M. (2007) 'Communication, Power and Counter-power in the Network Society', *International Journal of Communication*, 1, 238–266.

Castells, M. (2009) *Communication Power* (Oxford: Oxford University Press).

Castells, M. (2012) *Networks of Outrage and Hope: Social Movements in the Internet Age* (Cambridge: Polity Press).

Castieau, B. (2012) *SlutWalk Perth 2011 Organiser*, Personal Interview, 5 September.

Chai, S. (2014) 'Hundreds Protest in Tel Aviv: "End Rape Culture"', *Ynetnews*, 30 March, online.

Chandramowli, D. (2014) *SlutWalk Bangalore 2011 Organiser*, Personal Interview, 6 June.

Chateauvert, M. (2013) *Sex Workers Unite: A History of the Movement from Stonewall to SlutWalk* (USA: Beacon Press).

Chattopadhyay, S. (2011) 'Online Activism for a Heterogenerous Time: The Pink Chaddi Campaign and the Social Media in India', *Proteus*, 27(1), 63–67.

Chawki, M. and el Shazly, Y. (2013) 'Online Sexual Harassment: Issues and Solutions', *JIPITEC* 4(2), 71–86.

Chen, K. (2012) '150 Join Ottawa's SlutWalk to Protest "Victim-blaming" Attitudes', *Ottawa Citizen*, 19 August, online.

Chidgey, R. (2012) 'Hand-Made Memories: Remediating Cultural Memory in DIY Feminist Networks', in E. Zobl and R. Drueke (eds.) *Feminist Media: Participatory Spaces, Networks and Cultural Citizenship* (Germany: Transcript), 87–97.

Chloe (2011) 'The Un-funny, Unfair and Un-feminist thing About Victim Blaming', *Feministing*, 5 April, online.

Church, E. (2011) 'SlutWalk Sparks Worldwide Movement', *Globe and Mail*, p. A6.

Clark, K. (1992) 'The Linguistics of Blame: Representations of Women in The Sun's Reporting of Crimes of Sexual Vviolence', in M. Toolan (ed.) *Language, Text and Context: Essays in Stylistics* (London and New York: Routledge), 208–26.

Clarke, J. (2011) 'Perth "Sluts" Prepare to Walk Despite Lack of Support', *Canberra Times Online*, 2 December, online.

Clay, A. (2011) 'Endorsing a Critique of Slutwalk', *Queer Black Feminist*, 5 October, online.

Cochrane, K. (2013) 'The Fourth Wave of Feminism: Meet the Rebel Women', *The Guardian*, 10 December, online.

Cole, A.M. (2007) *The Cult of True Victimhood: From the War on Welfare to the War on Terror* (Stanford: Stanford University Press).

Colleen (2012) 'SWTO Speech from the 2012 National Sexual Assault Conference in Chicago', *SlutWalk Toronto*, 11 September, online.

come again? (2011) 'NZ Media Asking for It', *Come Again?* 24 June, online.

Conboy, M. (2006) *Tabloid Tales: Constructing a Community Through Language* (Abingdon: Routledge).

Consent Workshop #1 (2012) 'SlutWalk Singapore', *Facebook*, online.

Conway, T. (2014) 'NBA to Review Domestic Violence Policies: Latest Details, Comments and Reaction', *Bleacher Report*, 22 September, online.

Coote, A. and Campbell, B. (1982) *Sweet Freedom: The Struggle for Women's Liberation* (London: Pan Books Ltd.)

Coren, V. (2011) 'Are Slutwalkers Losing their Way?', *The Observer*, 19 June, online.

Corinna, H. (2011) 'This is What a SlutWalk (Really) Looks Like', *Scarleteen*, 26 July, online.

Corrigan, R. (2013) *Up Against A Wall: Rape Reform and its Failures and Successes* (New York and London: NYU Press).

Costain, A.N., Braunstein, R., and Berggren, H. (1997) 'Framing the Women's Movement', in P. Norris (ed.) *Women, Media and Politics* (New York: Oxford University Press), 205–20.

Cottle, S. (2003) *Media Organisation and Production* (London, Thousand Oaks, and New Delhi: Sage Publications).

Cottle, S. (2009) 'Journalism and Globalisation', in K. Wahl-Jorgensen and T. Hanitzsch (eds.) *The Handbook of Journalism Studies* (New York and Abingdon: Routledge), 341–56.

Couldry, N. (1999) 'Disrupting the Media Frame at Greenham Common: A New Chapter in the History of Mediations?' *Media, Culture and Society*, 21(3), 337–58.

Cox, L. (2013) ' "Don't Get Drunk, Don't Be Sick in the Gutter and Don't Stagger about in the Wrong Clothes at Midnight": Fury as Ab Fab's Patsy Warns Girls they are Putting THEMSELVES at Risk of Rape', *Daily Mail Online*, 24 January, online.

Creedon, P.J. (1993) 'Framing Feminism-A Feminist Primer for the Mass Media', *Media Studies Journal*, 7(1/2), 69–80.

Crenshaw, K. (1989) 'Demarginalizing the Intersection of Race and Sex: A Black Feminist Critique of Antidiscrimination Doctrine, Feminist Theory, and Antiracist Critique', *University of Chicago Legal Forum*, 139–67.

Cress, D.M. and Snow, D.A. (2000) 'The Outcomes of Homeless Mobilization: The Influence of Organization, Disruption, Political Mediation, and Framing', *American Journal of Sociology*, 105(4), 1063–104.

Crown Prosecution Service (2013) 'Charging Perverting the Course of Justice and Wasting Police Time in Cases Involving Allegedly False Rape and Domestic Violence Accusations', *Crown Prosecution Service*, online.

Crunktastic (2011a) 'SlutWalk vs. Ho Strolls', *Crunk Feminist Collective*, 23 May, online.

Crunktastic (2011b) 'I Saw the Sign but Did We Really Need a Sign?: SlutWalk and Racism', *Crunk Feminist Collective*, 6 October, online.

Cuklanz, L. (1996) *Rape on Trial: How the mass media construct legal reform and social change* (Philadelphia: University of Pennsylvania Press).

Cuklanz, L. (2000) *Rape in Prime Time: Television, Masculinity and Sexual Violence* (Philadelphia: University of Pennsylvania Press).

Cuervo, I. (2011) 'Toronto "SlutWalk" Spreads to US', *CBC*, 6 May, online.

Currie, D., Kelly, D., and Pomerantz, S. (2009) *'Girl Power:' Girls Reinventing Girlhood* (New York: Peter Lang).

D'Acci, J. (2005) 'Cultural Studies, Television Studies, and the Crisis in the Humanities', in L. Spigel and J. Olsson (eds.) *Television After TV: Essays on a Medium in Transition* (Durham, NC: Duke University Press), 418–46.

da Cunha, D. (2002) *Singapore in the New Millennium: Challenges Facing the City-State* (Singapore: Institute of Southeast Asian Studies).

Darmon, K. (2014) 'Framing SlutWalk London: How Does the Privilege of Feminist Activism in Social Media Travel into the Mass Media?', *Feminist Media Studies*, 14(4), 700–04.

de Castella, T. and Brown, V. (2011) 'Trolling: Who Does it and Why?', *BBC*, 14 September, online.

de Haan, F., Allen, M., Purvis, J. and Daskalova, K. (2013) *Women's Activism: Global Perspectives from the 1890s to the Present* (Abingdon and New York: Routledge).

Deacon, D., Pickering, M., Golding, P., and Murdock, G. (1999) *Researching Communications: A Practical Guide to Methods in Media and Cultural Analysis* (London: Arnold).

Dean, J. (2010) 'Feminism in the Papers: Contested Feminisms in the British Quality Press,' *Feminist Media Studies* 10(4), 391–407.

Deanna (2012) *SlutWalk Winnipeg 2011 & 2012 Organiser*, Personal Interview, 30 November.

Delgado, L. (2014a) *SlutWalk Seattle 2013 & 2014 Organiser*, Personal Interview, 17 May.

Delgado, L. (2014b) *SlutWalk Seattle 2013 & 2014 Organiser*, Personal Interview, 7 September.

Della Porta, D. and Diani, M. (2006) *Social Movements: An Introduction, 2nd ed.* (Malden MA: Blackwell Publishing).

Dhillon, A. (2011) 'It Mock India's Real Issues', *Globe and Mail*, 29 July, A13.

Diani, M. and McAdam, D. (2003) *Social Movements and Networks* (Oxford: Oxford University Press).

Digby, T. (1998) *Men Doing Feminism* (New York and London: Routledge).

Dines, G. (2010) *Pornland: How Porn has Hijacked Our Sexuality* (Boston: Beacon Press).

Diondra (2013) *SlutWalk Victoria, B.C. Organiser 2013*, Personal Interview, 17 April.

Dodd, V. (2014) 'Metropolitan Police's Handling of Rape Allegations to be Reviewed', *The Guardian*, 9 June, online.

Douglas, S. (1994) *Where the Girls Are: Growing up Female with the Mass Media* (New York: Three Rivers Press).

Douglas, S. (2010) *The Rise of Enlightened Sexism: How Popular Culture Took us from Girl Power to Girls Gone Wild* (New York: St. Martin's Griffin).

Dow, B.J. (1996) *Prime-Time Feminism: Television, Media Culture, and the Women's Movement Since 1970* (Philadelphia: University of Pennsylvania Press).

Dow, B. J. (1999) 'Spectacle, Spectatorship, and Gender Anxiety in the Television Coverage of the 1970 Women's Strike for Equality', *Communication Studies*, 50, 143–57.

Dow, B.J. and Wood, J.T. (2014) 'Repeating History and Learning From It: What Can SlutWalks Teach Us About Feminism?', *Women's Studies in Communication*, 37(1), 22–43.

Downing, J. (2000) *Radical Media: Rebellious Communications and Social Movements* (Thousand Oaks: Sage Publications).

Downing, J. (2008) 'Social Movement Theories and Alternative Media: An Evaluation and Critique', *Communication, Culture & Critique*, 1, 40–50.

Drezner, D.W. and Farrell, H. (2008) 'The Power and Politics of Blogs,' *Public Choices*, 134(1–2), 15–30.

Driscoll, C. (2002) *Girls: Feminine Adolescence in Popular Culture and Cultural History* (New York: Columbia University Press).

Durham, M.G. (2013) 'Vicious Assault Shakes Texas Town', *Journalism Studies*, 14(1), 1–12.

Echo Zen (2012) 'Feminist Advocacy and Social Media (or How We Achieved Critical Mass)', *AlterNet*, 28 April, online.

Editorial (2011) 'The Overcoming of Stigma', *Globe and Mail*, 12 May, A16.

'Egypt Keeping Women Out: Sexual Violence Against Women in the Public Sphere' (2014) *FIDH, Nazra for Feminist Studies, New Women Foundation, & Uprising of Women in the Arab World*, http://www.fidh.org/IMG/pdf/egypt_women_final_english.pdf, date accessed 6 June 2014.

Ericson, R.V., Baranek, P.M., and Chan, J.B.L. (1987) *Visualising Deviance: A Study of News Organization* (Milton Keynes: Open University Press).

Facebook (2014a) 'Facebook Reports First Quarter 2014 Results', *Facebook*, online.

Facebook (2014b) 'Groups', *Facebook*, https://www.facebook.com/about/groups, date accessed 20 September 2014.

Fairclough, N. (1995) *Critical Discourse Analysis: The Critical Study of Language* (New York: Longman).

Faludi, S. (1992) *Backlash: The Undeclared War against Women* (Chatto and Windus: London).

FAQs (n.d.a) *SlutWalk Seattle*, http://slutwalkseattle.com/faqs, date accessed 3 July 2014.

FAQs (n.d.b) *SlutWalk Toronto*, http://www.slutwalktoronto.com/about/faqs, date accessed 2 July 2014.

Feeney, K. (2011) 'Proud to be a "Slut"', *Sydney Morning Herald*, 9 June, online.

Feminist Catalyst (2011) 'Why I SlutWalk(ed)', *Feminist Catalyst*, 16 May, online.

Fenton, N. (2010) 'News in the Digital Age', in S. Allan (ed.) *The Routledge companion to News and Journalism* (Routledge: Abingdon), 557–67.

'Fight rape, join first SlutWalk in G'Town' (2011) *Daily Dispatch*, 28 October, 16.

Fitzwater, A.J. (2012) 'Walking Off the Anger: SlutWalk Christchurch 2012', *Pickled Think*, 20 May, online.

Flanagan, C. (2011) 'The Trouble with SlutWalks: They Trivialize Rape', *Daily News Online*, 4 August, online.

Fondas, N. (2013) 'Rape, Steubenville, Social Media: How About Another Sort of Super Bowl Sunday?', *Ms. Magazine*, 2 February, online.

FORCE (n.d.) 'Pink Loves Consent', *FORCE: Upsetting Rape Culture*, http://upsettingrapeculture.com/pinklovesconsent.php, date accessed 6 June 2014.

FORCE (2014) 'About FORCE', *FORCE: Upsetting Rape Culture*, http://upsettingrapeculture.com/, date accessed 18 September 2014.

Forestell, N.M. and Moynagh, M. (2014) 'Introduction', in N.M. Forestell and M. Moynagh (eds.) *Documenting First Wave Feminisms: Volume II* (Toronto, Buffalo, and London: University of Toronto Press), xvii–xxi.

Foucault, M. (1980) *Language, Counter-memory, Practice: Selected Essays and Interviews By Michel Foucault* (Ed. D. Bouchard) (Cornell, NY: Cornell University Press).

Frank, A.G. and Fuentes, M. (1987) 'Nine Theses on Social Movements', *Economic & Political Weekly*, 22(35), 1503–09.

Franklin, B. (1997) *Newszak and News Media* (London: Arnold).

Franklin, B. (2008a) 'Introduction', in B. Franklin (ed.) *Pulling Newspapers Apart: Analysing Print Journalism* (London and New York: Routledge), 1–34.

Franklin, B. (2008b) *Pulling Newspapers Apart: Analysing Print Journalism* (London and New York: Routledge).

Fraser, N. (1990) 'Rethinking the Public Sphere: A Contribution to the Critique of Actually Existing Democracy', *Social Text*, 25/26, 56–80.

Fraser, S. (2011) 'An Issue that Deserved Some Solid Feminism', *Rabble.ca*, 17 May, online.

Freeman, B. (2001) *The Satellite Sex: The Media and Women's Issues in English Canada, 1966–1971* (Waterloo: Wilfred Laurier Press).

Freeman, J. (1972) 'The Tyranny of Structurelessness', *Berkeley Journal of Sociology*, 17, 151–64.

Frye, M. (1983) *The Politics of Reality: Essays in Feminist Theory* (New York: Crossing Press).

Galtung, J. and Ruge, M.H. (1965): 'The Structure of Foreign News. The Presentation of the Congo, Cuba and Cyprus Crises in Four Norwegian Newspapers,' *Journal of Peace Research*, 2, 64–91.

Gambino, L. (2014) 'NFL Toughens Policy on Domestic Violence after Criticism of Ray Rice Ban', *The Guardian*, 28 August, online.

Gamson, W.A. (1990) *The Strategy of Social Protest*, 2nd ed. (Belmont, CA: Wadsworth Publishing).

Gangoli, G. (2007) *Indian Feminisms: Law, Patriarchies and Violence in India* (Aldershot: Ashgate).

Gavey, N. (2005) *Just Sex? The Cultural Scaffolding of Rape* (Hove and New York: Routledge).

Genz, S., and Brabon, B.A. (2009) *Postfeminism: Cultural Texts and Theories* (Edinburgh: University of Edinburgh Press).

'George Galloway attacked over Assange "rape" comments', (2012) *BBC*, 20 August, online.

Gerbaudo, P. (2012) *Tweets and the Streets: Social Media and Contemporary Activism* (London: Pluto Press).

Gill, R. (2007) *Gender and the Media* (Cambridge: Polity).

Gill, R. and Scharff, C. (2011) *New Femininities: Postfeminism, Neoliberalism and Subjectivity* (London: Palgrave).

Gitlin, T. (2003) *The Whole World is Watching: Mass Media and the Making and Unmaking of the New Left* (London: University of California Press).

Global Media Monitoring Project (2010) 'Who Makes the News?' *World Association for Christian Communication*, http://whomakesthenews.org/images/stories/restricted/national/UK.pdf, date accessed 29 January 2013.

Goddu, J. (1999) '"Powerless, Public-Spirited Women", "Angry Feminists", and "The Muffin Lobby": Newspaper and Magazine Coverage of Three National Women's Groups from 1980–1995', *Canadian Journal of Communication*, 24(2), 105–26.

Goff, K. (2011) 'Dear Feminists, Will You also be Marching in N***erwalk? Because I won't', *Huffington Post (USA)*, 3 October, online.

Goldenberg, E. (2014) '80% Of Central American Women, Girls Are Raped Crossing Into The U.S', *Huffington Post*, 12 September, online.

Gornick, J.C. and Meyer, D.S. (1998) 'Changing Political Opportunity: The Anti-Rape Movement and Public Policy', *Journal of Policy History*, 10(4), 367–98.

Gorton, K. and Garde-Hansen, J. (2013) 'From Old Media Whore to New Media Troll: The Online Negotiations of Madonna's Ageing Body', *Feminist Media Studies*, 13(2), 288–302.

Gottipati, S. (2012) 'Delhi Starts Women's Hotline' *India Ink*, 31 December, http://india.blogs.nytimes.com/2012/12/31/delhi-starts-womens-hotline/?_php=true&_type=blogs&_r=0, date accessed 5 June 2014.

Govender, U. (2011) 'From the "Chief Slut" Herself...', *Mail & Guardian*, 24 August, online.

Govender, U. (2014) *SlutWalk Cape Town 2011 Organiser*, Personal Interview, 24 April.

Gramsci, A. (1971) *Selections from the Prison Notebooks* (Lawrence and Wishart Limited: London).

Gray, A. (2014a) *SlutWalk Melbourne 2012 & 2013 Organiser*, Personal Interview, 27 May.

Gray, A. (2014b) *SlutWalk Melbourne 2012 & 2013 Organiser*, Personal Interview, 8 September.

Gray, L. (2014) *SlutWalk Newcastle 2011–2013 Organiser*, Personal Interview, 19 May.

Gregg, M. (2006) 'Posting with Passion: Blogs and the Politics of Gender', in A. Bruns and J. Jacobs (eds.) *Uses of Blogs* (New York: Peter Lang) 151–60.

Griffin, M. (2011) 'SlutWalk may Damage Women's Rights Cause, Professor Says', *Sydney Morning Herald*, 13 May, online.

Grigoriadis, V. (2014) 'Meet the College Women Who Are Starting a Revolution Against Campus Sexual Assault', *New York Magazine*, 21 September, online.

Groeneveld, E. (2009) ' "Be a Feminist or Just Dress like One": BUST, Fashion and Feminism as Lifestyle', *Journal of Gender Studies*, 18(2), 179–90.

Groth, N. (2001 [1979]) *Men Who Rape: The Psychology of the Offender* (New York: Plenum Press).

Gwynne, J. (2013) 'SlutWalk, Feminist Activism and the Foreign Body in Singapore', *Journal of Contemporary Asia*, 43(1), 173–85.

Gwynne, J. and Muller, N. (2013) *Postfeminism and Contemporary Hollywood Cinema* (New York: Palgrave MacMillan).

Habermas, J. (1989) *The Structural Transformation of the Public Sphere: An Inquiry into a Category of Bourgeois Society* (Malden, MA: Polity Press).

Hall, S., Critcher, C., Jefferson, T., Clarke, J.N., and Roberts, B. (1978) *Policing the Crisis: Mugging, the State and Law and Order* (Basingstoke: Palgrave Macmillan).

Hamad, R. (2011) 'Expect No Good from SlutWalk', *Sydney Morning Herald*, 25 May, online.

Hamilton, C. (2011) '"SlutWalk" Hits Saskatoon', *CBC*, 28 May, online.

Han, K. (2011) 'No Need to Get your Knickers in a Twist', *SlutWalk Singapore*, 27 December, online.

Hancox, G. (2012) 'Marital Rape in South Africa', *Open Society Initiative for South Africa*, http://www.osisa.org/buwa/south-africa/marital-rape-south-africa, date accessed 11 June 2014.

Hanson, K. (2012) 'Slutwalk: Whatever We Wear, Wherever We Go, Yes Means Yes and No Means No!', *The F-Word*, online.

Harassmap (2013) 'How and Why We Began', *Harrassmap*, http://harrassmap.org/en/who-we-are/how-and-why-we-began/, date accessed 19 June 2014.

Harcup, T. and O'Neill, D. (2001) 'What Is News?: Galtung and Ruge Revisited', *Journalism Studies*, 2(2), 261–80.

Hare, B. (2011) 'Roman Polanski Apologises to Victim in Documentary', *CNN*, 29 September, online.

Harlow, S. (2011) 'Social Media and Social Movements: Facebook and an Online Guatemalan Justice Movement that Moved Offline', *New Media & Society*, 14(2), 225–43.

Harp, D., Loke, J. and Bachmann, I. (2014) 'Spaces for Feminist (Re)Articulations: The Blogosphere and the Sexual Attack on Journalist Lara Logan', *Feminist Media Studies*, 14(1), 5–21.

Harris, A. (2004a) *Future Girl: Young Women in the Twenty-first Century* (New York: Routledge).

Harris, A. (2004b) *All About the Girl: Culture, Power, and Identity* (New York: Routledge).

Harris, A. (2008a) *Next Wave Cultures: Feminism, Subcultures, Activism* (New York: Routledge).

Harris, A. (2008b) 'Young women, late modern politics, and the participatory possibilities of online cultures', *Journal of Youth Studies*, 11(5), 481–95.

Hart, R. (2012) 'Jill Meagher, SlutWalk and Reclaim the Night Sydney Road', *Dangers Untold and Hardships Unnumbered*, 28 September, online.

Harzewski, S. (2011) *Chicklit and Postfeminism* (Charlottesville and London: University of Virginia Press).

Hasinoff, A.A. (2009) 'It's Sociobiology, Hon!: Genetic Gender Determinism in *Cosmopolitan* Magazine', *Feminist Media Studies*, 9(3), 267–84.

Haugen, M. (2014) *SlutWalk Vancouver 2013 & 2014 Organiser*, Personal Interview, 11 April.

Heather (2011) 'From the Ground Up: A Response to an Open Letter and the Beginning of an Action Plan for Better Work with our Communities', *SlutWalk Toronto*, 17 October, online.

Hemmings, C. (2005) 'Telling Feminist Stories' *Feminist Theory*, 6(2), 115–39.

Henry, A. (2004) *Not My Mother's Sister: Generational Conflict and Third-Wave Feminism* (Bloomington & Indianapolis: Indiana University Press).

Hepola, S. (2012) 'A Woman Like no Other', *New York Times*, 8 March, 9–10.

Herman, D.F. (1978) 'The Rape Culture,' in J. Freeman (ed) *Women: A Feminist Perspectives* (Mountain View, CA: Mayfield), 41–63.

Herring, S., Scheidt, L.A., Kouper, I., and Wright, E. (2002) 'Longitudinal Content Analysis of Blogs: 2003–2004', in M. Tremayne (ed.) *Blogging, Citizenship and the Future of Media* (London and New York: Routledge), 3–19.

Heywood, L. and Drake, J. (1997) *Third Wave Agenda: Being Feminist, Doing Feminism* (Minneapolis and London: University of Minnesota Press).

Hill Collins, P. (2000) *Black Feminist Thought: Knowledge, Consciousness and the Politics of Empowerment, 2nd ed.* (New York and London: Routledge).

Hinds, H. and Stacey, J. (2001) 'Imaging Feminism, Imaging Femininity: The Bra-Burner, Diana, and the Woman Who Kills', *Feminist Media Studies*, 1(2), 153–77.

Hine, C. (2000) *Virtual Ethnography* (London: Sage).

Ho, C. (2014) 'U of C Bar Trains Staff in Sexual Assault Prevention', *The Calgary Herald*, 1 October, online.

Ho, V. (2012) *SlutWalk Singapore 2011 & 2012 Organiser*, Personal Interview, 6 December.

Hole, J. and Levine, E. (1971) *The Rebirth of Feminism* (New York: Quadrangle).

Hollaback! (2014) 'About', *Hollaback!* http://www.ihollaback.org/about/, date accessed 19 June 2014.

Hollows, J. and Moseley, R. (2006) *Feminism in Popular Culture* (New York: Berg Publisher).

Holman, R. (2013) 'The Rise and Fall of America's Most Infamous "Male Feminist": Hugo Schwyzer', *The Telegraph*, 27 September, online.

Holzman, C.G. (1994) 'Mulicultural Perspectives on Counselling Survivors of Rape,' *Journal of Social Distress and the Homeless*, 3(1), 87–97.

hooks, b. (1984) *Feminist Theory: From Margin to Centre* (Cambridge, MA: South End Press).

hooks, b. (1989) *Talking Back: Thinking Feminist, Thinking Black* (Boston, MA: Southend Press).

hooks, b. (2000) *Feminism is for Everyone: Passionate Politics* (New York and London: Routledge).

Hope, E. (2011) 'Rally to Counter Sexual Aassault', *Hobart Mercury*, 11 November, 15.

Ideologically Impure (2012) 'What did You Expect, Wearing Trackpants like That?', *Ideologically Impure*, 7 May, online.

'India's "Slutwalk" Brings Tamer, Smaller Crowd' (2011) *CBC*, 31 July, online.

'India "Slutwalk" Sex Harassment Protest in Delhi' (2011) *BBC*, 31 July, online.

It's On Us (2014) *It's On Us*, http://itsonus.org, date accessed 24 September 2014.

Izrael, J. (2011) 'I Am Amber Cole's Father', *Jezebel*, 25 October, online.

Jacquet, C. (2010) ' "Where are All the Feminists?" The Joan Little Case and Anti-Rape Activism During the 1970s', *Thinking Gender Papers* (Los Angeles: UCLA Centre for the Study of Women).

Jaggar, A.M. (1983) *Feminist Politics and Human Nature* (New Jersey: Rowman & Allanheld).

Jamel, J. (2014) 'Do the Print Media Provide a Gender-Biased Representation of Male Rape Victims?', *Internet Journal of Criminology*, http://www.internet-journalofcriminology.com/Jamel_Print_Media_Representation_of_Male_Rape_Survivors_IJC_Jan_2014.pdf, date accessed 26 June 2014.

Jane, E.J. (2014) '"Your a Ugly, Whorish Slut": Understanding E-bile', *Feminist Media Studies*, 14(4), 531–46.

Järvinen, J., Kail, A., and Miller, I. (2008) *Hard Knock Life: Violence Against Women – a Guide for Donors and Funders* (London: New Philanthropy Capital).

Jarvis, H. (2012) *SlutWalk Toronto Co-Founder and 2011–2014 Organiser*, Personal Interview, 7 December.

Jasper, J.M. (1997) *The Art of Moral Protest: Culture, Biography, and Creativity in Social Movements* (Chicago: University of Chicago Press).

Jaworska, S. and Krishnamurthy, R. (2012) 'On the F Word: A Corpus Based Analysis of the Media Representation of Feminism in British and German Press Discourse, 1990–2009', *Discourse & Society*, 23(4), 401–31.

Jayawardena, K. (1986) *Feminism and Nationalism in the Third World* (London: Zed Books).

Jefferson, W. (2011) 'A Glimpse at SlutWalks Across the Globe', *Jezebel*, 3 October, online.

Jenni (2010) 'Feminist Self-Defence', *Bad Reputation*, 8 December, online.

Jones, J. and Saad, L. (2013) 'TV Is Americans' Main Source of News' *Gallup Politics*, 8 July, online.

Jones, L. (2011) 'Class is the Real Problem, Sisters, Not Slutty Clothes', *Mail on Sunday*, 6 June, online.

Joseph, A. (2005) *Making News: Women in Journalism* (Delhi: Konark Publishers).

Juris, J.S. (2008) *Networking Futures: The Movements Against Corporate Globalization* (Durham, NC: Duke University Press).

Juris, J.S. (2012) 'Reflections On #Occupy Everywhere: Social Media, Public Space, and Emerging Logics of Aggregation', *American Ethnologist*, 39(2), 259–79.

Kaaber, E.S.O. (2014) 'Eleven Thousand Attend Fourth Annual SlutWalk', *Iceland Review Online*, 28 July, online.

Kapur, R. (2012) 'Pink Chaddis and SlutWalk Couture: The Postcolonial Politics of Feminism Lite', *Feminist Legal Studies*, 20(1), 1–20.

Karlsson, L. (2007) 'Desperately Seeking Sameness: The Processes and Pleasures of Identification in Women's Diary Blog Reading,' *Feminist Media Studies*, 7(2), 137–53.

Keller, J.M. (2011) 'Virtual Feminisms', *Information, Communication & Society*, 15(3), 429–47.

Keller, J.M. (2013) '"Still Alive and Kicking": Girl Bloggers and Feminist Politics in a "Postfeminist" Age', PhD Dissertation (Austin: University of Texas at Austin).

Keller, J.M. (2015) *Girls' Feminist Blogging in a Postfeminist Age* (New York: Routledge).

Keller, J.M. (forthcoming 2016) 'Making Activism Accessible: Exploring Girls' Blogs as Sites of Contemporary Feminist Activism', in C. Mitchell and C. Rentschler (eds.) *The Politics of Place: Contemporary Paradigms for Research in Girlhood Studies* (New York: Berghahn Books).

Kingkade, T. (2014) 'Yes, Rape Culture Is Real, And Here is What It Looks Like', *Huffington Post*, 31 March, online.

Kingsley, P. (2014) 'Egypt Criminalizes Sexual Harassment for the First Time', *BBC*, 6 June, http://www.theguardian.com/world/2014/jun/06/egypt-criminalises-sexual-harassment, date accessed 6 June 2014.

Kitchens, C. (2013) 'The Rape "Epidemic" Doesn't Actually Exist', *US News*, 24 October, online.

Kitchens, C. (2014) 'It's Time To End "Rape Culture" Hysteria', *Time*, 20 March, online.

Kitzinger, J. (2009) 'Rape in the Media', in M. Horvath and J. Brown (eds.) *Rape: Challenging Contemporary Thinking* (Cullompton, UK and Portland, USA: Willan Publishing), 74–98.

'Kiwis Plan to Join "SlutWalk" Crusade' (2011) *Sunday Star-Times*, 8 May, online.

Kolesova, E.K. (2013) 'Defending Pussy Riot Metonymically: The Trial Representations, Media and Social Movements in Russia and the United States', MA Dissertation (Austin: University of Texas at Austin).

Kozinets, R.V. (2010) *Netnography: Doing Ethnographic Research Online* (London, Thousand Oaks and New Delhi: Sage).

Kraus, K. (2011) 'SlutWalk: Changing a "Don't Get Raped" Culture to a "Don't Rape" Culture', *Rabble.ca*, 5 April, online.

Krippendorff, K. (2004) *Content Analysis: An Introduction to Its Methodology* (Thousand Oaks: Sage Publications).

Kwan, R. (2011) 'Don't Dress Like a Slut: Toronto Cop', *Excalibur*, 8 February, http://www.excal.on.ca/dont-dress-like-a-slut-toronto-cop/, date accessed 5 June 2014.

Lady News (2011a) 'Blame the Rapist', *Lady News*, 26 May, online.

Lady News (2011b) 'SlutWalk' *Lady News*, 24 June, online.

Lazar, M. (2005) *Feminist Critical Discourse Analysis: Gender, Power and Ideology in Discourse* (Basingstoke: Palgrave MacMillan).

Lazar, M. (2011) 'The Right to Be Beautiful: Postfeminist Identity and Consumer Beauty Advertising', in R. Gill and C. Scharff (eds.) *New Femininities: Postfeminism, Neoliberalism and Subjectivity* (Basingstoke and New York: Palgrave), 37–51.

Laïcité (2011) 'Reclaiming the Word "Slut"', *SlutWalk Singapore*, 16 October, online.

Levy, A. (2005) *Female Chauvenist Pigs: Women and the Rise of Raunch Culture* (New York: Free Press).

Lewis, H. (2012) 'Game Theory: Making Room for Women', *The New York Times*, 25 December, online.

Lim, J. (2011) 'Slutty? We're Just Sexy', *The New Paper*, 31 October, online.

Lim, M. (2013) 'Many Clicks But Little Sticks: Social Media Activism in Indonesia', *Journal of Contemporary Asia*, 43(4), 636–57.

Lim, T. (2011) 'When Naïve Girls Would be Sluts', *The Strait Times*, 20 June, n.p.

Lind, R.A. and Salo, C. (2002) 'The Framing of Feminists and Feminism in News and Public Affairs Programs in U.S. Electronic Media', *Journal of Communication*, 52(1), 211–27.

Lipsticklori (2011) 'Let's Talk about Slutwalk London', *Rarely Wears Lipstick*, 14 June, online.

Lisak, D. (1994) 'The Psychological Impact of Sexual Abuse: Content Analysis of Interviews with Male Survivors', *Journal of Traumatic Stress*, 7(4), 525–48.

Lisak, D., Gardinier, L., Nicksa, S.C., and Cote, A.M. (2010) 'False Allegation of Sexual Assault: An Analysis of Ten Years of Reported Cases', *Violence Against Women*, 16(12), 1318–34.

Little, A. (2103) '#FBrape Campaign Takes on Facebook Misogyny and Wins!', *Ms. Magazine*, 30 May, http://msmagazine.com/blog/2013/05/30/fbrape-campaign-takes-on-facebook-misogyny-and-wins/, date accessed 19 September 2014.

London Feminist Network (2014) 'Reclaim the Night', *London Feminist Network*, http://londonfeministnetwork.org.uk/lfn-events/reclaim-the-night, date accessed 11 June 2014.

MacAskill, A. (2013) 'Defence Lawyer in New Delhi Rape Case Blames Victim; Claims he's Never Heard of "Respected" Lady Getting Raped in India', *National Post*, 9 January, online.

MacDonald, C. (2014) *SlutWalk Vancouver 2013 & 2014 Organiser*, Personal Interview, 11 April.

Macdonald, M. (1995) *Representing Women: Myths of Femininity in the Popular Media* (London and New York: Edward Arnold).

MacDonald, S. (2014) *SlutWalk Cape Town 2011 Organiser*, Personal Interview, 17 May.

Mackay, F. (2012) *Reclaim the Night London Organiser*, Personal Interview, 6 September.

Mackay, F. (2014) 'Mapping the Routes: An Exploration of Charges of Racism Made Against the 1970s UK Reclaim the Night Marches', *Women's Studies International Forum*, 44(May-June), 46–64.

MacKinnon, A. (2011) 'Misogynist Social Attitude' *Toronto Star*, 1 April, A18.

Maddison, S. (2013a) 'SlutWalking: Where is the Next Generation of Feminists?', in S. Maddison and M. Sawer (eds.) *The Women's Movement in Protest, Institutions and the Internet: Australia in Transnational Perspective* (Abingdon and New York: Routledge), 132–48.

Maddison, S. (2013b) 'Discursive Politics: Changing the Ttalk and Raising Expectations', in S. Maddison and M. Sawer (eds.) *The Women's Movement in Protest, Institutions and the Internet: Australia in Transnational Perspective* (Abingdon and New York: Routledge), 37–53.

Madianou, M. (2013) 'Humanitarian Campaigns in Social Media', *Journalism Studies*, 14(2), 249–66.

Maggie (2011) 'SlutWalk and the Legacy of White Feminism', *Where Is Your Line?* 7 November.

Maggie (2012) 'SlutWalk and the Legacy of White Feminism', *Where Is Your Line?* 11 July, online.

Maitse, T. (1998) 'Political Change, Rape, and Pornography in Post-apartheid South Africa', *Gender and Development*, 6(3), 55–9.

Mahajan, E., and Roy Chowdhury, S. (2011) '"Sluts" Walk for Safer Delhi', *Times of India*, 1 August, n.p.

Mandell, N. (2011) '"SlutWalks" Fight Back against Stigma Surrounding Sexual Assault and Rape Victims', *Daily News Online*, 6 May, online.

Manning, B. (2013) 'Roast Busters: Protest Today Aims to "Bust Rape Culture"', *New Zealand Herald*, 16 November, http://www.nzherald.co.nz/nz/news/article. cfm?c_id=1&objectid=11158233, date accessed 6 June 2014.

Marmura, S. (2008) 'A Net Advantage?: The Internet, Grassroots Activism and America-Middle Eastern Policy', *New Media & Society*, 10(2), 247–71.

Marturano, M. (2013) *SlutWalk NYC Organiser 2011*, Personal Interview, 12 April.

Marwick, A.E., and boyd, d.m. (2011) 'To See and Be Seen: Celebrity Practice on Twitter', *Convergence*, 17(2), 139–58.

Matthews, N. (1989) 'Surmounting a Legacy: The Expansion of Racial Diversity in a Local Anti-Rape Movement', *Gender & Society*, 3(4), 518–32.

Matthews, N. (2005) *Confronting Rape: The Feminist Anti-rape Movement and the State* (London and New York: Routledge).

Mayne, A. (2003) 'Feminism and the Anti-Rape Movement', in D.E.H. Russell (ed.) *Lives of Courage: Women for a new South Africa* (Lincoln, NE: iUniverse).

McArthur, G. (2011) 'Women Walk the Talk after Officer's Offending "Slut" Remarks', *Globe and Mail Online*, 4 April, online.

McCaughey, M. (1997) *Real Knockouts: The Physical Feminism of Women's Self-defense* (New York: NYU Press).

McCormack, C. and Prostran, N. (2012) 'Asking for It: A First-hand Account from SlutWalk', *International Feminist Journal of Politics*, 14(3), 410–14.

McDuff, R., Pernell, D., and Saunders, K. (1977) 'Letter to the Anti-rape Movement', *Off Our Backs*, 7(5), 9–10.

McKinley, J.C. (2011) 'Vicious Assault Shakes Texas Town', *The New York Times*, 8 March, online.

McKinney, D. (2006) 'Reporting on Rape Trauma', in R. Simpson and W.E. Cote (eds.) *Covering Violence* (New York: Columbia University Press), 201–21.

McManus, J. and Dorfman, L. (2005) 'Functional Truth or Sexist Distortion? Assessing a Feminist Critique of Intimate Violence Reporting', *Journalism*, 6(1), 43–65.

McNair, B. (2008) 'I, Columnist', in B. Franklin (ed.) *Pulling Newspapers Apart: Analysing Print Journalism* (London and New York: Routledge), 112–20.

McNickle Rose, V. (1977) 'Rape as a Social Problem: A By-product of the Feminist Movement', *Social Problems*, 25(1), 75–89.

McNicol, L. (2012) 'SlutWalk is "Kind of Like Feminism": A Critical Reading of Canadian Mainstream News Coverage of SlutWalk', MA Thesis (Kingston: Queens University).

McNicol, L. (2015) 'A Critical Reading of SlutWalk in the News: Reproducing Postfeminism and Whiteness', in K. Silva and K. Mendes (eds.) *Feminist Erasures: Challenging Backlash Culture* (Basingstoke: Palgrave), 235–57.

McRobbie, A. (2007) 'Postfeminism and Popular Culture: Bridget Jones and the New Gender Regime', in Y. Tasker and D. Negra (eds.) *Interrogating Post-Feminism* (Durham and London: Duke University Press), 27–39.

McRobbie, A. (2009) *The Aftermath of Feminism: Gender, Culture and Social Change* (Los Angeles, London, New Delhi, Singapore and Washington, D.C.: Sage).

McVeigh, T. (2011) 'SlutWalk – Wrong Message, Poor Taste, or Great Idea?', *The Observer*, 15 May, 24.

Meagher, T. (2014) 'The Dangers of the Monster Myth', *White Ribbon Campaign*, 17 April, online.

Media Insight Project (2014) 'The Personal News Cycle: How Americans Choose to Get their News', *American Press Institute*, 17 March, online.

Mendes, K. (2011a) *Feminism in the News: Representations of the Women's Movement Since the 1960s* (Basingstoke: Palgrave).

Mendes, K. (2011b) 'The Lady is a Closet Feminist!: Discourses of Backlash and Postfeminism in British and American Newspapers', *International Journal of Cultural Studies*, 14(6), 1–17.

Mendes, K. (2012) '"Feminism Rules! Now, Where's My Swimsuit?" Re-evaluating Feminist Discourse in Print Media 1968–2008', *Media, Culture & Society*, 34(5), 554–70.

Mendes, K. (2015) 'SlutWalk, Feminism and News', in K. Silva and K. Mendes (eds.) *Feminist Erasures: Challenging Backlash Culture* (Basingstoke: Palgrave MacMillan), 219–34.

Mendes, K., Ringrose, J. and Keller, J.M. (2014) 'Documenting Digital Feminist Activism: Mapping Online Misogyny and Rape Culture', *AHRC Grant*.

Meyer, A. (2010) '"Too Drunk to Say No": Binge Drinking, Rape and the *Daily Mail*', *Feminist Media Studies*, 10(1), 19–34.

Meyer, H. (2011) 'Why I'm Marching in the Slutwalk: Time for New York's Women to Speak out Against Rape', *Daily News*, 1 October, online.

Meyers, M. (1997) *News Coverage of Violence Against Women* (Thousand Oaks: Sage).

Meyers, M. (2006) 'News of Battering', *Journal of Communication*, 44(2), 47–63.

Midgley, C. (2013) 'I don't Give a Monkey's …', *The Times*, 23 February, M14.

Mills, K. (1997) 'What Difference Do Women Journalists Make?', in P. Norris (ed.) *Women, Media and Politics* (New York: Oxford University Press), 41–56.

Miranda (2011a) 'Chicagoans Organize Around Cases of Police Violence', *Where Is Your Line?* 14 June, online.

Miranda (2011b) 'Why We Need SlutWalk', *Where Is Your Line?* 15 May, online.

Miriam (2011) 'SlutWalk in Mexico City: We Have Many Reasons to March', *Feministing*, 29 June, online.

Mitchell, A., Kiley, J., Gottfried, J., & Guskin, E. (2013) 'The Role of News on Facebook', *PEW Research Journalism Project*, 24 October, http://www.journalism.org/2013/10/24/the-role-of-news-on-facebook/, date accessed 12 September 2014.

Mitchell, C. and Reid-Walsh, J. (2004) 'Girls' Web Sites: A Virtual "Room of One's Own"?' in A. Harris (ed.) *All About the Girl: Culture, Power, and Identity* (New York: Routledge), 173–82.

Mitra, A. (2013) *Voices of Privilege and Sacrifice from Women Volunteers in India: I Can Change* (Lanham: Lexington Books).

'MLB Meets with Groups on Domestic Violence Policy' (2014) *Yahoo News*, 24 September, online.

Moffett, H. (2006) 'These Women, They Force Us to Rape Them: Rape as Narrative of Social Control in Post-apartheid South Africa', *Journal of Southern African Studies*, 32(1), 129–44.

Mohanty, C.T. (2003) '"Under Western Eyes" Revisited: Feminist Solidarity through Anticapitalist Struggles', *Signs*, 28(2), 499–535.

Molotch, H.L. (1978) 'The News of Women and the Works of Men', in G. Tuchman, A.K. Daniels, and J. Bennett (eds.) *Hearth and Home: Images of Women in the Mass Media* (New York: Oxford University Press).

Moodie, D. (2011) 'Getting Past the Word "Slut"', *Huffington Post*, 7 October, online.

Moore, S. (2011) 'Being a Slut, to My Mind, was Mostly Fun – Wearing and Doing What you Liked', *The Guardian Online*, 14 May, online.

Moore, S.E.H. (2011) 'Tracing the Life of a Crime Category', *Feminist Media Studies*, 11(4), 451–65.

Moorti, S. (2002) *Color of Rape: Gender and Race in Television's Public Sphere* (New York: State University of New York Press).

Morrell, S. (2011) 'Protest is Misplaced in PC Fervour', *Herald Sun*, 27 May, 35.

Morris, M.B. (1973a) 'The Public Definition of a Social Movement: Women's Liberation', *Sociology and Social Research*, 57(4), 526–43.

Morris, M.B. (1973b) 'Newspapers and the New Feminists: Black-Out as Social Control?' *Journalism and Mass Communication Quarterly*, 50(1), 37–42.

Mowles, J.M. (2008) 'Framing Issues, Fomenting Change, "Feministing": A Contemporary Feminist Blog in the Landscape of Online Political Activism', *International Reports On Socio-Informatics*, 52, 29–49.

Mposo, N. (2011) 'SlutWalk is Coming to SA', *Daily News*, 6 June, 5.

Munford, R. and Waters, M. (2014) *Postfeminism and Popular Culture: Investigating the Postfeminist Mystique* (London and New York: I.B. Tauris).

Murphy, M. (2011a) 'Grasping at Straws: Comparing SlutWalk an Occupy Wall Street', *Feminist Current*, 16 October, online.

Murphy, M. (2011b) 'SlutWalk NYC: More of the Same', *Feminist Current*, 3 October, online.

Murphy, M. (2011c) 'A Progressive Dialogue: Building a Progressive Feminist Movement in Neo-liberal Times', *Rabble.ca*, 28 October, online.

Murphy, M. (2012a) 'SlutWalk One Year Later: A Movement or a Moment?', *Rabble.ca*, 1 June, online.

Murphy, M. (2012b) 'Safer strolls: A New, Progressive Way to Blame the Victim?', *Feminist Current*, 14 March, online.

Murphy, M. (2012c) 'Breaking! SlutWalk is About Spectacle, Individual Empowerment, Wearing Sexy Lingerie, Says Everyone with Eyes and Brains', *Feminist Current*, 9 August, online.

Murphy, M. (2012d) 'The Naked Protestor (or, How to Get the Media to Pay Attention to Women)', *Feminist Current*, 31 January, online.

Murphy, M. (2012e) 'Liberal Feminists Realize that Feminism is a Movement after All. Confusion Ensues', *Feminist Current*, 26 June, online.

Murphy, M. (2012f) 'SlutWalk Vancouver Keeps it Real', *Feminist Current*, 5 July, online.

Murtha, T. (2013) 'SlutWalk Philly Changes Protest Name to "A March to End Rape Culture"', *RH Reality Check*, 26 September, online.

Nair, Y. (2012) 'Is Slutwalk the End of Feminism?', *Yasmin Nair*, 6 June, online.

Ndlovu, Z. (2011) 'Why I Won't be at SlutWalk', *Mail & Guardian*, 22 August, online.

Negra, D. (2008) *What a Girl Wants? Fantasizing the Reclamation of Self in Postfeminism* (Abingdon and New York: Routledge).

Nelson, D. (2014) 'Delhi's Rape Hotline Faces Closure', *The Telegraph*, 4 March, http://www.telegraph.co.uk/news/worldnews/asia/india/10675511/Delhis-rape-hotline-faces-closure.html, date accessed 11 June 2014.

'New Delhi "SlutWalk" Brings Global Sexual Violence Protest Phenomenon to India' (2011) *Huffington Post*, 10 June, online.

Nicholson, Z. (2011) 'Anti-rape Campaign Coming to City Streets', *Cape Times*, 10 August, 6.

Nkosi, M. (2012) 'South Africa Mini Dkirt March in Protest Over Attacks', *BBC*, 17 February, online.

North L. (2009) *The Gendered Newsroom: How Journalists Experience the Changing World of Media* (New York: Hampton Press).

O'Brien, S. (2011) 'Ladies and Friends will Dress to Tramp Melbourne Joins Global Protests Over Violence Against Women', *Herald Sun*, 11 May, 5.

O'Keefe, T. (2011) 'Flaunting Our Way to Freedom? SlutWalks, Gender Protest and Feminist Futures', *New Agendas in Social Movement Studies*, Conference Proceedings, National University of Ireland Maynooth, 24–26 November.

Ogilvy Public Relations Worldwide (2011) 'Dynamics of Cause Engagement: Understanding the Impact of the Digital Revolution on Cause Engagement', *The Center for Social Impact Communications at Georgetown University*, http://www.slideshare.net/georgetowncsic/dynamics-of-cause-engagement-final-report, date accessed 4 September 2014.

Onstad, K. (2011) 'Feminism and Fashion: The Other Two Solitudes', *The Globe and Mail*, 16 April, L14.

Panahi, R. (2012) 'Slutwalk's Priorities Misplaced', *Herald Sun*, 5 September, 39.

Parkins, I. (2008) 'Building a Feminist Theory of Fashion', *Australian Feminist Media Studies*, 23(58), 501–15.

Pearce, M. (2014) 'Indiana Judge Assailed for Light Sentence in Husband-wife Rape Case', *LA Times*, 20 May, online.

Pearce, R. (2012) 'Speak out Against Rape with Slutwalk and Reclaim the Night', *Lesbilicious*, 25 August, online.

Penney, J. and Dadas, C. (2014) '(Re)Tweeting in the Service of Protest: Digital Composition and Circulation in the Occupy Wall Street Movement', *New Media and Society*, 16(1), 74–90.

Penny, L. (2013) *Cybersexism: Sex, Gender and Power on the Internet* (London: Bloomsbury Publishing, Kindle Edition).

Perlmutter, D.D. (2008) *Blog Wars* (Oxford: Oxford University Press).

Peterson, L. (2011) 'SlutWalk, Slutslurs and Why Feminism Still Has Race Issues', *Racialicious*, 6 October, online.

Petro, M. (2011) 'The H-Word: Who You Calling a Hooker?', *Bitch Media*, 3 November, online.

Phillips, M. (2011) 'These "SlutWalks" Prove Feminism is Now Irrelevant to Most Women's Lives', *Daily Mail*, 13 June, online.

Piepmeier, A. (2009) *Girl Zines: Making Media, Doing Feminism* (New York: NYU Press).

Pillay-Siokos, K. (2013) *SlutWalk Johanessburg 2013 Organiser*, Personal Interview, 25 May.

Pingree, S. and Hawkins, R.P. (1978) 'News Definitions and Their Effects on Women', in L.K. Epstein (ed.) *Woman and the News* (New York: Hasting House), 116–35.

Pinto, V. (2012) 'Slutwalk SF Says no to Victim Blaming', *Huffington Post*, 14 September, online.

Piven, F.F. and Cloward, R.A. (1977) *Poor People's Movements: How they succeed, how they fail* (USA: Vintage Books).

Plaid, A. (2011) 'Does Slutwalk Speak to Women of Color?', *Alternet*, 22 June, online.

Poindexter, P., Meraz, S., and Schmitt Weiss, A. (2008) *Women, Men and News: Divided in Disconnected in the News Media Landscape* (Abingdon and New York: Routledge).

Posadzki, A. (2012) 'Hundreds March in Toronto SlutWalk to Combat Sexual Violence', *Globe and Mail*, 25 May, online.

Postill, J. and Pink, S. (2012) 'Social Media Ethnography: The Digital Researcher in a Messy Web', *Media International Australia*, 145(November), 123–34.

Powell, K. (2011) 'When Skirts Break the Law', *The News With Nipples*, 18 May, online.

Projansky, S. (2001) *Watching Rape: Film and Television in Postfeminist Culture* (New York: New York University Press).

Projansky, S. (2007) 'Mass Magazine Cover Girls: Some Reflections on Postfeminist Girls and Postfeminisms' Daughters', in Y. Tasker and D. Negra (eds.) *Interrogating Post-Feminism* (Durham and London: Duke University Press), 40–72.

Prominski, J. (2012) '"Real Men Don't Rape": The Sexual Politics of Anti-rape Campaigns', *5th Annual Undergraduate Research Conference*, Conference Proceedings, Nippissing University, 23–24 March.

Puente, S.N. (2011) 'Feminist Cyberactivism: Violence Against Women, Internet Politics and Spanish Feminist Praxis Online', *Continuum: Journal of Media and Cultural Studies*, 25(3), 333–46.

Purcell, C. (2011) 'It's My Fault Because I Had a Drink? How Being Sexually Assaulted Introduced Me to Victim-Blaming Culture', *AlterNet*, 5 December, online.

RAINN (2009a) *RAINN*, https://www.rainn.org/get-help/national-sexual-assault-online-hotline, date accessed 11 June 2014.

RAINN (2009b) 'The Offenders', *RAINN*, https://www.rainn.org/get-information/statistics/sexual-assault-offenders, date accessed 16 September 2014.

'Rape and sexual assault: The hidden side of Egypt's protests' (2013) *Euronews*, 4 July, http://www.euronews.com/2013/07/04/rape-and-sexual-assault-the-hidden-side-of-egypts-protests/, date accessed 10 June 2014.

Rapp, L., Button, D.M., Fleufy-Steiner, B., and Fleury-Steiner, R. (2010) 'The Internet as a Tool for Black Feminist Activism: Lessons From an Online Antirape Protest', *Feminist Criminology*, 5(3), 244–62.

Reclaim the Night Australia (2014) *Reclaim the Night Australia*, http://www.isis.aust.com/rtn/, date accessed 11 June 2014.

Redfern, C. and Aune, K. (2010) *Reclaiming the F-Word: The New Feminist Movement* (London and New York: Zed Books).

Reed, J. (1997) 'Roseanne: A "Killer Bitch" for Generation X', in L. Heywood and J. Drake (eds.) *Third Wave Agenda: Being Feminist, Doing Feminism* (Minneapolis and London: University of Minnesota Press), 122–33.

Reese, S.D. (2001) 'Prologue – Framing Public Life: A Bridging Model for Media Research', in S.D. Reese, O.H. Gandy, and A.E. Grant (eds.) *Framing Public Life: Perspectives on Media and our Understanding of the Social World* (Mahwah, NJ: Lawrence Erlbaum Associates), 7–32.

Rentschler, C.A. (2014) 'Rape Culture and the Feminist Politics of Social Media', *Girlhood Studies*, 7(1), 65–82.

Rhode, D.L. (1995) 'Media Images, Feminist Issues,' *Signs: A Journal of Women, Culture and Society*, 20(3), 685–711.

Rii (2012) 'I Plan to Wear a Sari at the SlutWalk', *Times of India*, 24 May, online.

Ringrose, J. and Renold, E. (2012) 'Slut-shaming, Girl Power and "Sexualisation": Thinking Through the Politics of the International SlutWalks with Teen Girls', *Gender and Education*, 24(3), 333–43.

Robertson, R. (1995) 'Glocalization: Time-Space and Homogeneity-Heterogeneity', in M. Featherstone, S. Lash, and R. Robertson (eds.) *Global Modernities* (London, Thousand Oaks and New Delhi: Sage), 25–43.

Robertson, L. (2009) 'Whoopi on Roman Polansky: It wasn't "Rape-rape"', *Jezebel*, 28 September, online.

Robinson, V. (2011) 'Anti-rape Marchers Walk Tall', *Sunday Star-Times*, 26 June, 7.

Rogers, K. (2011) 'SlutWalk: Is a Woman's Body the Best Way to Get a Feminist Point Across?', *The Washington Post*, 6 June, online.

Rohlinger, D. (2002) 'Framing the Abortion Debate: Organizational Resources, Media Strategies, and Movement-Counter Movement Dynamics', *The Sociological Quarterly*, 43(4), 479–507.

Roiphe, K. (1994) *The Morning After: Fear, Sex & Feminism* (Boston: Back Bay Books).

Rosenthall, M. (2001) 'Danger Talk: Race and Empowerment in the New South Africa', in K.M. Blee, and T.F. Vinddance (eds.) *Feminism and Antiracism: International Struggles for Justice* (New York: New Your University Press), 97–124.

Ross, J. (2014) 'This Girl Was Sent Home From School For Her Outfit. Her Mom's Response Was Incredible', *Identities.Mic*, 16 June, online.

Ross, S. (2011) 'BadRep goes SlutWalking', *Bad Reputation*, 22 June, online.

Roy, J. (2014) 'Columbia Student will Carry a Mattress with her Everywhere she goes Until her Alleged Rapist is Expelled', *New York Magazine*, 2 September, online.

Roy, N.S. (2011) 'Ready or Not, New Delhi Gets a Women's Street Protest', *New York Times*, 14 June, online.

Rozee, P. (1999) 'Stranger Rape', in M.A. Paludi (ed.) *The Psychology of Sexual Victimization: A Handbook* (Westport, CT: Greenwood Press), 97–116.

Sanford, T. and Fetter, A. (1979) *In Defense of Ourselves* (Garden City, NY: Doubleday).

Sarkeesian, A. (2011) 'Feminist Critiques of SlutWalk', *Feminist Frequency*, 16 May, online.

Sawer, M. (2013) 'Finding the Women's Movement', in S. Maddison and M. Sawer (eds.) *The Women's Movement in Protest, Institutions and the Internet: Australia in Transnational Perspective* (Abingdon and New York: Routledge), 1–19.

Scharff, C. (2012) *Repudiating Feminism: Young Women in a Neoliberal World* (Farnham: Ashgate).

Schreiber, M. (2014) *American Postfeminist Cinema: Women, Romance and Contemporary Culture* (Edinburgh: Edinburgh University Press).

Schutte, G. (2011) 'Stop Telling Women What to Wear', *Cape Times*, 29 August, 9.

Schwartz, M. (2014) 'Why Feeding Online Trolls Only Feeds Online Trolling', *Huffington Post*, 8 September, online.

Schwyzer, H. (2011) 'SlutWalk LA: Brief Initial Recap', *Hugo Schwyzer*, 4 June, online.

Schwyzer, H. (2014) *SlutWalk LA 2011 Organiser*, Personal Interview, 9 April.

Scully, D. and Marolla, J. (1985) '"Riding the Bull at Gilley's": Convicted Rapists Describe the Rewards of Rape', *Social Problems*, 32(3), 251–63.

Searles, P. and Berger, R.J. (1987) 'The Feminist Self-Defence Movement: A Case Study', *Gender & Society*, 1(1), 61–84.

Seltzer, S. and Kelley, L. (2011) '"Hey Rapists, Go Fuck Yourselves": SlutWalk Arrives in NYC', *AlterNet*, 3 Oct., online.

Selva-Thomson, A. (2011) 'Yes Means Yes and No Means No, Whether I am Wearing a Thong or a Chastity Belt', *SlutWalk Singapore*, 22 October, online.

Sharma, S. (2014) 'Need for a Rape Crisis Centre!', *Feminia*, http://femina.in/lifestyle/in-the-news/need-for-a-rape-crisis-centre-1647.html, date accessed 11 June 2014.

Shaw, F. (2011) '(Dis)locating Feminisms: Blog Activism as Crisis Response', *Outskirts*, 24 May, http://www.outskirts.arts.uwa.edu.au/volumes/volume-24/shaw, date accessed 5 May 2013.

Shaw, F. (2012a) 'Discursive Politics Online: Political Creativity and Affective Networking in Australian Feminist Blogs', PhD Thesis (Sydney: University of New South Wales)

Shaw, F. (2012b) '"Hottest 100 Women": Cross-Platform Discursive Activism in Feminist Blogging Networks', *Australia Feminist Studies*, 27(74), 373–87.

Shaw, F. (2012c) 'The Politics of Blogs: Theories of Discursive Activism Online', *Media International Australia*, 142, 41–9.

Shaw, F. (2013) '"These Wars are Personal:" Methods and Theory in Online Feminist Research', *Qualitative Research Journal*, 13(1), 90–101.

Shaw, M. (2011) 'SlutWalk London June 2011: An Eyewitness Account', *Lesbilicious*, 12 June, online.

Sheridan, S., Magarey, S., and Lilburn, S. (2007) 'Feminism in the News', in J. Hollows and R. Moseley (eds.) *Feminism in Popular Culture* (New York: Berg Publisher), 25–40.

Shirky, C. (2011) 'The Political Power of Social Media', *Foreign Affairs*, January/February, online.

Shoemaker, P.J. and Reese, S.D. (1996) *Mediating the Message: Theories of Influences on Mass Media Content, 2nd ed.* (USA: Longman Publishers).

Shoesmith, K. (2014) 'Five Years Jail for Bricklayer Lee Setford Who "Lost Control" and Raped Drunken Woman at Beverley Home', *Hull Daily Mail*, 8 July, online.

Simmons, T. (2008) 'The Personal is Political? Blogging and Citizen Stories, the Case of Mum's Army', *Information Polity*, 13(1–2), 87–96.

'Singapore Allows SlutWalk' (2011) *News 24*, 30 November, online.

Sitrin, M. (2006) *Horizontalism: Voices of Popular Power in Argentina* (Oakland, CA and Edinburgh: AK Press).

Sitrin, M. (2012) 'Horizontalism and the Occupy Movements', *Dissent*, 59(2), 74–5.

Skelly, B. (2011) 'Letters', *The Sun*, 16 June, 49.

SlutTalk (2012) 'SlutTalk: The (Un)Conference – Hosted by SlutWalk Vancouver', *The Media Co-Op*, online.

'SlutWalk' (2011) *The Telegraph (India)*, 7 July, n.p.

SlutWalk Baltimore (2014) 'Timeline', *Facebook*, https://www.facebook.com/SlutWalkBaltimore, date accessed 18 September 2014.

SlutWalk Bangalore (2011) 'About', *Facebook*, https://www.facebook.com/slut-walkblore/info, date accessed 3 July 2014.

SlutWalk Birmingham (2011) 'About', *Facebook*, https://www.facebook.com/events/221317677886350/, date accessed 2 August 2014.

'SlutWalk Event Given Police go-ahead' (2011) *Straits Times*, 30 November, n.p.

'SlutWalk Goes Global' (2011) *Toronto Star*, 27 April, A2.

SlutWalk Grahamstown (2011) *Twitter*, 29 October, https://twitter.com/SlutWalkGHT, date accessed 4 November 2014.

'Slutwalk Hits the Streets of Hamilton' (2011) *Toronto Star*, 6 June, A8.

SlutWalk Johannesburg (2011) 'About', *Facebook*, https://www.face-book.com/slutwalk.india.3?fref=ts&ref=br_tf#!/pages/Slutwalk-Johannesburg/147836015284588?sk=info, date accessed 2 July 2014.

SlutWalk Johannesburg (2012) 'SlutWalk Slogans 2012', *SlutWalk Johannesburg*, http://slutwalkjhb.co.za/?p=221, date accessed 16 September 2014.

SlutWalk Johannesburg (2014a) 'SlutWalk Johannesburg 2014', *Facebook*, https://www.facebook.com/events/229955380544855/, date accessed 3 July 2014.

SlutWalk Johannesburg (2014b) *Facebook*, 25 August, https://www.facebook.com/pages/Slutwalk-Johannesburg/147836015284588, date accessed 8 September 2014.

SlutWalk LA (2014a) 'About', *Facebook*, https://www.facebook.com/laslutwalk/info, date accessed 3 July 2014).

SlutWalk LA (2014b) 'Profile Picture', *Facebook*, https://www.facebook.com/laslutwalk, date accessed 19 September 2014.

Slutwalk London (2012) 'Who Are We?', *Tumblr*, http://slutmeansspeakup.tum-blr.com/about, date accessed 2 August 2014.

'Slutwalk March Takes Place in Bristol' (2011) *BBC Online*, 1 October, online.

SlutWalk Melbourne (2012) *Twitter*, 1 September, https://twitter.com/SlutWalkMelb, date accessed 2 November 2014.

SlutWalk Melbourne (2014) *SlutWalk Melbourne*,http://slutwalkmelbourne.com.au/, date accessed 4 November 2014.

SlutWalk Newcastle (2014) *Facebook*, 16 June, https://www.facebook.com/pages/Slutwalk-Newcastle/113964255354656, date accessed 9 September.

SlutWalk NYC (2011) *Twitter*, https://twitter.com/SlutWalkNYC, date accessed 4 November 2014.

'Slutwalk NYC Causes Stir in Black Community' (2011) *Huffington Post*, 29 September, online.

SlutWalk Omaha (2014) *Twitter*, 2 September, https://twitter.com/SlutwalkOmaha/status/506944818635763712, date accessed 8 September 2014.

SlutWalk Orlando (2012) 'About', *Facebook*, https://www.facebook.com/SlutWalkOrlando/posts/240011986122092, date accessed 2 August 2014.

SlutWalk Perth (2012) 'Timeline', *Facebook*, 31 December, https://www.facebook.com/SlutWalkPerth, date accessed 9 September 2014.

SlutWalk Perth (2013) 'Timeline', *Facebook*, 30 October, https://www.facebook.com/SlutWalkPerth, date accessed 18 September 2014.

SlutWalk Perth (2014) 'Profile Picture', *Facebook*, https://www.facebook.com/SlutWalkPerth, date accessed 19 September 2014.

SlutWalk Philadelphia (2013) 'About', *Facebook*, https://www.facebook.com/slutwalkphiladelphia/info, date accessed 18 September 2014.

'SlutWalk Protest in New Delhi a first for Asia' (2011) *Toronto Star*, 1 August, A8.

'Slutwalk Protest Targets Dress Slur' (2011) *Sunday Star-Times*, 8 May, 3.

SlutWalk Seattle (2012) 'Timeline', *Facebook*, https://www.facebook.com/slutwalkseattle, date accessed 2 November 2014.

SlutWalk Seattle (2014) 'About', *Facebook*, https://www.facebook.com/slutwalkseattle/info, date accessed 2 August 2014.

SlutWalk Singapore (2011a) 'Interview with SlutWalk Bangalore', *SlutWalk Singapore*, 24 November, online.

SlutWalk Singapore (2011b) 'Interview with SlutWalk Hong Kong', *SlutWalk Singapore*, 16 October, online.

SlutWalk Singapore (2014) *Twitter*, 26 March, https://twitter.com/SlutWalkSG, date accessed 4 November 2014.

SlutWalk St. Louis (2013) *Twitter*, 28 August, https://twitter.com/SlutWalkSTL, date accessed 1 November 2014.

'SlutWalk sweeps Australia' (2011) *Daily Dispatch*, 12 May, n.p.

SlutWalk Toronto (2011) 'About', *SlutWalk Toronto*, http://www.slutwalktoronto.com/, date accessed 2 August 2014.

SlutWalk Toronto (2014) *Facebook*, 20 April, https://www.facebook.com/SlutWalkToronto, date accessed 8 September 2014.

'SlutWalk Vancouver' (2011) *Rabble.ca*, 15 May, online.

SlutWalk Vancouver (2012) 'SlutWalk Vancouver Keeping its Name ... for Now', *Facebook*, https://www.facebook.com/notes/384408591596053/, date accessed 10 November 2014.

SlutWalk Vancouver (2014) 'Timeline', *Facebook*, 20 June, https://www.facebook.com/slutwalkvancouver, date accessed 18 September 2014.

SlutWalk Victoria (2013) *Facebook*, 24 April, https://www.facebook.com/SlutwalkVictoriabc?fref=pb&hc_location=profile_browser, date accessed 8 September 2014.

SlutWalk Winnipeg (2014) 'Zine!', *Word Press*, http://slutwalkwinnipeg.wordpress.com/zine/, date accessed 9 September 2014.

'Slutwalks Brave Cold to Get Message Across' (2011) *New Zealand TV*, 25 June, online.

'"SlutWalks" go Worldwide' (2011) *Bust*, online.

'SlutWalks to Rally Against Shaming of Rape Victims' (2011) *New Zealand Herald*, 25 June, n.p.

Smullens, S.K. (2011) 'SlutWalk in Philly and Worldwide: Long Overdue Focus on the Blame and Shame of Women', *Huffington Post*, 11 August, online.

Sodhi, A. (2014) *SlutWalk Bangalore 2011 Organiser*, Personal Interview, 22 May.

Solomon, M. (2011) 'Our Sexual Expression is Our Choice', *Thought Leader*, 25 October, online.

Soothill, K. and Walby, S. (1991) *Sex Crime in the News* (London: Routledge).

Spackman, B. (2011) 'Cultivate Respect', *Calgary Herald*, 2 August, A9.

Spankhead, T. (2012a) 'Victim Blaming 101', *The Lady Garden*, 3 August, online.

Spankhead, T. (2012b) 'SlutWalk: This Weekend', *The Lady Garden*, 15 May, online.

Sparks, C. (2000) 'Introduction: The Panic Over Tabloid News', in C. Sparks and J. Tulloch (eds.) *Tabloid Tales: Global Debates Over Media Standards* (Lanham, MD: Rownan & Littlefield Publishers Inc), 1–40.

Staggenborg, S. (2008) *Social Movements* (Oxford: Oxford University Press).

'Statistics Shed Little Light on Rape Statistics' (2013) *The Wall Street Journal*, 30 August, online.

Steiner, L. (2005) 'The Feminist Cable Collective as Public Sphere Activity', *Journalism*, 6(3), 313–34.

Strauss, E. (2012) 'Do Men Belong in the Women's Movement', *AlterNet*, 13 February, online.

Street-Porter, J. (2011) 'Fighting for the Right to be a "Slut" Demeans Us All', *Daily Mail*, 16 May, online.

Strutt, S.M. (1994) *Framing Feminisms: Feminist Critiques of Patriarchal News Media*, MA Dissertation (Vancouver: Simon Fraser University).

Stringer, R. (2014) *Knowing Victims: Feminism, Agency and Victim Politics in Neoliberal Times* (Hove and New York: Routledge).

Sutton, S. (2014) *SlutWalk Chicago 2011 Organiser*, Personal Interview, 27 May.

T., E. (2011) 'The Slut Walks and Victim Blaming', *The FBomb*, 31 May, online.

'Tackling Sexual Violence' (2011) *Canberra Times*, 5 August, online.

Taft, J.K. (2004) 'Girl Power Politics: Pop-Culture Barriers and Organizational Resistance', in A. Harris (ed.) *All About the Girl: Culture, Power and Identity* (New York: Routledge), 69–78.

Taft, J.K. (2011) *Rebel Girls: Youth Activism & Social Change Across the Americas* (New York: New York University Press).

Take Back the Night (2014) 'History, *Take Back the Night*, http://takebackthenight.org/history/, date accessed 11 June 2014.

Take Back the Night Calgary (2014) 'History of Take Back the Night', *Take Back the Night Calgary*, http://takebackthenightcalgary.com/history-of-take-back-the-night/, date accessed 11 June 2014.

Tarrant, S. (2009) *Men and Feminism* (Berkeley, CA: Seal Press)

Tarrant, S. (2011a) 'Ending the Slutwars', *Huffington Post*, 6 October, online.

Tarrant, S. (2011b) 'It's a Dress, Not a Yes', *Ms. Magazine*, 4 November, online.

Tasker, Y. and Negra, D. (2007) *Interrogating Postfeminism* (Durham, NC: Duke University Press).

Taylor, K.L. (2014) *Survival* (Bloomington, IN: Author House)

Taylor, V. (1989) 'Social Movement Continuity: The Women's Movement in Abeyance', *American Sociological Review*, 54(5), 761–75.

The Everyday Sexism Project (2014) 'About', *The Everyday Sexism Project*, http://everydaysexism.com/index.php/about, date accessed 19 June 2014.

The White House (2014) '1 is 2 Many', *The White House*, http://www.whitehouse.gov/1is2many, date accessed 6 June 2014.

The White House Council on Women and Girls (2014) 'Rape and Sexual Assault: A Renewed Call for Action', *The White House*, http://www.whitehouse.gov/sites/default/files/docs/sexual_assault_report_1-21-14.pdf, date accessed 10 June 2014.

Thorpe, J. (2012) 'Why Men Can't Lead the Women's Movement', *FeministsSA*, 10 January, online.

Thorsen, E. (2009) 'Blogging the Climate Change Crisis from Antartica', in S. Allan and E. Thorsen (eds.) *Citizen Journalism: Global Perspectives* (Oxford: Peter Lang), 107–17.

tigtog (2011) 'An Open Challenge to Mainstream Media re SlutWalk Sydney', *Hoyden About Town*, 12 June, online.

To The Curb (2011) 'Slutwalk: A Stroll Through White Supremacy', *To The Curb*, 13 May, online.

'Toronto's Slutwalk Sparks Blogosphere Feminism Debate' (2011) *Toronto Star*, 9 April, IN2.

Townsend, C. (2011) 'Misconceptions about Rape', *The Wellingtonian*, 18 August, online.

Traister, R. (2014) 'Feminism has Conquered the Culture – Now Comes the Hard Part', *New Statesman*, 15 September, online.

Trew, B (2013) 'Egypt's Sexual Assault Epidemic', *Al-Jazeera*, 13 August, online.

Trixie Films (2011) '#slutwalk nyc 2011', *Vimeo*, https://vimeo.com/73893505, date accessed 31 October 2014.

Tuchman, G. (1978) *Making News: A Study of the Construction of Reality* (New York: The Free Press).

Tuchman, G., Daniels, A.K., and Bennett, J. (eds.) (1978) *Hearth and Home: Images of Women in the Mass Media* (New York: Oxford University Press).

Tumblr (2014) 'About', *Tumblr*, http://www.tumblr.com/about, date accessed 10 June 2014.

Turner, J. (2011) 'Slutwalks are Treading on Dangerous Ground', *The Times*, 14 May, 25.

Twitter (2014) 'About', *Twitter*, https://about.twitter.com/company, date accessed 5 June 2014.

UK Government (2014) 'Global Summit to End Sexual Violence in Conflict', *Gov.UK*, https://www.gov.uk/government/topical-events/sexual-violence-in-conflict/about, date acessed 10 June 2014.

UN (1992) 'Convention on the Elimination of All Forms of Discrimination Against Women', *United Nations Entity for Gender Equality and the Empowerment of Women*, http://www.un.org/womenwatch/daw/cedaw/committee.htm, date accessed 1 June 2014.

UN Human Rights (2014) 'Rape: Weapon of War', *UN Human Rights*, http://www.ohchr.org/en/newsevents/pages/rapeweaponwar.aspx, date accessed 2 August 2014.

Vagianos, A. (2014) '28 Famous Men Who Prove You Don't Need To Be A Woman To Be A Feminist', *Huffington Post*, 25 July, online.

Valenti, J. (2007) *Full Frontal Feminism* (Emeryville, CA: Seal Press).

Valenti, J. (2011) 'The New Feminists: As Slutty as We Want to Be', *The Washington Post*, 5 June, B01.

Valenti, J. (2014a) 'Elliot Rodger's California Shooting Spree: Further Proof that Misogyny Kills', *The Guardian*, 25 May, online.

Valenti, J. (2014b) 'Why is it Easier to Invent Anti-rape Nail Polish than Find a Way to Stop Rapists?', *The Guardian*, 26 August, online.

Valenti, J. (2014c) 'Beyoncé's "Flawless" Feminist Act at the VMAs Leads the Way for Other Women', *The Guardian*, 25 August, online.

Vallabhajosyula, R. (2011) 'SlutWalk, Besharmi Morcha? Thanks But not Thanks', *Just Femme*, 16 August, online.

Van Acker, E. (1999) *Different Voices: Gender and Politics in Australia* (Melbourne: Macmillan Education).

van Dijk, T. (2008) *Discourse and Power* (Houndsmills: Palgrave Macmillan).

van Zoonen, L.(1992) 'The Women's Movement and the Media: Constructing a Public Identity,' *European Journal of Communication*, 7(4), 453–76.

Van Zuydam (2011) 'SlutWalk Hits South Africa, Where Rape is National Crisis' *Huffington Post (USA)*, 20 August, online.

Varvus, M.D. (2002) *Postfeminist News: Political Women in Media Culture* (Albany: State University of New York Press).

Varvus, M.D. (2007) 'Opting Out Moms in the News,' *Feminist Media Studies* 7(1), 47–63.

Vasudev, S. (2011) 'It's All About the Clothes', *Indian Express*, 9 July, n.p.

Walia, H. (2011) 'Slutwalk – To March or Not to March', *Rabble.ca*, 18 May, online.

Walmsley, C. (2013) 'Comment: The Ban on "Blurred Lines"', *The National Student*, 23 September, online.

Walter, N. (2010) *Living Dolls: The Return of Sexism* (London: Virago).

Ward, C.A. (1995) *Attitudes Towards Rape: Feminist and Social Psychological Perspectives* (London, Thousand Oaks and New Delhi: Sage).

Wardle, C. (2004) *Monsters and Angels: A Comparison of Broadsheet and Tabloid Press Coverage of Child Murders from the US and UK, 1930–2000*, PhD Dissertation (Philadelphia: Pennsylvania State University).

Warner, M. (2002) *Publics and Counterpublics* (New York: Zone).

Weiner, M.F. (2011) 'All the News that's Fit to Print? Silence and Voice in Mainstream and Ethnic Press Accounts of African American Protest,' *Research in Social Movements, Conflicts and Change*, 31, 291–324.

Weiss, K.G. (2010) 'Too Ashamed to Report: Deconstructing the Shame of Sexual Victimization', *Feminist Criminology*, 5(3), 286–310.

Whelehan, I. (2000) *Overloaded: Popular Culture and the Future of Feminism* (London: The Women's Press).

White, A.M. (2001) 'I am Because We are: Combined Race and Gender Political Consciousness Among African American Women and Men Anti-rape Activists', *Women's Studies International Forum*, 24(1), 11–24.

Williams, K. (2003) *Understanding Media Theory* (London: Hodder Education).

Williams, R.H. (1995) 'Constructing the Public Good: Social Movements and Cultural Resources', *Social Problems*, 42(1), 124–44.

'Winnipeg "SlutWalk" participants mull name change' (2011) *CBC*, 8 September, online.

Wolburt Burgess, A., Lewis-O'Connor, A., Nugent-Borakove, M.E., and Fanflik, P. (2009) 'Victim Services and SANE/SART Programs', in R. Hazlewood and A. Wolbert Burgess (eds.) *Practical Aspects of Rape Investigations*, 4th ed. (Boca Raton: Taylor & Francis) 39–51.

Wolfson, T. (2012) 'From the Zapatistas to Indymedia: Dialectics and Orthodoxy in Contemporary Social Movements', *Communication, Culture & Critique*, 5, 149–70.

'Woman Gang Raped on Orders of a "kangaroo court" ' (2014) *BBC*, 23 January, http://www.bbc.com/news/world-asia-india-25855325, date accessed 2 August 2014.

Wood, E.J. (2006) 'Variation in Sexual Violence During War', *Politics & Society*, 34(3), 307–41.

WordPress (n.d.) 'About WordPress' *WordPress*, http://wordpress.org/about/, date accessed 25 June 2014.

Worthington, N. (2008) 'Progress and Persistent Problems: Local TV News Framing of Acquaintance Rape on Campus', *Feminist Media Studies*, 8(1), 1–16.

Worthington, N. (2010) 'Of Conspiracies and Kangas: Mail & Guardian's Online Construction of the Jacob Zuma Rape Trial', *Journalism*, 11(5), 607–23.

Wraith, D. (2013) *SlutWalk St. Louis 2012 Organiser*, Personal Interview, 28 April.

Wu, J.Q. (2011) 'Steps Toward Fighting a Culture of Blame', *Washington Times*, 14 August, C04.

Young, S. (1997) *Discourse, Politics and the Feminist Movement* (London and New York: Routledge).

Zaslow, E. (2009) *Feminism, Inc.: Coming of Age in Girl Power Media Culture* (New York: Palgrave MacMillan).

Zobl, E. and Drueke, R. (2012) 'Introduction', in E. Zobl and R. Drueke (eds.) *Feminist Media: Participatory Spaces, Networks and Cultural Citizenship* (Verlag, Bielefeld: transcript) 11–20.

Index

Printed and bound by CPI Group (UK) Ltd, Croydon, CR0 4YY